The Troubled Encounter:
The United States and Japan

AMERICA AND THE WORLD

The Troubled Encounter:

The United States and Japan

CHARLES E. NEU
Brown University

Charles E. Neu

John Wiley & Sons, Inc.
New York · London · Sydney · Toronto

Copyright © 1975, by John Wiley & Sons, Inc.

All rights reserved. Published simultaneously in Canada.

No part of this book may be reproduced by any means, nor transmitted, nor translated into a machine language without the written permission of the publisher.

Library of Congress Cataloging in Publication Data:

Neu, Charles E
    The troubled encounter: the United States and Japan

    (America and the world)
    Bibliography: p.
    1. United States—Foreign relations—Japan.
 2. Japan—Foreign relations—United States. I. Title.

E183.8.J3N367   327.73'052
ISBN 0-471-63190-6
ISBN 0-471-63191-4 (pbk)

Printed in the United States of America

10-9 8 7 6 5 4 3 2 1

To Dorothy Borg

Foreword

For over a century, the Japanese have symbolized the mysterious Orient for the American people. The image has been a strangely shifting one, from the polite creatures who greeted Commodore Perry to the brutal men who swept across the Pacific in World War II. Throughout the decades, Americans tended to assign Japan a secondary position in East Asia as they focused their thoughts, dreams, and ambitions on China. Indeed, Japan assumed greatest importance in American eyes when it threatened to overwhelm the open door policy and reduce China to an economic and political vassal. Pearl Harbor wrought a profound transformation in Japanese-American relations as the cauldron of war fused the antagonisms of the past into a terrible climax at Hiroshima, yet one that ultimately led to a new and friendlier relationship as MacArthur helped guide the Japanese toward democratic reform and economic rebirth. Today Japan stands out as America's leading ally in Asia, troubled by a new phase in the old American love affair with China and by serious trade conflicts, but still dependent on the United States for its national security.

Professor Neu traces the long sweep of Japanese-American relations with a broad approach that avoids excessive reliance on any single interpretive factor. He sees the major role of commercial ties without falling into the trap of economic determinism; he perceives the important but indirect role played by missionaries in shaping American attitudes toward Japan; he acknowledges the strategic rivalry that developed, especially on the part of American naval leaders; and he never neglects the vital cultural differences that contributed so heavily to the mutual misunderstandings that often troubled relations between the two nations. The result is a multifaceted study that provides both a coherent narrative and an incisive analysis of a major strand in American diplomatic history.

"Nippon and America, all the same heart," a Japanese official proclaimed in a toast to Perry back in 1854. Neu's book helps us understand both the hopeful promise and the ultimate inadequacy of this optimistic forecast of the future course of Japanese-American relations.

This book is one in a series of volumes tracing the history of American foreign policy toward those nations with which the United States has had significant relations over a long period of time. By stressing the continuity of diplomatic themes through the decades, each author seeks to identify the distinctive character of America's international relationships. It is hoped that this country-by-country approach will not only enable readers to understand more deeply the diplomatic history of their nation, but that it will also make them aware that past events and patterns of behavior exert a continuous influence on American foreign policy.

ROBERT A. DIVINE

Preface

Years ago, as an undergraduate, I became intrigued with the encounter between the United States and Japan. It seemed paradoxical that two nations that had interacted so continuously on the cultural, economic, and diplomatic levels should have understood one another so poorly and, ultimately, clashed in a great Pacific war. In this book I have attempted to explain the many facets of each government's policy, to explore the intellectual assumptions, bureaucratic perspectives, domestic political currents, and national aspirations that fused together to form official decisions. In the process I have tried to keep in mind the frequent confusion within each government and the extent to which statesmen, no matter how noble their intentions, seemed unable to transcend the values of their own culture and achieve the level of insight necessary to assert some control over the drift of events. I have emphasized the period from 1890 to 1941. Prior to 1890, contact between the two nations was slight; after 1941 contact was, of course, intense, but our knowledge is too superficial to allow the same depth of coverage as for previous years.

Like any synthesis, this one relies heavily on secondary works in the field of American-East Asian relations. Although this literature has become a large and rich one, it is stronger in some areas than in others, more satisfactory in explaining the dynamics of government policy than in analyzing the broad cultural and intellectual context out of which it emerged. Hopefully this book will tell us where we stand and suggest, through its failures of explanation, where we have to go. I hope, too, that it will give scholars outside the speciality of American-East Asian relations some understanding of the conclusions of a mass of published and unpublished material and, most important, that it will provide beginning students with a sense of the drama, complexity, and pathos of this particular segment of the past.

Many institutions, friends, and scholars eased the burden of writing this book and helped to make it a better one. The Charles Warren Center for Studies in American History offered a year of ideal working conditions, during which much of the research and writing were done. Robert A. Divine not only suggested that I undertake this study but patiently waited for its completion and made thoughtful suggestions for revising it. I am grateful to Richard W. Leopold for his careful reading of the manuscript and for introducing me to the excitement of history as an undergraduate. Edwin O. Reischauer shared his knowledge of the recent past with me, Akira Iriye, Ernest R. May, and Shumpei Okamoto each contributed to the improvement of the text. My former colleague, Louis Galambos, scrutinized the prose as only he can. My wife Deborah, along with Hilary and Douglas, sustained me with the most important but least tangible form of support. Finally, Karen Mota and Madeline Gross typed the manuscript cheerfully and efficiently. Portions of Chapter Three are reprinted with the permission of Harvard University Press from my essay in Ernest R. May and James C. Thomson, Jr., eds., *American-East Asian Relations: A Survey* (Cambridge, Mass., 1972). I have dedicated this book to Dorothy Borg, in recognition of the integrity of her scholarship and the warmth of her humanity. She has set an example for us all and has given the field of American-East Asian relations a special sense of community.

Providence, Rhode Island, 1974   CHARLES E. NEU

Contents

CHAPTER I

Pacific Vistas

D URING THE FIRST HALF OF THE NINETEENTH CENTURY the intellectual and physical horizons of the American people continued to expand, as they had since the birth of the republic. Americans felt the pull both of distant lands across the sea and of their own vast, largely unexplored continent. They set forth as merchants, explorers, and missionaries to participate in a great age of exploration and discovery, impelled by a remarkable messianic zeal to extend the landed and oceanic frontiers of the young nation. Some looked inward, uncertain of how the republic would relate to the great space to the west, while others believed that the vitality of the nation depended on maritime commerce. Confronted with a closed mercantile system in Europe, Americans searched for commercial opportunities in lesser known parts of the world. They saw commerce as not only essential for national survival, but also as a key to the advancement of liberal institutions. A growing national self-consciousness and confidence led Americans to believe more than ever before that a benign providence presided over the nation's destiny and imposed a duty on the nation to extend the blessings of liberty to other peoples and lands. As early as 1810, New England clergymen formed the American Board of Commissioners for Foreign Missions, and American missionaries soon appeared in India and Ceylon, then in Hawaii and the Middle East, convinced they would play a major role in the evangelization of the world.

Various government expeditions furthered this restless expansionist impulse. From 1838 to 1842 Lieutenant Charles Wilkes, commander of the United States Exploring Expedition, roamed the Pacific and charted the frozen coasts of the Antarctic. Another naval officer led a group down the Jordan River to the Dead Sea. Much earlier, Meriwether Lewis and William Clark had sketched in the broad outlines of the continent, and subsequent expeditions had penetrated farther into the West. By the late 1820s the army had completed its exploration of the Sante Fe trail and opened the path to the Rocky Mountains as far as the Great Salt Lake. In the 1830s government expeditions had laid out clear trails to Oregon and California. By the early 1840s, as William H. Goetzmann writes, "the West was no longer an unknown wilderness, a stepping stone on the road to India. . . . It had become . . . a place to move into—to occupy and settle and develop."[1] This progressive opening of the West inspired visions of continental expansion and settlement and brought the intermingling of the older notion of a maritime empire with the newer one of a landed empire stretching from the Atlantic to the Pacific.

Some Americans—particularly Eastern Whigs—saw the movement across the continent to the Pacific Coast as a part of the commercial advance into East Asia. Since the 1780s, when the China trade began, Asia had been a part of this expanding American horizon. China exercised a particular fascination because of its vast population and ancient culture. The growing trade with China in the first half of the nineteenth century reinforced beliefs that the course of empire was westward and that the destiny of the nation lay in the Pacific. As Henry Nash Smith remarks, "the idea of a passage to India, with its associated images of fabulous wealth, of ivory and apes and peacocks, led a vigorous existence on the level of the imagination entirely apart from its practicability."[2]

In the 1840s Americans gave considerable thought to East Asia. The Opium War between China and Great Britain, extending from 1839 to 1842, ended the humiliating arrangements under which foreigners had conducted their trade with China. The settlement brought the opening of new ports, the granting of extraterritorial privileges, and the beginnings of the whole complex of legal rights

---

[1]William H. Goetzmann, *Exploration and Empire: The Explorer and the Scientist in the Winning of the American West* (New York, 1967), p. 179.
[2]Henry Nash Smith, *Virgin Land: The American West as Symbol and Myth* (Cambridge, Mass., 1950), p. 23.

known as the treaty system. Although the United States stood aside in the Anglo-Chinese struggle, it acquired in the Treaty of Wanghia (1844) the privileges won by the British. This new situation brought a larger American presence in China that, in turn, stimulated popular interest. Americans viewed the peoples of China and Japan as dominated by oppressive governments and burdened with degrading customs. They wanted to extend commerce and lead the nations of East Asia into the mainstream of human progress.

Initially China dominated the American image of East Asia, while Japan existed on the edge of the nation's consciousness, in the shadow of China, as a way station to the riches of the mainland of Asia. There had, of course, been earlier contacts with Japan. Around 1543 the first European traders had reached Japan, and soon Jesuit missionaries had followed. Initially responsive to the West, Japanese leaders in the early seventeenth century had suppressed Christianity and virtually closed their nation to all foreign intercourse, leaving only a carefully supervised Dutch trading post in Nagasaki harbor. Japan had slipped from the European horizon and remained isolated for over 200 years. By the late eighteenth century, however, increased Western activity in China had stimulated a renewed curiosity about Japan, and Western ships had begun to appear in Japanese waters. In 1791 the first American vessel had entered a Japanese harbor and, during the Napoleonic Wars, the Dutch had chartered American ships to carry their annual cargo to Nagasaki. After 1807, 25 years had passed before an American ship visited Japan, but American clipper ships bound for China had passed close to the islands, and American whalers had sometimes ran ashore on Japan's rugged, uncharted coasts. Shipwrecked sailors had brought back tales of their confinement and stimulated public concern and resentment. By the 1830s interest in Japan had grown and, in the 1840s, with the rapid expansion of the China trade, the opening of Japan became inevitable.

Americans had previously considered breaking down Japan's barriers. As early as 1815 Captain David Porter urged President James Madison to inaugurate commercial relations. Porter emphasized national glory and commerce, but others believed it was the Christian duty of the United States to bring Japan within the circle of civilized nations. In 1832 the Jackson administration commissioned Edmund Roberts to negotiate commercial treaties with several Asian nations, including Japan, but Roberts failed to reach Japan on his first mission and died in 1836 before he could complete his second. Other attempts followed. In 1837 an American merchant, Charles W. King, sent a vessel to Japan to return Japanese seamen. Both commercial and religious motives underlay King's effort and, although it failed, he was convinced that an official expedition could end Japan's seclusion.

More and more the American government came to feel the same way. In 1846 and again in 1849, American navy ships entered Japanese harbors. The first expedition, commanded by Commodore James Biddle, sought to establish commercial relations, but received humiliating treatment at the hands of the Japanese; the second, commanded by Commodore James Glynn, assumed a much more belligerent attitude and secured the release of captured American seamen. Glynn felt contemptuous of the Japanese and concluded that only through a display of force could the United States "convert their selfish government into a liberal republic."[3] Glynn's attitude reflected a growing desire among Americans to expose Japan to the allegedly beneficent influence of Western civilization.

This heightened interest in Japan took place against the backdrop of the 1840s, a decade that brought a culmination of expansionist fervor. It was a decade of confidence and ambition, full of frantic activity and of the exuberance of a people on the move, fascinated by what Walt Whitman described as the "enormous untravelled plains and forests" of the West.[4] Imaginations soared as men contemplated the glorious destiny of their nation. America now stood, so it seemed to men at the time, at the center of Western civilization, on the cutting edge of progress. Commerce thrived, geographical barriers vanished, and the vision of a repub-

---

[3]Quoted in William L. Neumann, *America Encounters Japan: From Perry to MacArthur* (Baltimore, 1963), p. 24.
[4]Quoted in Fred Somkin, *Unquiet Eagle: Memory and Desire in the Idea of American Freedom, 1815-60* (Ithaca, 1967), p. 93.

lic stretching from the Atlantic to the Pacific became common-place. Often, however, it was a troubled vision, for many in the North already believed, as Senator William H. Seward proclaimed, that slavery was "incompatible with all . . . the elements of the security, welfare, and greatness of nations."[5] The bitter conten-tion surrounding the Mexican War revealed the depth of these feelings and the way in which they could become entangled with aspects of continental expansion. Nevertheless, the nation moved west and, by the end of the decade, gazed across the Pacific.

Americans looked not only across the Pacific but in other direc-tions as well, and it is important to keep the American interest in East Asia in perspective. Involvement in the Mediterranean world —the birthplace of Western civilization and Christianity—was of longer duration and far more substantial. From 1801 to 1815 United States naval forces sporadically fought the Barbary states to free American commerce; in subsequent years America's mer-centile-missionary stake in the Mediterranean grew rapidly. In the 1830s the eastern Mediterranean surpassed the Hawaiian Islands as the largest field of missionary endeavor and, in the next two decades, it not only retained that position, but also led all other areas in rate of growth. In 1850, for example, the missionary effort in China had only one fifth the budget of that in the Levant. As early as 1830 the United States signed a commercial treaty with the Ottoman Empire and, as American commerce and missions thrived, the Mediterranean Squadron became the most sought after command, the pinnacle of a naval career. Prior to his accept-ance of the expedition to Japan, Commodore Matthew C. Perry had served in the Mediterranean, on the west coast of Africa, and in the Caribbean. These were the areas that formed his experience and shaped his imagination.

By the late 1840s a shift had begun to occur in American percep-tions of the outside world. The United States had achieved a large trade in the Atlantic, and now East Asia beckoned more strongly than ever before. Herman Melville caught the popular curiosity

---

[5]Quoted in Eric Foner, *Free Labor, Free Soil, Free Men: The Ideology of the Republican Party Before the Civil War* (New York, 1970), p. 51.

when he wrote of "unknown Archipelagoes and impenetrable Japans."[6] To some missionaries, naval officers, and adventurers, East Asia seemed more challenging than areas in which the American presence was older and better established. Japan in particular seemed a mysterious archipelago, a land of paradox. Filled with an intelligent and frugal people, it was governed by a cruel despotism, one that practiced barbarism, duplicity, and treachery. This image of Japan aroused the intense curiosity of some Americans. Moreover, the acquisition of new Pacific Coast possessions, the development of isthmian routes, and the talk of a transcontinental railway excited expansionists who had for decades dreamed of making the American West the passage to India. Senator Thomas Hart Benton believed that "the European merchant, as well as the American, will fly across our continent on a straight line to China,"[7] while Secretary of the Treasury Robert J. Walker claimed that "Asia has suddenly become our neighbor with a placid, intervening ocean inviting our steamships upon the track of a commerce greater than that of all Europe combined."[8]

By the middle of the nineteenth century, then, changes in the expansionist mood gave a new impetus to a Japan expedition. While many Americans felt that duty compelled the United States to open Japan to the commerce and civilization of the West, more specific interests also urged an American expedition. Naval officers hoped to win prestige for themselves and their nation; the American whaling industry wanted ports of refuge and protection for shipwrecked seamen; some commercial interests, impressed by the growth of the China trade in the 1840s, dwelled on the commercial possibilities of Japan; and those determined to establish a Pacific steamship line to China believed that Japan, with its allegedly rich coal deposits, would be an essential stopping point. In Congress, too, agitation grew. Although only a handful of men actively pushed for it, many felt, as the *Democratic Review* put it, that "the

---

[6]Quoted in Foster Rhea Dulles, *Yankees and Samurai: America's Role in the Emergence of Modern Japan, 1791-1900* (New York, 1965), p. 56.

[7]Quoted in Smith, *Virgin Land*, p. 30.

[8]Quoted in Neumann, *America Encounters Japan*, p. 23.

opening of commerce with Japan is demanded by reason, civilization, progress and religion."[9] It was no surprise when, in early
1851, President Millard Fillmore decided to send a naval force to
Japan to secure "friendship, commerce, a supply of coal and provisions, and protection for our shipwrecked people."[10]

The President's aims were modest. He saw the end of Japanese
isolation as a way to enlarge peacefully both American prestige
and commerce in East Asia. Although the area was of peripheral
concern, he wished for the expedition's success and took great care
in the selection of its commander, Matthew C. Perry. Commodore
Perry had developed some interest in the Pacific after the Mexican
War, but he agreed to assume command of the East India Squadron only after assurances by the administration that he would
preside over a sizable force with ample funds for equipment and
gifts. Once committed to the enterprise, Perry prepared for it with
vigor. He talked with whalers at New Bedford, read European
books on Japan, and concluded that only an ominous display of
force combined with a haughty, distant attitude would bring success. Perry viewed the Japanese as "weak and semi-barbarous,"
"deceitful," and "vindictive in character."[11] In dealing with
them, the ordinary rules of discourse among civilized peoples did
not apply. Only extraordinary measures would convince their rulers to receive the President's letter and to grant American demands. Perry was far less reluctant than the President to use force
to achieve these ends and far more conscious of past humiliations
inflicted on American vessels by the Japanese government.

Perry's leadership endowed the expedition with a loftier purpose than the Fillmore administration had intended. Already a
fervent advocate of Manifest Destiny, he came to view the opening of Japan as the great object of his life and proclaimed the
inevitability of American expansion into the Pacific. Predicting an
Anglo-American struggle for control of that ocean, Perry sought
strategic outposts to strengthen America's position. His wide dis-

[9]*Democratic Review,* CLXVI (April 1852), p. 332.
[10]Frank H. Severance, ed., *Millard Fillmore Papers,* 2 vols. (Buffalo, 1907), I, p. 395.
[11]Quoted in Neumann, *America Encounters Japan,* p. 31.

cretionary powers and the slowness of communications provided many opportunities to pursue these larger aims.

When Perry reached the Pacific in the spring of 1853, he began to act on his broad vision of the nation's destiny. He visited the Ryūkyūs and the Bonins, forced concessions from the rulers of those islands, and even contemplated the bases that both island chains could provide for America's Pacific empire. On July 8 his four "black ships" arrived in what is today the Bay of Tokyo (then Edo Bay), prepared for determined resistance from the Japanese. Perry decided, as he had done years before at Naples, to make his demands and depart, promising to return with a more imposing force. But, before leaving, Perry intimidated the Japanese by moving his ships closer to Tokyo, the capital of the Tokugawa Shogunate, than any other foreign vessels had dared to advance. Purposefully remote and sensitive to the slightest affronts to his dignity, he finally brought his first visit to a culmination by delivering the President's letter to Japanese authorities in an elaborate ceremony on the shores of Tokyo Bay. Full of a sense of historic purpose, he wrote in his journal that "we pray God that our present attempt to bring a singular and isolated people into the family of civilized nations may succeed without bloodshed."[12]

In March 1854 Perry returned to Japan with an enlarged squadron to negotiate the Treaty of Kanagawa. His tactics were typical of the era. He warned the Japanese of the fate of Mexico, threatened to assemble an even larger force, and made it clear that he intended to achieve his aims at whatever cost. Despite his bluster, however, Perry dropped his demand for commercial relations and settled for a treaty that provided for the protection of the crews of shipwrecked vessels, the opening of two ports where American ships could obtain coal, wood, water and supplies, and the right to station consular officials in these ports. Perry knew that he had made only a small beginning, but he confidently expected others to carry forward the great work that he had launched.

Perry's belligerency and desire for territorial aggrandizement

---

[12]Quoted in Samuel Elliot Morison, *"Old Bruin": Commodore Matthew C. Perry, 1794-1858* (Boston, 1967), p. 324.

worried the American government and brought out what was to become a persistent dichotomy in American East Asian policy. Most American diplomats in China and Japan were restless and impatient, inspired by a vision of an American empire of commerce and religion in East Asia. As men on the spot, they were influenced by the course of events and by the attitudes of their European colleagues. Their activism contrasted sharply with the passivity of their government. More often than not, the American government was indifferent to their needs and programs; officials in Washington had a far narrower vision of American interests in East Asia. The government negotiated treaties to open China and Japan to Western influence and to encourage the growth of commerce. But these objectives, once achieved, satisfied leaders in Washington, who wished to avoid further involvement. When difficulties arose over commercial rights and the protection of missionaries and other Westerners, the United States usually responded cautiously. In the 1850s events in Japan temporarily obscured the fact that in East Asia the United States was a minor power, without the resources or the will to sustain major policy initiatives. For men in Washington, as for most Americans, Asia remained an abstract idea, a distant area that was only one part of a worldwide commercial empire. American representatives in China and Japan seldom shared this attitude and, because of the lag in communications, often pursued their private goals.

Full of grandiose objectives in East Asia, Perry was inevitably disappointed on his return to the United States in early 1855. He received a warm but not overwhelming reception, and the Democratic administration of Franklin Pierce seemed cool toward Perry's elaborate vision of the nation's Pacific destiny. Perry proclaimed that the Treaty of Kanagawa was "a mere commencement" in "bringing a mighty Empire into the family of nations and within the influence of our benign religion."[13] The government did, to be sure, follow up Perry's achievement with the dispatch of Townsend Harris as the first American consul in Japan but, by this time, the nation's leaders were absorbed in more pressing foreign and domestic problems.

---

[13]Quoted in Morison, "*Old Bruin*", p. 417.

American interest in East Asia—which peaked during the 1840s and early 1850s—began to wane. The lure of Asia had always been a subordinate theme in American expansionism, serving as one of many justifications for the conquest of the continent. Those who saw the American West more as a bridge to Asia than as an area to be settled and developed in its own right were understandably excited by the vistas unveiled by expansion to the Pacific and the opening of Japan. For most Americans, however, the vision of the American West as a passage to India was never the central motive for the westward movement and became even less compelling in the 1850s as they turned more decisively inward. Gradually the American people had grasped the potential resources and enormous dimensions of the West. The acquisition of California and Oregon, although it gave a brief impetus to the thrust into East Asia, presented Americans with the reality of a continental empire and coalesced feelings about the abundance of the West. It brought a shift of consciousness as men began to think, far more than previously, in terms of a great internal, landed empire to be peopled and tamed. The theme of the West as a passage to India gave way to the theme of the West as the "garden of the world," [14] a vast, interior space that would shape the promise and define the meaning of American life.

In the 1850s the nature of this internal domain became more and more controversial. Southerners believed that their peculiar institution must expand or perish and yearned for a Caribbean slave empire; Northerners were equally convinced that their free society must grow and disturbed by the domestic and international implications of slavery. During the decade internal disorder deepened, and many Republicans concluded that slavery dimmed the radiance of America and prevented the nation from fulfilling its historic mission to spread freedom throughout the world. Abraham Lincoln remarked in 1854 that slavery "deprives our republican example of its just influence in the world—enables the enemies of free institutions to taunt us as hypocrites."[15] As the

---

[14]Smith, *Virgin Land,* p. 34.
[15]Quoted in Foner, *Free Labor, Free Soil, Free Men,* p. 72.

ordeal of the union intensified, East Asia receded even farther toward the periphery of men's minds.

Nevertheless, American activities in Japan retained a certain momentum and, in 1856, Townsend Harris arrived to establish the first American consulate in the remote port of Shimoda. The State Department instructed Harris to secure a commercial treaty that would open Japan to foreign trade on terms similar to China. Harris, who had considerable experience in the Orient, had ardently sought this mission in an effort to make his mark on history. Highly conscious of the precedents he set, he proved to be an argumentative and tenacious representative. Unlike Perry, however, he had little choice but to proceed peacefully. He was neglected by the American government and never possessed naval force to back up his demands. "The absence of a man-of-war," he recognized, " . . . tends to weaken my influence with the Japanese."[16] He could only issue veiled threats and adjust to the realities of his lonely position. But there was also an element of idealism in Harris' conduct. He valued many of the unique qualities of Japanese life and saw himself as that nation's sympathetic friend, as a tutor for Japan's emergence from centuries of seclusion.

Harris proved to be a man of endurance and courage. He waited 14 months, largely isolated from the outside world, before receiving permission to proceed to Tokyo to begin treaty negotiations. Once there, he warned the Japanese that if they should fail to sign a moderate treaty with the United States, a British expedition would soon appear to impose harsh terms. Harris emphasized the distinctiveness of American policy and the unique American friendship with Japan. His approach was highly personal, partly because he possessed only the most general of guidelines. American statesmen had vague and scattered views about Asia; to them the further opening of Japan was a small event in the expanding American commercial empire. As a result, American representatives in the 1850s frequently pursued the most contradictory policies in East Asia. In Japan Harris operated on his own and talked

---

[16]Mario Emilio Cosenza, ed., *The Complete Journal of Townsend Harris, First American Consul General and Minister to Japan* (New York, 1930), p. 357.

peace and friendship, while in China American diplomats formulated risky, aggressive schemes, often in collaboration with the European powers. In both nations American diplomats pursued a highly independent course.

In July 1858, Harris concluded, after tedious negotiations, a commercial treaty that set the pattern for the relationships between all of the foreign powers and Japan. It provided for freedom of trade and the opening of new ports, for American residence in these ports and in Tokyo, and for a schedule of tariff rates along with extraterritorial rights. Finally, it stipulated that the President, at the request of Japan, would act as a friendly mediator in any dispute between Japan and a European power. In 1859 Harris, who was eager to inaugurate the new era in Japanese-American relations, became the first American minister to Japan and opened an American legation in Tokyo.

II

This new Western presence upset the delicate balance of internal forces in Japan and had a shattering impact on that country. For over two centuries Japan's hierarchical, feudal society had been ruled by the Tokugawa Shoguns, who governed a large central domain and possessed only an indirect control over certain semiautonomous clans. By the 1850s the Shogunate had become a lethargic, indecisive bureaucracy, weakened by domestic unrest and by economic changes that had gradually eroded its authority. The threat of domestic crises and decades of foreign intrusions had alarmed the Shogunate, along with many other educated Japanese. In fact, for over 50 years prior to Perry's arrival, they had been pondering their relationship with the West and rethinking their world view. In the process, they had learned much about Western history and technology.

By the midnineteenth century the Shogunate realized the superior power of the West and feared that Japan might suffer the fate of China if it did not make some concessions. Thus, the Shogunate bent before Western pressure and permitted the establishment of a foreign foothold in Japan. But these controversial concessions—made in the face of virulent antiforeignism and presumably in violation of the wishes of the Emperor—brought a

renewed interest in national politics among court nobles and feudal lords. The result was a deepening of the domestic crisis. After
1858 the Shogunate was trapped between the demands of the
West and the demands of powerful domestic opponents. Unable
to satisfy either, its hold on the nation weakened.

Resentment against the intrusion of foreigners was genuine and
widespread, but antiforeignism also became a way of attacking the
power of the Shogunate. Some powerful clans held strong, traditional animosities against the Tokugawa Shogunate and also
wished to give the Emperor a more central position in the political
system (one that had been lost centuries before). In the decade
after 1858 Western interests, including those of the United States,
became enmeshed in a complex struggle among the Shogunate, the
Imperial Court, and feudal fiefs such as Chōshū and Satsuma.
Although the Shogunate controlled the more economically and
socially advanced areas of the nation, this proved to be a disadvantage. In these regions the traditional feudal class structure had
eroded far more than in the more remote domains of the opposing
clans. These clans—particularly Chōshū and Satsuma—possessed
a feudal cohesiveness and a unity and purpose that allowed them
to act effectively. They came to be led by a remarkable group of
young samurai (an upper class of warrier-administrators) who,
once they understood the enormous military superiority of the
West, quickly shed their antiforeignism and absorbed themselves
in the task of strengthening the nation. They emerged triumphant
in a civil war that ended in 1868 with the restoration of the titular
sovereignty of the young Meiji Emperor.

Between 1858 and 1868, however, Japan experienced a decade
of chaos. The appearance of foreigners in the open ports and in
Tokyo, along with the economic dislocations brought by expanded trade with the West, provoked some samurai to commit
acts of violence against foreign merchants and diplomats and
against the officials of the Shogunate. In 1861 these rebellious
samurai killed the secretary of the American legation; later in the
year they attacked the British legation in Tokyo. All of the foreign
representatives, with the exception of Harris, withdrew to the
comparative safety of Yokohama. Antiforeignism was so powerful
that the Shogunate attempted to obstruct the growth of foreign

trade and, in December 1862, even promised the Emperor that it would expel the foreigners. In 1863 Chōshū, acting on its own initiative, bombarded foreign ships and temporarily closed the Straits of Shimonoseki.

III

The tumult in Japan created repeated crises between the Western powers and the Shogunate. Foreign diplomats, although puzzled by the complex political crosscurrents of the 1860s, were determined to preserve their foothold and to punish the Japanese government for its failure to discharge its treaty obligations. Harris was more sympathetic toward the Japanese than the European ministers. By 1860 he realized that he had underestimated the difficulties of ending Japan's seclusion and concluded that the Japanese were still a semicivilized people. Harris still believed, however, that the Japanese government wished to carry out its treaty commitments, although rampant antiforeignism sometimes prevented it from doing so, and he continued to counsel patience and restraint. Conscious of the recent experience of China, he hoped that Japan might prove to be the "one spot in the Eastern world [where] the advent of Christian civilization did not bring with it its usual attendants of rapine and bloodshed."[17]

Harris' benign attitudes were largely personal. Although Secretary of State William H. Seward deferred to his minister's judgments, he preferred a more aggressive defense of American interests in collaboration with the European powers. The Secretary of State—a long-standing advocate of expanding America's influence in Asia—fear that attacks on foreigners and the neglect of treaty obligations would damage Western prestige. Like so many outsiders, he saw the domestic conflict in Japan in terms of a struggle between the liberal, pro-Western Shogunate and the reactionary, antiforeign feudal groups gathered around the Emperor. Seward believed that a forceful response would strengthen the position of the Shogunate. In 1861 he proposed to the powers a joint naval

---

[17]Quoted in Payson J. Treat, *Diplomatic Relations Between the United States and Japan, 1853-1905,* 3 vols. (Stanford, 1932-1938), I, p. 109.

expedition to suppress antiforeign activities, while 1 year later the new American minister, Robert H. Pruyn, advocated a naval demonstration and even a march on Kyōto to force the Emperor to ratify the commercial treaties. Pruyn observed that "the silent but no less potent utterances of bayonet and wide-mouthed cannon burst away the barriers of isolation, and our foothold here can be maintained only by a firm attitude and with the hand on the sword."[18] In 1864 an American warship helped to reopen the Straits of Shimonoseki and when, the next year, a squadron took foreign representatives to Osaka to negotiate with the Shogun, the American minister arrived on a British man-of-war.

In their demands on the Shogunate, most American ministers were more restrained than their British or French counterparts. But this moderation was primarily a reflection of weakness, accentuated in the early 1860s by America's absorption in the Civil War. As a minor Asian power, the United States lacked the military strength to implement a highly vigorous policy. In both China and Japan the United States belonged to a Western community dominated by Great Britain and benefited from a complex system of rights and privileges largely maintained by others. The onus of this task fell on the major European powers, not on the United States, and this fact, combined with the sense of a unique American mission, allowed Americans to sustain the myth that their policy in East Asia was uniquely pure and benevolent.

The achievements of Perry and Harris did, for a time, bring American ascendancy in Japan. But the American government had no taste for the sustained commitments necessary to preserve this position. Its brief period of leadership was an historic anomaly that ended in the 1860s when tranquility in China and India allowed the British to devote more attention to Japan. The British possessed every advantage—a commanding presence in China, an elaborate commercial network in East Asia, and ample diplomatic, naval, and military resources. From the start, Britain had more residents and firms in Japan than any other power and dominated trade with that nation. But the government in London—although

---

[18] *Papers Relating to Foreign Affairs: 1863,* 2 vols. (Washington, D. C., 1864), II, p. 1046.

concerned with trade and prestige—had little interest in Japan and allowed its representatives in Tokyo much discretion. These men, guided by previous experience in China, pursued a vigorous policy. Sir Harry S. Parkes, the British minister from 1865 to 1883, surrounded himself with students of Japanese language and culture who established close ties with the leaders of Chōshū and Satsuma. As a result, the British understood well before the Meiji restoration the superficiality of the antiforeignism of these clans and their profound desire to overthrow the Shogunate and create a strong national government under the aegis of the Emperor. The British supported these goals and, after 1868, Parkes became the most influential foreign diplomat in Japan.

After Harris' departure in 1862, the British ministers dominated their American counterparts. In the 1860s American ministers, lacking experience in East Asia and an adequate diplomatic establishment, could not penetrate the surface confusion of Japanese politics. Pruyn complained that "everything seen [is] in palpable open conflict with what is heard,"[19] while his successor confidently predicted in 1868 that "the movement to unite the whole of Japan under the sceptre of the Mikado is not a bona fide one, and there is not the remotest prospect of the people being benefited by the results."[20] As late as 1871 the American minister wrote pessimistic assessments of the prospects facing the new imperial regime.

With the end of the American Civil War Seward sought to revive the expansionism of the prewar years. He returned to the theme of the westward flow of empire and predicted the spread of America's commerce and ideology over the entire globe. The nations of the Western hemisphere, he believed, would steadily gravitate toward the United States and one day enter the Union. Although he hoped to secure island outposts to protect the growing American empire, he did not advocate expansion by force or desire colonies in distant lands. In East Asia, Seward considered China, not Japan, the center of American concern because of the

---

[19]Quoted in Treat, *Diplomatic Relations Between the United States and Japan,* I, p. 215.
[20]Ibid., I, p. 336.

superiority of its civilization and its unlimited commercial potential.

Seward achieved little of his expansionist program. Although the United States acquired Alaska and Midway Island, the nation displayed far less enthusiasm for Manifest Destiny than it had in the 1840s and 1850s. In the years after the Civil War America turned inward. The vast, unsettled spaces of the West exerted a powerful claim on men's energies and imaginations, as did the startling alterations in the fabric of American society. In an era of widespread dislocation, the expansionism of the first half of the century lost its force.

Seward never fully understood these changes in the nation's mood, although he did realize that the postwar years would not be a time of spectacular gains for his program. "How sadly," he observed, "domestic disturbances of ours demoralize the national ambition."[21] Even the bulk of his own energies were focused on the liquidation of Napoleon III's adventure in Mexico and the settlement of Civil War claims against Great Britain, and he could only hope to lay the foundation for a future, more outward-oriented generation.

IV

Seward left office in 1869, on the eve of extraordinary changes in Japan. The Meiji restoration of 1868 inaugurated a remarkable period of modernization, one that revolutionized the country's economic, political, and social makeup. In less than half a century a small ruling oligarchy—driven by its fervent desire for equality and national security—transformed a feudal society into a modern nation. Japan's leaders centralized governmental power and promoted national unity and patriotism, steadied the nation's finances, and greatly increased its military and industrial capabilities. They instituted military conscription and imposed sweeping legal and educational reforms on the Japanese people. The resulting social turmoil was acute but, in 1877, the government success-

---

[21]Quoted in Glyndon G. Van Deusen, *William Henry Seward* (New York, 1967), p. 530.

fully repressed a major rebellion and proceeded, in the 1880s, to introduce representative political institutions gradually. In 1889 this process culminated with the Meiji Constitution, which guaranteed many popular rights and created a Diet with a popularly elected lower house. Although the lower house possessed severely restricted powers and was based on a limited franchise, Japan had gone much further in the process of westernization than most had expected. Meiji leaders had begun the new era determined to end their nation's shameful weakness and to emulate the Western powers. While pursuing these goals, they had altered the nation's social structure far beyond their original intentions. They had also placed Japan, toward the end of the century, in a position to achieve a new standing among the nations of the world.

V

This great transformation soon altered the American image of Japan. In the 1850s Americans saw a friendly, curious people dominated by a despotic, cruel government. In the 1860s the Shogunate seemed more and more receptive to westernization, while powerful feudal clans stood in opposition. Americans viewed the Meiji restoration as a setback for progressive forces in Japan. As late as 1871 the American minister, Charles E. DeLong, deplored the fact that the Japanese people, "naturally brave, charitable, and kind, who pant for freedom, must remain enslaved in a thraldom of physical and mental servitude of the most revolting nature."[22] In the 1870s this attitude faded, as Americans came to believe that both government and people had joined hands to throw off the trappings of a feudal, medieval society. Americans concluded that Japan was becoming more like the West and discussed Japan's progress in terms of Western historical analogies. Only the few who studied Japan deeply had any misgivings about the impact of the West upon Japan or about Japan's future as a westernized, Asiatic power. Instead, in the 1870s and 1880s travelers, missionaries, and diplomats viewed Japan through a romantic haze. They praised the physical beauty of the land and the recep-

---

[22]Quoted in Treat, *Diplomatic Relations Between the United States and Japan,* I, pp. 391-392.

tiveness of its people and government to constructive change. The paeans to the new Japan were endless. The American minister from 1873 to 1885, John A. Bingham, reported in 1880 that "seldom, if ever, in the history of civil administration, had any other ruler done so much within so brief a period for the reformation and well-being of a people,"[23] while 9 years later his successor, Richard B. Hubbard (1885 to 1889), concluded that Japan's progress "is not a short-lived or experimental thing, nor a thin veneering of Western civilization . . . but rather proof of a solid and permanent triumph over the past of her history."[24]

Some Americans developed an appreciation of Japanese art and architecture; others sought personal involvement in Japan's metamorphosis. Beginning in the 1870s, American agricultural experts, engineers, and specialists in law and diplomacy traveled to Japan to assist the government. It was as educators, however, that Americans made their greatest impact. The schools and universities established by American missionaries had a profound effect on the Japanese educated classes and, by 1872, between 200 and 300 Japanese students were studying in the United States. Like the British, French, and Germans, Americans played a significant part in the modernization of Japan.

As the image of Japan brightened, that of China dimmed. In the 1870s and 1880s Americans in Japan fell under that nation's spell and conveyed a favorable impression to their countrymen at home. As a consequence, Japan took on a new importance as Americans contrasted the "awakening of Japan" with China's "deadening conservatism."[25] They warmly welcomed Japanese statesmen and students, but became more and more hostile to Chinese immigrants, who were of a much lower class. By the early 1870s a potent anti-Chinese movement had developed along the Pacific Coast. To more and more Americans, Japan held the key to the future of East Asia.

---

[23] *Papers Relating to the Foreign Relations of the United States: 1880* (Washington, D. C., 1880), p. 690.

[24] *Papers Relating to the Foreign Relations of the United States: 1889* (Washington, D. C., 1890), p. 536.

[25] Quoted in Akira Iriye, *Across the Pacific: An Inner History of American-East Asian Relations* (New York, 1967), pp. 21, 26.

Missionaries played a crucial role in altering the American image of Japan's position in Asia. Initially American missionaries saw few possibilities for Christian activity in Japan but, with the signing of Harris' treaty in 1858, this view changed, and a year later the first Protestant missionaries from the United States reached Japan. For over a decade their impact was minor. Harris had failed to open Japan to Christianity and had only secured the right of foreigners to practice their own religion within the treaty ports. Confined to these small areas and confronted with popular and governmental hostility, American missionaries concentrated on the study of Japanese and the translation of religious tracts and the Bible in an effort to lay the foundations for future growth. But the prospects for expansion seemed so remote that the American Board of Commissioners for Foreign Missions—the most prominent American missionary organization—did not send a representative to Japan until 1869. The previous year the Emperor had renewed the ban on Christianity, and the new government began to persecute a small group of Japanese Christians who had kept the faith over the centuries. The United States, along with the other powers, strongly protested. Secretary of State Seward warned that "when one foreign Christian shall have suffered martyrdom in Japan for his faith, Christendom will be shocked to its center."[26] Two years later Secretary of State Hamilton Fish sought the cooperation of Great Britain, France, and Germany in imposing restraints on the Japanese government. Although Britain rejected Fish's overtures, the American initiative indicated how seriously the government viewed the question of toleration. It was responding not only to the complaints of missionaries, but also to the widespread feeling that Christianity and modernization must proceed hand in hand.

The fears of the American government soon passed. Japanese leaders came to grasp the importance of toleration, and in 1873 the Emperor repealed the anti-Christian edict. Although Christianity was given no legal status, government neutrality now brought new opportunities and a new interest in Japan among Western chur-

---

[26]*Papers Relating to Foreign Affairs: 1868,* 2 vols. (Washington, D. C., 1869), I, p. 828.

ches. In the 1870s Christianity spread slowly, but the 1880s were the great decade for Christianity in Japan, a decade of unparalleled growth and hope. Church membership rose from 4000 to 39,000, while the number of missionaries increased from 145 in 1883 to 363 at the end of the decade. Missionaries held revivalistic mass meetings in large urban areas and gathered much support from Japanese converts. Although Christianity remained an urban movement with close ties to Japan's social, political, and intellectual elites, the progress of the 1880s was so great that some missionaries spoke of the conversion of Japan within a generation. Missionaries felt that Japan was the model for the rest of Asia, the "Key to the Orient"[27] and that, if Christianity could succeed there, the task facing them in other Asian nations—especially China—would be far less formidable.

In both China and Japan missionaries played a pivotal role in forming the American image of each nation but, in most ways, their positions among the two peoples differed. In China their efforts provoked bitter resistance and often required government support; in Japan, after the early 1870s, missionaries encountered little overt popular hostility and did not need their government's diplomatic assistance. The apparent responsiveness of the Japanese to the Christian message led missionaries to regard them as superior to other Asian people—particularly the Chinese—and to sympathize with the dilemmas of their government. They often urged the United States to modify the humiliating treaties imposed on Japan. In China missionaries served as interpreters, consular officials, and even ministers; in Japan they never achieved such a striking position as intermediaries between the two governments. Instead, they were absorbed in the conquest of a nation. It was only at the end of the 1880s that a resurgence of Japanese nationalism forced American missionaries to understand, for the first time, the powerful cultural forces with which they would have to contend.

---

[27]Quoted in Masaya Yamamoto, "Image-Makers of Japan: A Case Study in the Impact of the American Protestant Foreign Missionary Movement, 1859-1905" (Ph.D. dissertation, Ohio State University, 1967), p. 314.

In the decades after the Civil War American trade with Japan, like the American missionary presence, grew rapidly, surpassing the China trade by 1890 and, by 1897, representing about 2 percent of the nation's total foreign commerce. Even then, America's position was weak compared to that of Great Britain. In 1863 Britain's share of Yokohama's total trade of $14 million was $11 million, while that of the United States, which stood next to Britain, was less than $1 million. As the years passed, the United States improved its relative position because of its absorption of a large share of Japanese exports (42 percent in 1880). Britain, however, stayed far ahead in the export of manufactured goods to Japan, with 53 percent of the market. The United States ranked a poor third with a mere 7 percent. Nearly every statistic reflected British commercial dominance.

Whatever the future promise of Japanese-American trade, in the nineteenth century it was much more important to Japan than to the United States. East Asia occupied a remote position on the American economic horizon. The completion of the Union Pacific Railway in 1869 did not make the United States the passage to India, for the Suez Canal provided a cheaper and shorter route for European exporters. America's China trade, which had peaked in the late 1850s, steadily receded until by 1897 it made up less than 2 percent of the nation's foreign commerce. Famous American mercantile houses in China either declined or failed. In the decades after the Civil War American businessmen, protected by a high tariff, concentrated upon the problems of domestic industrial expansion and struggled to adjust to the economy's mysterious and frightening gyrations. For most, this internal market seemed almost infinite and it did, in fact, absorb more manufactured goods than American factories could normally produce. American exports consisted largely of agricultural staples that flowed across the traditional North Atlantic trade route to the nations of Europe. Only occasionally was it necessary for the American government to take action to protect these European agricultural markets or to promote commercial relations with Latin America.

Among those few Americans concerned with foreign lands, the relative position of East Asia improved in the 1870s and 1880s. It could not, of course, compete with the Caribbean and Latin

America, where Americans fretted over control of any isthmian canal and feared European encroachments into the Western hemisphere. But involvement in Asia finally surpassed that in the eastern Mediterranean. Americans had lost their once bright hope in the Ottoman Empire and, although the Levant remained the center of missionary activity, the momentum shifted to the Orient. China and Japan became the fastest growing missionary fields. In the 1850s the expenditures of the American Board of Commissioners for Foreign Missions in East Asia amounted to only one sixth of those for the Levant; by the 1870s they were one half; and by 1890 the two areas received equal amounts. Together they accounted for more than half of the American Board's total budget.

The concern of the American government, however, seldom extended across the Pacific. It was, to be sure, deeply interested in the fate of Hawaii and Samoa and, in 1871, sanctioned a naval expedition to Korea. It responded, too, to the needs of China missionaries. But neither businessmen nor missionaries sought an active American policy in Japan, and the government continued to view events in that nation, as in the whole of East Asia, with its customary "complacent detachment."[28]

The dichotomy persisted between a passive government at home and active representatives abroad. American presidents and secretaries of state had only the vaguest impressions of Japan and saw there no sizable national interest at stake. Concerned with treaty rights, commerce, and peace, they assumed that the modernization and westernization of Japan were simultaneous processes and took a benign if aloof attitude toward Japanese territorial expansion in the 1870s and 1880s. Japan negotiated with Russia over the Kuriles and Sakhalin, sent a punitive expedition to Formosa in 1874 and, imitating Perry, opened Korea in 1876. Sino-Japanese relations became tense because of conflicting claims to the Ryūkyūs and a struggle for dominance in Korea. It was a measure of the contempt for China and the admiration of Japan that so few Americans disapproved of Japan's policy. In fact, many Americans in East Asia identified with Japan's aspirations. Minis-

---

[28]Iriye, *Across the Pacific*, p. 32.

ter DeLong believed that Japan was the key to East Asia and a "power to be welcomed as an ally and to be dreaded as a foe."[29] Fearing an alliance between China and Japan, he encouraged aggressive Japanese policies toward China, Formosa, and Korea and, in 1872, even went so far as to introduce a notorious American adventurer, General Charles LeGendre, to the Japanese government. Japan employed LeGendre as an adviser for its military operations against Formosa.

Events in Korea revealed the gap between Washington and its representatives in East Asia. After the failure of an American naval expedition in 1871, the opening of Korea became the intense personal ambition of Commodore Robert W. Shufeldt. His importunities convinced the American government to authorize another attempt in 1878 that, after prolonged effort, produced a commercial treaty 4 years later. This achievement brought an apathetic response from the American government, for it had never been seriously interested in the project. Secretary of State James G. Blaine had made this clear in instructions to Shufeldt in 1881, when he wrote that "no political or commercial interest renders such a treaty urgent."[30] Blaine agreed to another effort because of his hope that an easy success would bring prestige to the United States. But Blaine, like other American statesmen of his time, had little interest in Korea or the whole of East Asia. Throughout the 1880s, when Korea was the center of repeated crises, American missionaries and diplomats in Seoul, along with the Korean government, sought to involve the United States. But Washington successfully resisted their efforts. The United States did recognize the independence of Korea—a policy that favored Japan—but it never pondered the implications of the Sino-Japanese tension there or considered America's national interest affected by the outcome of the contest.

Americans continued to believe that their government pursued an idealistic policy toward Japan, one that functioned separately from that of the European powers. Many Americans and Japanese

---

[29] Quoted in Tyler Dennett, *Americans in Eastern Asia* (New York, 1922), p. 438.
[30] *Irid.*, p. 461.

regarded the United States as Japan's special friend. As Minister Bingham put it, "the Emperor and people of Japan look with a confiding trust to our government and people."[31] When former President Ulysses S. Grant visited Japan in 1879, he received an unprecedented welcome, including a personal call by the Emperor. Japan's material progress and westernization fascinated Grant, who warned the Japanese of the threats to their independence from the European powers and urged Japan and China to remain at peace. Events such as Grant's visit and the return of the Shimonoseki indemnity (extracted from Japan in 1863 when Chōshū fired on foreign ships in the Straits of Shimonoseki) helped to sustain the notion of a special relationship and even endowed it with a grain of truth. It was, however, largely a myth, for the two nations were so remote from one another that no real clash of interests had occurred to strain the friendship and test the intentions of statesmen on either side of the Pacific.

During the 1870s and 1880s treaty revision proved to be the major test of American goodwill. For over two decades it was the central issue between the powers and Japan, one filled with exceptional difficulties because changes in extraterritorial rights or the tariff required unanimity among the powers. The Japanese came to believe that the treaties were a stigma of inequality, a national humiliation implying racial inferiority. By the late 1880s the unequal treaties had become an explosive issue in Japanese politics.

Japan's efforts to alter the unequal treaties began in 1871. Initially the powers, particularly Great Britain, were reluctant to make concessions, for Japan's legal system was still in the early stages of westernization and remained an unformed and untested instrument. Moreover, the powers wished to trade concessions on extraterritoriality for the complete opening of Japan to commerce and travel. The United States shared these attitudes, although it had always been more moderate in its application of its own extraterritorial privileges. Secretary of State Fish feared that a separate settlement might imperil equality of commercial oppor-

---

[31]*Papers Relating to the Foreign Relations of the United States: 1879* (Washington, D. C., 1879), p. 685.

tunity and the security of American citizens in Japan. After Fish left office, the influence of the American minister, John A. Bingham, increased. Like many other Americans, Bingham was impressed by Japan's dazzling progress and disturbed by the manifest inequality of the treaty system. He resisted instructions calling for joint action with the other powers and argued for an independent American course. Washington partly accepted his views when, in 1878, it signed a separate tariff convention with Japan. Although the new convention granted Japan tariff autonomy, it was to take effect only when other nations concurred. This would not happen for many years.

During the 1880s the United States drifted back toward a policy of cooperation with the powers, whose reluctance to make concessions on extraterritoriality gradually weakened. At a treaty revision conference in 1882 most were willing to accept a Japanese proposal for a transitional period in which foreign judges would participate in a system of mixed courts. Britain's adamant opposition killed this proposal but, by 1886, when another conference convened, the British were more moderate. The Japanese, however, would no longer settle for their previous terms, and the conference broke down. Japan returned to a policy of separate negotiations that, for a time, seemed certain to succeed. In 1889 the United States and Germany signed treaties granting tariff autonomy and phasing out extraterritorial rights on terms more favorable to Japan. Just as the other powers were about to follow, popular opposition in Japan split the cabinet and again prevented a settlement.

As it turned out, this development suited the United States. In 1889 a new American minister, John Franklin Swift, arrived in Japan. A native of California, Swift had strong prejudices against Orientals and, during the 1880s, had been actively involved in efforts to limit Chinese immigration. He found Japan backward, its judicial system crude, and its people unprepared for the sudden influx of foreigners that the new treaties would bring. The treaty of 1889, Swift argued, was seriously flawed, particularly because it would open the door to Japanese immigration. Apparently Swift's objections convinced James G. Blaine, the Secretary of State in the Harrison administration, that better terms must be won before a treaty could be submitted to the Senate. When Britain signed a treaty in 1894 ending extraterritoriality, the United States soon followed with a similar agreement. But the American government now included a clause that gave it the power to regulate Japanese immigration.

Swift's attitudes were not typical of those American ministers who preceded or followed him. But they did suggest that an era of untroubled relations was drawing to a close. In the final decade of the nineteenth century the climate of international relations changed and, in the process, the distance between Japan and the United States lessened, producing new fears and tensions in each nation.

CHAPTER II

The First Confrontation

As the nineteenth century drew to a close, some Americans reassessed the position of their nation in world affairs. Influenced by the ideological currents of European imperialism and by the spread of feverish great power rivalries in distant areas of the globe, those concerned with foreign policy pondered the implications of these new thoughts and stirring events. In the 1880s expansionists such as John Fiske and Josiah Strong had propagated the mystique of Anglo-Saxonism and had heralded the benevolent spread of an Anglo-Saxon world order. They had seen the world moving toward a new level of spiritual awareness and peaceful interdependence. As the turn of the century neared, however, the optimism of Fiske and Strong gave way to a darker and more doubtful vision of the future of Western civilization. Brooks Adams and Alfred Thayer Mahan portrayed a Western world at bay, in danger of losing its momentum and facing the staggering task of assimilating millions of semicivilized peoples who inhabited the waste spaces of the globe. Much of the earlier complacency about the essential unity of mankind vanished, to be replaced by new concepts of fixed, biologically determined racial categories and by a new awareness of racial and cultural diversity. Racist assumptions brought worries over the intermingling of superior and inferior peoples and focused attention on the need to maintain the strength of the West. They encouraged the development of an acute historical consciousness, of a conviction that Western civilization had reached a critical juncture and that the United States, because of its great power, must play a major role in resolving the dilemma.

During the 1890s East Asia loomed ever larger in the minds of Americans. Earlier it had been only an abstraction; now it seemed much closer and somewhat threatening. Convinced that the world was growing smaller, Americans also became more aware of the difficulties of transplanting Western culture to the Orient and perceived the possibility of an industrialized, hostile Asia turning against the West. As Mahan observed, "civilizations on different planes of material prosperity and progress, with different spiritual ideals, and with very different political capacities, are fast closing together." Mahan believed that the world stood at the beginning of a period that would decide the dominance of Eastern or Western civilization. "The great task now before the world of civilized Christianity," he wrote, " . . . is to receive into its own bosom and raise to its own ideals those ancient and different civilizations by which it is surrounded and outnumbered."[1]

Missionary activity provides one index of the growing popular involvement in East Asia. The 1890s brought a new sense of urgency among American missionaries. In 1888 the Student Volunteers for Foreign Missions was organized to channel the energies of young people into the Christian crusade. Much of this effort was directed toward East Asia, particularly China. The number of missionaries there doubled during the decade as churchmen sought to guide China along the paths of democracy and Christianity.

American churches remained fascinated with Japan, but the 1890s proved to be a discouraging decade. The exciting momentum of the Christian movement there flagged as Christianity entered a period of decline in the face of a mounting tide of nationalism. Nevertheless, American missionaries in Japan still considered that nation pivotal for the future of Christianity in the Orient and for the creation of a harmonious relationship between East and West. A Christianized, modernized Japan would serve as a model for its less advanced neighbors and perhaps take the lead in the conversion of the whole of East Asia. As the most developed nation in that region, Japan must also be the most Christian. Whatever the current setbacks, this belief endowed missionary activities there with a peculiar importance. But the discrepancy

---

[1] Alfred Thayer Mahan, *The Interest of America in Sea Power, Present and Future* (Boston, 1897), pp. 243, 263.

between Japan's modernization and Christianization was puzzling. Missionaries could only conclude that Japan had somehow accepted the values of Western civilization without accepting its more formal religious beliefs.

China also proved a powerful magnet for some sectors of the American business community. In 1895 a group of American financiers formed the American China Development Company to seek investment opportunities there, and 3 years later businessmen and others interested in the China market formed a pressure group, the American Asiatic Association. One railway builder, James J. Hill, believed that the success of the Northern Pacific depended on the expansion of trade with Asia. Business journals, however, displayed no great concern with the Japanese market, although trade with Japan continued to exceed that with China and to grow more rapidly. Instead, a handful of businessmen began to fear that rapid industrialization would allow the Japanese to compete with Western goods on the Asian mainland.

The implications of this new awareness of East Asia were unclear for American policymakers, as was the widespread concern over falling prices and economic depression. The depression produced confusion among economists and businessmen, who could reach no consensus on a remedy. Those who urged economic expansion abroad were only one of many groups. Moreover, even a turn toward foreign markets did not necessarily imply an aggressive foreign policy, for American money and goods flowed in a separate stream, often unconnected with government policy. In the late nineteenth and early twentieth centuries American foreign trade grew rapidly, as did direct and indirect investment in other lands. Europe took most American exports although, with the gradual shift from agricultural to manufactured goods, the percentage absorbed by Europe gradually declined. Many of the largest American corporations became multinational enterprises whose leaders thought in international terms. These firms, however, were interested in industrialized or industrializing nations, where there were markets for their products. Or, if they were engaged in the extraction of raw materials, they mostly did so in nearby regions. Their activities focused on Western Europe, Canada, and Mexico and, to a lesser extent, on other portions of

Latin America. The Orient was a distant and relatively unknown area; those manufacturing firms that did invest there did so in Japan, not China.

Government leaders always extolled economic expansion abroad, but felt little need to act on their public statements. They did, to be sure, seek to protect markets for American agricultural goods in Europe and to assist corporations that had invested in unstable, backward areas—especially the Caribbean. Generally, however, they had little inclination to intervene and remained passive spectators of the growing involvement of the American economy in the world.

In the 1890s, the very vagueness of expansionist ideology lessened its impact on foreign policy. Talk of the need for foreign markets, or of expanding fields of Anglo-Saxon civilization or Protestantism, pointed in no obvious direction. Only a few expansionist spokesmen proposed a concrete agenda. But those directing American foreign policy were not prepared to listen. The new currents of thought had largely passed them by; their vision of America's relation to the world was traditional, unaffected by the anxiety over the decline of Western civilization or the impending conflict of races. The Monroe Doctrine, the tradition of neutrality, and the concept of America as the symbol of democracy and freedom—these were the principles on which they relied. Knowing little about the world around them, foreign events appeared as fragmented, isolated incidents. Foreign policy was episodic; only a minuscule State Department bureaucracy existed to transfer the scattered ideas of one administration to the next. Even if presidents had wished to act, they lacked the military, naval, and diplomatic establishments that would have allowed them to proceed with confidence.

Leaders in the 1890s were, however, aware of the growth of American industrial power and of an erratic public concern with foreign issues. Nor could they shut out the clamor of those with a special interest in foreign policy. When, at times, foreign issues touched their sense of patriotism or principle or political expediency, they would move with surprising aggressiveness. In general the restiveness of the public, its unpredictability and irrationality, frightened them, as did the domestic currents of the decade. Like

so many Americans, they were bewildered by the massive alterations in the structure of their society. The speed and magnitude
of social change outpaced the ability of men to comprehend it and,
combined with the violence of the nineties, produced a sense of
alarm and desperation, a spreading crisis psychology. All of these
troubling changes turned statesmen inward, not outward, depriv-
ing them of the ability to innovate in foreign or domestic policy.

Faced with uncertain times, men in power often clung to old
truths. When they looked beyond America's shores, they did so
largely in a defensive way, for they had no concept of the national
interest that pointed to a significant American stake in any area of
the world outside of the Western hemisphere or the Eastern Pacific. They watched from afar as the European powers, deadlocked
on the continent, turned their energies toward areas of the globe
such as Africa, Central Asia, the Middle East and, later in the
decade, East Asia. But they feared European expansion into the
Western hemisphere and the decline of American influence there.
It is significant that the major crises of the decade involved Chile,
Cuba, Hawaii, and Venezuela. Although some Americans dwelled
on the implications of the encounter between East and West, this
confrontation of two diverse civilizations seemed remote to those
in power. Only toward the end of the decade did such concerns
begin to have a noticeable impact on American foreign policy.

II

Japan's oligarchs shared none of the detachment that American
leaders felt toward world events. Still economically and militarily
weak, threatened by growing imperialist rivalries, they felt profoundly insecure, acutely conscious of Japan's unique position in
East Asia. Uncertainty and fear increased the sensitivity of Japan's
rulers and people to the new trends in international thought and
politics. Impressed with the example of Western nations, by the
1890s Japan had developed a dynamic expansionism. One strain
was directed toward the Asiatic mainland and the establishment
of predominance in Korea and spheres of influence in China. Japan's victory in the Sino-Japanese War launched the nation on the
road to formal empire with the acquisition of Taiwan and greater
influence in Korea. It nourished dreams of a far larger role on the

continent of Asia and strengthened a second strain of expansionism, one that emphasized the flow of emigrants and trade across the Pacific. It seemed essential for a vigorous, growing nation to spread its people and culture over a wide area of the globe. Peaceful expansionism would relieve population pressures and enrich the nation through the creation of Japanese colonies abroad. The Japanese believed that, unlike the Chinese, their settlers would be welcomed in California, Latin America, and the islands of the Pacific. Japanese expansionist literature dwelled on California's abundance and mild climate. Expansion on the continent of Asia was essential for national security, but the American Pacific Coast seemed far more promising as an area to settle. Whatever its geographic focus, the Japanese viewed expansion as a attribute of national greatness.

III

Most Americans had no objection to Japanese expansion on the Asiatic continent, even if it was at the expense of China. When tension over Korea led to war between China and Japan in 1894, Americans identified so strongly with Japan that some bitterly criticized their government's initial coolness toward Japan's cause. The Cleveland administration pursued a traditional policy of noninvolvement, avoiding cooperation with the other powers and offering good offices only if both belligerents accepted. Neither President Grover Cleveland nor Secretary of State Walter Q. Gresham believed that the struggle affected any vital American interest.

Japan's unexpectedly decisive triumph only increased American admiration and seemed to mark another stage in the new Asian power's remarkable progress. Secretary of the Navy Hilary A. Herbert announced that "Japan has leaped, almost at one bound, to a place among the great nations of the earth,"[2] while the American Minister to China, Charles Denby, expressed the feelings of many Americans when he wrote that "Japan is now doing for

---

[2]Quoted in William L. Neumann, *America Encounters Japan: From Perry to MacArthur* (Baltimore, 1963), p. 106.

China what the United States did for Japan. She has learnt western civilization and she is forcing it on her unwieldy neighbor. The only hope in the world for China is to take the lesson, rude as it is, to heart."[3]

Inevitably, however, the interests of the two expanding nations were bound to clash. In 1897 the first serious Japanese-American crisis erupted over Hawaii. The American stake in Hawaii had gradually deepened over the course of the nineteenth century and, with the Hawaiian Revolution of January 1893, it was natural that many Americans should approve of annexation. Hawaii seemed a vital p\rt of the nation's Pacific sphere of influence and an important waystation to the markets of the Orient. Annexation failed in 1893, for President Cleveland disapproved of the revolutionaries' methods and was immune to imperialistic rhetoric, with its emphasis on race and civilization and its calls for territorial expansion. He stood for an older tradition that stressed the peaceful, unobstrusive growth of America's moral and economic influence.

Nevertheless, American expansionists retained a strong interest in the fate of the new Hawaiian Republic, one that was fed by the dilemma of its white leaders. In the mid-1880s their need for labor on the sugar plantations had led them to encourage Japanese immigration and, by the middle of the 1890s, they ruled uneasily over a polyglot nation with an ominously large Japanese population. Japan's victory in the Sino-Japanese War increased their fear of being overwhelmed by a confident and powerful Asian nation. In early 1897 they moved to halt the growth of Japan's influence by turning back its emigrants. The Japanese government reacted sharply, dispatching a warship and a strong note of protest. Hawaii was a crucial test of Japan's ability to expand peacefully into the Pacific; Japan's psychological commitment there ran far beyond its material interests.

Hawaii also had a larger meaning for American imperialists, who viewed annexation as a symbol of the nation's determination to expand into the Pacific. They displayed a remarkable sensitivity

---

[3]Quoted in Payson J. Treat, *Diplomatic Relations Between the United States and Japan, 1853-1905,* 3 vols. (Stanford, 1932-1938), II, p. 525.

to the Japanese threat to Hawaii; Assistant Secretary of the Navy Theodore Roosevelt wanted the American navy to seize the islands immediately. In May 1897 he asked the Naval War College to plan for a conflict that involved the defense of Hawaii against Japan and the liberation of Cuba from Spanish rule. Although the navy did not expect war, it instructed the commander of the American cruiser in Pearl Harbor to proclaim a provisional protectorate if Japan seemed likely to employ force. Concern over Japan's intentions reached all the way to President William McKinley and was a significant although not a determining factor in his decision to submit a treaty of annexation to the Senate in June 1897.

Japan sought to block American annexation by drawing the European powers into a joint protest. When this move failed, Japan informed the United States that annexation would upset the status quo in the Pacific and endanger Japanese rights in Hawaii. Japan was unwilling, however, to go beyond this initial protest. After receiving American assurances that the United States would respect Japanese interests in Hawaii, Japan withdrew its note and reconciled itself to the inevitability of American annexation. The alarm in Washington quickly passed, but it left behind a new awareness of Japan's power and a small but potent residue of fear over a future encounter between Japanese and American expansionism in the Pacific.

Momentous events soon overshadowed the brief crisis over Hawaii. The United States emerged from the Spanish-American War with a new colonial empire, the most distant portion of which was the Philippines. The Japanese government reacted cautiously to America's territorial advance into East Asia. Its leaders had hoped for no change in the status of the Philippines; if change must occur, they preferred American control over that of any other nation. Although American expansion into the Philippines blocked off one more area for Japan's empire, the Japanese government had no taste for another challenge to the United States. With the breakup of China imminent, Japan needed American cooperation to prevent the disintegration of that nation. Japan welcomed the Open Door Notes of September 1899, along with American participation in the international expedition that defeated the Boxers and freed the foreign community in Peking in 1900. But the extension of American power into East Asia had some ominous implications. Although the Open Door Notes were in part an expression of the domestic needs of the McKinley administration, they also signified a belief that the United States was an Asian power with a special role to play in that region.

By the turn of the century Americans had developed a new level of concern over events in East Asia. The acquisition of Hawaii and the Philippines, the Open Door Notes, and the dramatic relief of the legations in Peking temporarily broadened the foreign policy public and gave East Asia a more central position in the works of expansionist thinkers. In *Expansion Under New World Conditions* (1900) Josiah Strong heralded the enlarged sense of destiny with which the American people had emerged from the war and predicted that the Pacific would be the Mediterranean of the twentieth century. There the struggle for dominance would focus on China, where the Anglo-Saxon powers, led by the United States, would confront the encroachments of the Slavs, led by Russia. Other thoughtful observers of American foreign policy shared this concern for Russian expansion on the mainland of Asia. In *The Problem of Asia* (1900) Alfred Thayer Mahan portrayed a vast drama in which Russia, the dominant land power, was moving on two flanks—through Central Asia and North China—toward the vital Yangtze Valley. The sea powers—including Japan—must join hands to prevent the Russian absorption of China, for the fate of China would determine the future of Western civilization.

In September 1901 these expansionist thinkers applauded Theodore Roosevelt's accession to the presidency. Roosevelt was one of their own, a close student of American and British imperialist thought and a forceful advocate of America's responsibility to the world. He fused unusual intellectual gifts with an ability to act. Here was a man who could lead the nation toward its new destiny.

But the early years of the century brought a rapid change in the nation's mood. There had never been a solid imperialist consensus in the United States; circumstances more than ideology explain the acquisition of Hawaii and the Philippines. After 1900 the glamor of imperialism faded rapidly both in Europe and America. The Boer War shook the certitudes of even British imperialists, and the bitter struggle to suppress the Philippine insurrection proved a dismal sequel to the heroic moments of the Spanish-American War. However much Roosevelt might admire the achievements of Great Britain and its proconsuls, imperialism in America was placed on the defensive. The question was not one of extending America's colonial empire, but of simply retaining and properly governing what had already been acquired.

The election of 1896, the ebbing of populism, the Spanish-American War and, above all, the return of prosperity, brought an end to the acute anxieties of the 1890s. The restoration of confidence encouraged the growth of a more moderate kind of reformism, as did the emergence of a new middle class, one that had achieved a secure professional identity and was now confidently prepared to project its models of professionalization and bureaucratization onto a disordered, chaotic society and ultimately onto the world itself. This new middle class had no taste for the global conflicts of the American geopoliticians; instead it envisaged a harmonious world order from which wasteful conflict would be banished. In fact, its rise coincided with and undoubtedly reinforced the growth of a powerful domestic peace movement. After the turn of the century more and more Americans became convinced of the decency of modern, civilized man and of the steady improvement of the world. As civilization developed, war would become less likely, it seemed, because the democratization of societies would increase the influence of the people. As backward areas were gradually assimilated into the mainstream of Western civilization, the primary source of international conflict would disappear. Most men agreed about the futility of war among civilized powers and discerned a worldwide trend toward interdependence and cooperation. They placed less emphasis on the role of force and more on a coalescence of mankind into one pacific, international community.

The new power and prestige of the peace movement revealed the concern of many Americans about international affairs. While they did not believe events in Europe could imperil the nation's security, they did feel that the United States must cooperate more with other nations in the quest for peace. Their concept of greater international involvement, however, did not include entanglement in the power politics of Europe but, instead, the purification of the world through the spread of American institutions and principles, particularly those of a legal or judicial character. Thus, prominent Americans emphasized the promise of arbitration, the Hague conferences, and the creation of a world court. The peace movement was an expression of American nationalism and ethnocentrism, not an indication that the American people would actively participate in world politics.

The assumptions of peace advocates alarmed power-oriented thinkers. In general these men perceived the stake of the United States in the stability of the world and ardently hoped that America would throw its weight into the struggle to preserve and expand the influence of Western civilization. But they mixed valid insight with dubious abstractions and misleading historical analogies. "The fantasies of power," Robert H. Wiebe writes, "with nations as tokens on a worldwide board, led most of them to dream . . . about shadowy thrusts and counterthrusts."[4] Many of their speculations bordered on the absurd. Brooks Adams offered as proof of the decay of England the lack of frontal attacks by British troops during the Boer War and argued that control of the mineral wealth of North China was crucial for the continuing dominance of the Anglo-Saxon powers. Mahan feared that Oriental hordes would overwhelm Western civilization, just as the barbarians had once overwhelmed the Roman Empire. Those who belonged to this circle reveled in a rich, imaginative life full of grand schemes and hypothetical wars.

Theodore Roosevelt participated vigorously in these fantasies; he played the game of world strategist with a feverish zest. He filled his correspondence with sweeping comments on the interplay of nations and civilizations and often indulged in alarming conversations with Baron Hermann Speck von Sternberg, the German Ambassador to America from 1903 to 1908. Historians have often, however, taken Roosevelt's theorizing too seriously, forgetting that he occupied a position of political power that encouraged him to confront the realities of domestic and international politics. The speculations of the American geopoliticians were, after all, far

---

[4]Robert H. Wiebe, *The Search for Order, 1877-1920* (New York, 1967), p. 235.

removed from the intense, immediate atmosphere of the presidency. Upon reading *The Problem of Asia,* Roosevelt wrote Mahan that, while he agreed with his argument, "I do not have to tell you, with your wide and profound historical research that while something can be done by public men in leading the people, they cannot lead them much further than public opinion has prepared the way."[5] The public was not ready for a major initiative in East Asia; during the early years of his presidency, Roosevelt found himself preoccupied with problems closer to home. He had to grapple with the Alaskan boundary dispute, secure a route for an isthmian canal, and define the nature of American hegemony in the Caribbean. Most important, Roosevelt had to win control of his own party, establish his leadership with the American people, and achieve reelection in 1904. He had neither the energy nor the inclination for adventures in East Asia.

Roosevelt did wish, however, to throw the full weight of the United States into the maintenance of the existing European balance of power. Whatever impression one might derive from his letters to Adams, Mahan, and others, it was the activities of the great European powers that absorbed his attention. But even where Europe was involved, the President discovered that he could only dabble in world affairs, for domestic restraints confined the United States to a minor role outside of the Western hemisphere. The tension between Roosevelt's ambitions and the public's apathy produced frustrations that found their outlet in fantasies that had little relation to the policies he actually pursued.

East Asia had never really engaged the President's attention. Roosevelt entered office with little knowledge of that area and little inclination to enlarge it. Sharing the assumptions of Secretary of State John Hay, he left East Asian policy in Hay's control. Neither man saw any connection between events there and American security. China was a weak and formless nation, a minor market for American goods, and a nation whose fate, in the foreseeable future, seemed far removed from American national inter-

---

[5]Elting E. Morison, ed., *The Letters of Theodore Roosevelt,* 8 vols. (Cambridge, Mass., 1951-1954), III, p. 23.

ests. Roosevelt and Hay had no intention of defending its integrity against Russian encroachments. In fact, they were willing to recognize Russia's special position in Manchuria if only that nation would withdraw its troops and open Manchurian treaty ports to trade. Russia's failure to meet these terms brought diplomatic protests, but never the suggestion that the United States would seriously press them. The President and Secretary of State eluded British and Japanese attempts to draw the United States into an anti-Russian coalition. For a time Roosevelt toyed with a stronger policy and talked of "going to an extreme" with Russia, but this was bluster.[6] He believed that it was Japan's task to contain Russian expansion on the Asiatic mainland and watched with fascination as the two empires drifted toward war.

IV

Japan had long lived in the shadow of Russian power in East Asia and had, since the mid-1890s, considered Russia the major threat to its vital interests. Japanese leaders agreed that a free hand in Korea was essential for the nation's security and insisted that Russia recognize Japan's hegemony there. Some felt that the Russian occupation of Manchuria undermined Japan's special position in Korea and hoped to place limits on the Russian sphere of influence in Southern Manchuria. The negotiation of the Anglo-Japanese Alliance in 1902—neutralizing France in the event of a Russo-Japanese War—gave Japan's rulers an opportunity, through war if necessary, to protect the nation's security needs on the continent of Asia.

In Meiji Japan the decision-making process in foreign policy involved fewer groups than in domestic policy. The Meiji Constitution had provided an important if limited role for the public in domestic affairs, where decisions were reached through bargaining among the various elites—the genro, the civil bureaucracy, the military services, the political parties and, to a lesser extent, the great business combines, or zaibatsu. But the Diet and political parties were excluded from foreign policy decisions. There the

---

[6] *Ibid., III,* p. 520.

genro or elder statesmen and their allies in the civilian and military bureaucracies ruled supreme. The genro, governing in the name of the Emperor, had guided the development of Meiji Japan into the twentieth century. They brought unity out of diversity, creating the consensus among the various elites that was essential for continued progress.

Despite differences over the relationship between the government and the political parties, the genro shared important attitudes. As young men they had lived through the chaos surrounding the Meiji Restoration, and they vividly remembered the turmoil of those years. Although pleased with Japan's great advance, they were sharply aware of its weakness and cautious and realistic in their pursuit of foreign policy objectives. By the early years of the new century, however, the genro had become old men, and their hold on national politics had imperceptibly loosened. A symbolic turning point came in 1901 when Yamagata Aritomo's protégé, Katsura Tarō, formed the government that was to lead Japan into war against Russia. In the future few elder statesmen would head cabinets; they had largely retired from active politics. Although Katsura and his Foreign Minister, Komura Jutarō, conferred with the genro closely on domestic and foreign matters, they represented a second generation of oligarchic leadership with somewhat different views. Younger and more optimistic, without the rich personal experience of their elders, they were more impressed with Japan's power and more confident and aggressive in their foreign policy. Katsura and Komura were less adverse to a showdown with Russia and less willing to make concessions to Russia in Manchuria. In late 1903 the genro insisted on more moderate Japanese terms, but Russian intransigence ended all hope for a diplomatic settlement and united Japan's leadership behind the decision for war.

The American people overwhelmingly approved Japan's challenge of Russia. Prior to 1905, the fears of a confrontation between East and West had not taken hold of the popular imagination. Most Americans still regarded Japan as an extraordinary protégé of the West and believed that Japan, not Russia, was advancing the cause of Western civilization in East Asia. Theodore Roosevelt caught the popular mood when he wrote that "Japan is playing our game."[7] American missionaries in Japan believed that a Japanese victory would ensure an open door for Christian enterprise on the Asiatic continent.

The Japanese government did not anticipate such strong support in the United States nor did it expect substantial loans from American financiers. Originally it feared possible American sympathy for Russia and dispatched a special envoy, Kaneko Kentarō, to combat the idea of a yellow peril. Kaneko soon discovered that the President—far from being hostile to Japan—was intensely sympathetic and eager to play a part in the settlement of the conflict. Initially Japan put Roosevelt off but, after the battle of Mukden in March 1905, most Japanese military and civilian leaders desired peace. They had never wanted a long war and now realized that they had underestimated Russian power. By the spring of 1905 Japan's military and financial position was critical, although the government concealed the nation's weakness from the public and all but a few of the party politicians. The government-controlled press reported one great victory after another and portrayed a Russia in turmoil, on the edge of disintegration. These dazzling triumphs over Japan's traditional enemy elated the masses, helped them to endure the very real sacrifices of the war, and encouraged them to form exaggerated expectations of the postwar settlement.

Within the oligarchy there were different opinions about peace making. The leaders of the younger generation of decision makers —Katsura and Komura—were more reluctant than their elders to initiate peace moves and hoped for tougher terms. These differences were only partly resolved when, in May 1905, Japan decided to seek peace and turned to Roosevelt as the neutral leader who could bring the two belligerents together.

The President was eager to oblige. Before the war began, Roosevelt had attempted to use his good offices to avoid a conflict. As the struggle progressed, he made no secret of his desire to help and worked to build the foundations for effective action at a later date. He kept in close contact with Japanese representatives and gave

---

[7]Morison, *The Letters of Theodore Roosevelt,* IV, p. 724.

profuse assurances of his friendship for Japan. The yellow peril, he told Kaneko, was nothing more than a "crafty fabrication," and he confided that he had "come to love Japan and the Japanese."[8] Moreover, Roosevelt worried about German involvement and expressed his determination to prevent any intervention that would deprive Japan of the fruits of victory. He also advised the Japanese on the terms of a settlement and talked expansively of Japan's great future in East Asia, comparing Japan's position in the Yellow Sea to that of the United States in the Caribbean. Japan would play the major role in leading China toward a higher level of civilization. Roosevelt had no serious reservations even about Japan's more extreme demands for an indemnity and cession of Sakhalin Island; he counseled moderation only when it seemed that the peace negotiations at Portsmouth, New Hampshire in August 1905 would fail.

V

Historians have often speculated on the reasons for Roosevelt's good offices. They have concluded that he wished to end a major war between two civilized powers and that, more importantly, he took to heart the theories of American geopoliticians concerning the critical importance of China. Determined to keep China open to the influence of the Anglo-Saxon powers, he acted to prevent either Japan or Russia from winning a decisive victory and to preserve a balance of power on the Asiatic mainland.

Roosevelt's letters are, to be sure, full of references to the need for maintaining tension between Japan and Russia. If such, however, was his motive for interceding, it raises certain puzzling questions. It is by no means clear why Roosevelt would have exerted himself to maintain balanced antagonisms on the Asiatic mainland when neither he nor his chief adviser believed that the nation had any significant interests there. The whole course of the American-East Asian policy prior to 1905 indicated that Roosevelt and Hay felt the mainland of Asia was extremely remote from the

---

[8]Quoted in Hikomatsu Kamikawa, ed., *Japan-American Diplomatic Relations in the Meiji-Taisho Era* (Tokyo, 1958), p. 207.

needs of American security. In fact, during the war Roosevelt repeatedly encouraged Japan's continental ambitions, urging Japanese hegemony in Korea and readily accepting Japan's demands for the cession of Russian rights on the Liaotung Peninsula and for a sphere of influence in Southern Manchuria. He had scant respect for Chinese sovereignty there and obviously expected it to be no more than nominal. At times Roosevelt seemed to envisage a greater role for Japan in China than even Japanese leaders were prepared to accept.

The President encouraged Japanese continentalism in an effort to limit Japanese ambitions in the Pacific. The real danger of conflict between the two nations, he believed, would not come from Japanese expansion onto the continent of Asia, which involved only a minor change in the status quo, but from racial and cultural differences, exacerbated by Japanese immigration to Hawaii and the United States. Roosevelt hoped to distract Japan, to turn its expansive energies in a direction that would involve little chance of tension with the United States. Pro-Japanese good offices were one way to establish a deep and lasting cordiality between the two nations; they also reflected Roosevelt's irresistible impulse to play a dramatic role on the world stage. Normally his ruthless realism held this impulse in check. During the Russo-Japanese War, however, those inner barriers to quixotic adventures weakened because action made some sense as a means of fulfilling Roosevelt's strategy for Japanese-American amity.

In 1905 the maintenance of cordial relations between the two nations was very much on Roosevelt's mind. He approved the renewal of the Anglo-Japanese Alliance and sent his Secretary of War, William Howard Taft, to Japan to engage in friendly discussion with Prime Minister Katsura. This exchange of views confirmed Japan's recognition of American hegemony in the Philippines and American recognition of Japan's predominance in Korea, and brought a pledge of American cooperation with Great Britain and Japan in East Asia.

Roosevelt also sought to raise the status of American representatives in Tokyo, agreeing to an exchange of ambassadors in the autumn of 1905 and seeking to find a prominent American to fill the post. Between 1892 and 1905, four men of moderate accomplishment had served as minister to Japan: Frank L. Coombs, a California lawyer and politician; Edwin Dun, an agricultural adviser to the Japanese government in Hokkaidō and secretary of the American Legation; Alfred E. Buck, an Alabama businessman and Republican party stalwart; and Lloyd C. Griscom, the son of a well-connected Philadelphia shipping magnate whom Roosevelt regarded as one of the rising stars of the foreign service. Upon leaving Japan in 1905, Griscom went to Brazil and concluded his career as American Ambassador to Italy. Hoping to replace Griscom with a person of great eminence, Roosevelt offered the ambassadorship to Joseph H. Choate, one of the leading American lawyers of his generation and a former ambassador to Great Britain. Choate declined the position and Roosevelt had to turn to a man of lesser stature. He chose Luke E. Wright, a Tennessee Democrat who had bolted his party in 1896 to support McKinley and who later became Governor-General of the Philippines. After Wright's brief tenure, Roosevelt shifted a Michigan lawyer, Thomas J. O'Brien, from Denmark to Japan. Throughout the Roosevelt years, the Japanese embassy remained in competent hands, but it never achieved the status of the missions to the great European powers or drew men as distinguished as those who went to China.

No doubt Roosevelt took so many steps to cement Japanese-American friendship because, like the American people, he was uneasy over the future. Japan's astonishing victory over a major European power raised the whole question of that nation's destiny to a new level of prominence. Fears of a yellow peril, previously half dormant, emerged in a virulent form. Many American war correspondents, angered by the harsh restrictions imposed by the Japanese military, returned with an anti-Japanese animus. Other Americans who directly experienced the Japanese conquerors underwent a transformation in their attitudes. "Come to Korea and see, . . . " Willard Straight wrote a friend, "the real yellow man. Not the pleasant fellow you meet at Harvard, not the very likeable men I knew in Tokyo, in the Foreign Office, but the real Jap, the kind there are pretty nearly thirty million of."[9] Japan's power in

---

[9] Quoted in Akira Iriye, *Pacific Estrangement: Japanese and American Expansion, 1897-1911* (Cambridge, Mass., 1972), p. 109.

East Asia had a profound psychological impact upon some Americans. They now saw an aggressive, heavily armed Japan, seething with a militarist spirit and rabidly hostile toward all white men, ready to unite with China in a mighty challenge to Western supremacy.

The traditional notion of the harmonious partnership between Japan and the United States remained powerful, however, and was often voiced in influential journals. Missionaries played a key role in preserving this faith in Japanese-American friendship. Despite the setbacks of the 1890s, American churches remained deeply involved with Japan. In 1905, 583 American missionaries lived there; only three other areas—Africa, China, and India—received more student volunteers. In the late 1890s some American missionaries had developed fears of Japanese chauvinism, but these passed away after the turn of the century, when a modest revival of interest in Christianity reaffirmed the missionaries' belief in Japan's responsiveness to the West. When tension between Japan and Russia arose, American missionaries had no doubts about the righteousness of Japan's cause, and later they became deeply concerned over the growing antagonism between Japan and the United States. They tried to combat the idea of a yellow peril and to convince their countrymen that there was no fundamental difference between East and West. One of the foremost American missionaries in Japan, Daniel Crosby Greene, believed that Japan ought to become the leader among Oriental nations. But it would be a calamity, he prophetically observed, if Japan "should be forced to the conviction that her interests are antagonistic to those of the West. . . . The natural trend of affairs here is toward a sympathetic unity of thought and feeling with the West. If the trend is overcome it will chiefly, if not altogether, be the fault of the West."[10]

These efforts to alter the drift of American public opinion failed.

---

[10]Quoted in Evarts Boutell Green, *A New-Englander in Japan: Daniel Crosby Greene* (Boston, 1927), p. 327.

They do, however, throw some light on the elusive and largely unstudied influence of American missionaries, who at times seem to have had a substantial impact on the public's image of Japan. They wrote articles for popular magazines, spoke frequently during their home leaves, dominated American scholarship on Japan, and corresponded with important men in government and politics. But missionaries in Japan, in contrast to those in China and the Middle East, did not form a powerful interest group, and their influence on both policymakers and the public was, after the Russo-Japanese war, extremely limited. No amount of talk, no number of articles, could relieve those inner tensions that spawned racism in America.

The President and his new Secretary of State, Elihu Root, shared some of the less extreme stereotypes of the yellow peril. Roosevelt feared that Japan "might get the 'big head' and enter into a general career of insolence and aggression." He was upset by reports from the Orient indicating that the Japanese lumped all Westerners together "as white devils inferior to themselves."[11] In his personal dealings with Japanese diplomats he sensed a cultural gap and felt uncertain of what Japan might do in the future. Despite these doubts, however, Roosevelt admired Japan's achievements as a nation, as did Root, and hoped that flattering assurances combined with astute diplomacy would keep the peace. His common sense told him that there was no tangible reason for conflict so long as Japan's expansionist thrust focused on the continent of Asia. In the summer of 1905, however, he fretted over anti-Japanese outbursts in California that could, he recognized, bring trouble between the two nations. Roosevelt felt a need to be vigilant in dealing with potentially explosive issues.

The mounting agitation in California understandably worried the President. The physical isolation of the Pacific Coast, combined with the long tradition of anti-Chinese feeling, made Americans there particularly sensitive to changes in Japan's world position. Although only a handful of Japanese had settled in California by the early 1890s, the concern was great enough to influ-

---

[11]Morison, *The Letters of Theodore Roosevelt*, IV, pp. 830, 1085-86.

ence Japanese-American negotiations over treaty revision. During that decade the Japanese government had attempted to restrict the flow of laborers to the Pacific Coast and, after Californians staged their first significant anti-Japanese protest in 1900, Japan further tightened its regulations. These restrictions were, however, only partly effective in controlling even the direct flow of laborers from Japan to the continental United States, and they left untouched the primary source of Japanese immigrants, Hawaii. Large numbers of Japanese laborers arrived there yearly and some moved on to the American Pacific Coast. In 1904 about 15,000 Japanese entered the United States. Californians feared a postwar influx of Japanese that would bring frightening social problems and further weaken the fragile cohesion of their society. Unlike the Chinese, Japanese immigrants were aggressive and backed by a powerful, victorious government. All of these considerations gave a new impetus to the anti-Japanese movement, particularly in San Francisco, where Japanese newcomers concentrated. There the municipal government, dominated by a Union-Labor Party, had much to gain by exploiting anti-Japanese feeling. It did so on October 11, 1906, when the Board of Education segregated Japanese children in the city's primary schools.

VI

The Japanese government and people were ill-prepared to cope with this striking example of American hostility. The Russo-Japanese War had brought them a continental empire and strengthened the people's feeling that their nation was a model for the rest of Asia. It had also released new energies for peaceful expansion throughout the Pacific. Despite the attractions of Japan's new Manchurian sphere, the interest in emigration to Hawaii and the American Pacific Coast remained high. Many Japanese believed that movement into these areas would prove that the peoples of the East and the West could live peacefully together. They could not close the gap between their benign image of America and the harsh reality of the racist feeling there.

Japan's oligarchs, primarily concerned with continental expansion, were more flexible in dealing with the hostility in America. They drew a fine line between the spread of commerce and of people and were unwilling to force the latter on the United States. Nonetheless, they found it difficult to grasp the depth of anti-Japanese sentiment in California and were slow to reassess their assumptions about Japanese-American relations. They were also conscious of Japan's new prestige among the Western powers and determined to protect it. Initially it seemed that only a handful of extremists were behind the agitation in California and that the Roosevelt administration could easily suppress them. Japan's leaders had taken Roosevelt's many assurances of friendship and admiration at face value and had no idea of the President's ambivalence toward Japan. In short, they assumed that Roosevelt would act decisively to right the wrong inflicted on Japanese school children in San Francisco.

It is only with this context in mind that one can understand the sharp protest delivered through Ambassador Aoki Shūzō in late October 1906. Japan contended that school segregation was a violation of the Japanese-American treaty of 1894 and warned that "the hostile demonstration in San Francisco has produced among all classes of people in Japan a feeling of profound disappointment and sorrow. Happily that feeling up to this time is unmixed with any suggestion of retaliation because it is firmly believed that the evil will be speedily removed."[12]

VII

The Japanese government had no intention of precipitating a serious crisis with the United States. It did not view Japanese and American interests as clashing on the Asiatic continent or in the Pacific and counted on American friendship in a future struggle with Russia. But Washington viewed the Japanese protest from a much different perspective. The President feared that racial discrimination in California was precisely the kind of issue that might have explosive repercussions in Japan. His views were reflected in a memorandum by Root, who described the Japanese as a "proud, sensitive, warlike" people who were so "ready for war" that they

---

[12]Quoted in Charles E. Neu, *An Uncertain Friendship: Theodore Roosevelt and Japan, 1906-1909* (Cambridge, Mass., 1967), p. 31.

could take the Philippines Islands, the Hawaiian Islands, and "probably the Pacific Coast" from the unprepared United States. "The subject," wrote Root, "is not one of some far distant, possible evil, but is an immediate and present danger to be considered and averted now, today."[13]

Both the President and the Secretary of State were determined to remove Japan's legitimate complaints about discrimination in California as quickly as possible. Initially they underestimated the scope and tenacity of anti-Japanese feeling there and did not anticipate any particular difficulty in ending San Francisco school segregation. Soon they were forced to take a more somber view. They learned that the most-favored-nation clause in the Japanese-American Treaty of 1894 would not provide an adequate basis for legal action against San Francisco officials. Moreover, reports from politicians and labor leaders in California revealed the surprising intensity of anti-Japanese emotions. The school segregation order could not be repealed until Japanese immigrants were barred from the Pacific Coast.

The President could have accepted the advice of several subordinates and asked the Congress for an amendment to the immigration laws allowing the government to prohibit the movement of laborers from Hawaii to the continental United States. This, after all, was the primary route used by the Japanese. After consulting with Root, however, he devised another strategy, the negotiation of a treaty of reciprocal exclusion in which each nation would be given the right to exclude the other's laborers. Apparently Roosevelt calculated that a treaty would serve his domestic needs better than an informal understanding combined with domestic legislation. A formal, concrete immigration agreement with Japan would increase the prestige of the President and his party in California and simplify negotiations with San Francisco authorities for repeal of the school segregation order.

Roosevelt viewed Japan's leaders as safe, sane men with whom he could deal and believed that he had credit with them on which he could not draw. But his treaty plan revealed a patronizing

---

[13]*Ibid.*, p. 35.

attitude, as did his strategy for imposing it on the Japanese government. In his December 1906 annual message Roosevelt extrava-
gently praised Japan's achievements as a nation, assuming that
such flattery would prepare the way for an unpalatable treaty. In
January 1907 Root proposed a treaty of reciprocal exclusion that
he claimed would solve the immigration problem and make congressional legislation unnecessary.

VIII

The Japanese government quickly rejected the American plan.
It was a patently unequal and humiliating arrangement, offensive
to the pride and patriotism of the oligarchy. Already opponents
were attacking the government for its timid, indecisive diplomacy
in the immigration dispute; in discussions with the United States,
the Japanese constantly emphasized the restiveness of public
opinion and the danger of a vicious outburst from the highly
nationalistic groups that had rioted against the Treaty of Portsmouth. Arguments of this sort, however, were disingenuous, for
the ruling elite felt little need to appease those who were deeply
committed to Pacific expansion. Japan's leaders had long been
bitterly criticized by various groups far from the centers of power
for their alleged weakness in handling the nation's foreign problems. But they had consistently ignored this criticism, providing
neither explanations nor justifications for the government's policies. Their duty, so they reasoned, was to pursue the nation's
interests abroad without consulting the Diet; they felt both contempt and anger toward the chauvinistic excesses of the Japanese
people, unaware of the fact that Japan's system of elitist rule
contributed to an ill-informed and volatile foreign policy public.

In January 1906 Prime Minister Katsura had transferred the
premiership to Saionji Kimmochi, the leader of the largest party
in the Diet, the Seiyūkai. Saionji had won the premiership by
faithfully supporting the Katsura ministry during the war and by
resisting pressure from the party's rank and file to oppose the
Treaty of Portsmouth. Saionji's eagerness for power overrode any
lingering responsiveness to public opinion; he entered office
pledged to continue Katsura's policies. Neither Saionji nor other
members of the oligarchy had learned much from the riots of the

previous year. They knew, of course, that the public was aroused by discriminatory acts in the United States, and they no doubt wished to avoid further trouble. But, given the oligarchy's concept of its responsibility in foreign policy, it is unlikely that any sensitivity to public opinion seriously affected its course. If a treaty of reciprocal exclusion had seemed essential, Japan's leaders would have disregarded the public's protests. It was obvious to the Japanese government, however, and to many in the American government, that such a treaty was not necessary. Japan had already suggested, as had Roosevelt's subordinates, that the administration secure congressional legislation giving it the power to prohibit the movement of Japanese laborers from Hawaii to the mainland.

IX

The initiative now lay with the United States. Roosevelt and Root, however, did not pick up the alternative plan until February 1907. The President had called the mayor of San Francisco and his board of education to Washington in early February to convince them of the urgency of the crisis and of the importance of repealing the school segregation order. He needed, however, to offer some sort of assurance that Japanese immigration would be restricted and, when the treaty plan died, he turned to the other proposal by having administration forces in the Senate attach an amendment to an immigration bill in Congress.

With the passage of this bill and the revocation of the school segregation order, the first phase of the Gentlemen's Agreement was concluded. It combined a cessation of Japanese immigration from Hawaii to the mainland with assurances from Foreign Minister Hayashi Tadasu that Japan would not, with a few minor exceptions, allow the emigration of laborers directly to the continental United States. Roosevelt and Root regarded this as only a temporary solution, but they felt they had acquired some breathing space in which to observe the arrangement. Although Californians were suspicious, most of the American press applauded the Gentlemen's Agreement as a reaffirmation of Japanese-American friendship. It looked as if the crisis with Japan had been solved painlessly, without disrupting the surface cordiality between the two nations.

In May 1907, however, Japanese-American relations again deteriorated. A street-railway strike in San Francisco created conditions that produced more violence against Japanese and their businesses, and the virtual paralysis of the city government did not offer much hope for improvement. Roosevelt sympathized with the racial sentiments of Californians and believed, as they did, that Japanese and Americans could not live together. But their reckless talk and offensive actions appalled the President and greatly deepened his concern over the future of Japanese-American relations. He still believed that Japan regarded Russia as its real enemy and that there would not be serious trouble in his own time, but he realized that his inability to eradicate dangerous incidents in California would produce continuing tension between the two nations. The possibility of a conflict with Japan, however remote, led him to shift his estimate of the prudent level of military and naval power needed by the nation. More battleships would strengthen the hand of the nation's diplomats and bring victory in the Pacific if war should come.

Developments in Europe, unrelated to Japanese-American relations, also spurred Roosevelt's determination to increase the navy. The completion in December 1906 of the H.M.S. Dreadnought—superior in size and armament to any battleship afloat—revolutionized naval construction and began a new era of naval competition between England and Germany.

During his first term Roosevelt had secured such impressive increases in naval appropriations and construction that in early 1905 he had called a halt to the further growth of the American navy. Roosevelt had already achieved so much of his original objective that he was unwilling to fight the mounting public opposition to further naval expansion. By the late spring of 1907, however, the growing crisis with Japan persuaded the President to seek four large battleships from the next Congress. He knew that the nation was more and more absorbed in the ferment of progressive reform, and that a four-battleship program would be extraordinarily difficult to obtain. With this coming struggle in mind, in early June 1907 Roosevelt decided to send the American battle fleet around the world as the most effective way to whip up American patriotism and "big navy" sentiment. He also set in motion plans to bring the army up to its authorized strength and to improve defenses in the Philippines.

The President calculated that the cruise of the fleet would serve other domestic purposes. Californians who felt neglected and defenseless would be reassured; those who regarded the administration's position as pro-Japanese would see the cruise as a bold assertion of American power in the Pacific. The Republican party would no longer suffer because of the administration's policies. Over the summer, as his suspicions of Japan deepened, Roosevelt came to view the voyage of the battle fleet as a means of impressing Japan with American power and quieting jingoes there. Whatever Roosevelt's claims in retrospect, initially he had directed the cruise toward the American instead of the Japanese people.

Roosevelt's decision to dispatch the fleet, however shrewd in terms of domestic politics, was full of risks. Such a conspicuous transfer of a large naval force into the Pacific was bound to arouse suspicions in Japan and to make future diplomatic dealings more difficult. Ambassador Aoki correctly observed that Roosevelt was "playing a dangerous game" by using the cruise to strengthen his political position in California.[14] Normally Roosevelt might have proceeded more cautiously, but the glamor of the cruise and the excitement of military and naval preparations against Japan appealed strongly to the President's imagination. This was the sort of high international politics he had always longed to direct—the alarms of war, the global strategic and diplomatic calculations. In June 1907 Roosevelt revealed his own excitement when he told a council of military and naval advisers that "if war does come after I am out of the presidency, I have decided just what sort of a regiment I shall raise of rifle men from the Rockies."[15] He could not exorcise his fascination with war. In conversations with the German ambassador he speculated on a Japanese invasion of the Pacific Coast and the crushing initial defeat the American army would suffer. But Roosevelt was convinced it would ultimately be victorious. In some deep, subconscious way the President relished

---

[14] Quoted in Neu, *An Uncertain Friendship*, p. 114.
[15] *Ibid.*, p. 105.

the crisis with Japan, which fed his half-suppressed fantasies of martial glory. While such fantasies did not have a major impact on most of his policies, they seem to have influenced his decision to send the fleet around the world.

In the early summer of 1907 anti-Japanese incidents in California sparked a war scare in the United States. Rumors filled the sensational press and reminded some observers of the atmosphere preceding the Spanish-American War. The more respected American newspapers and journals denounced the activities of the yellow press, but the preoccupation with a Japanese-American clash ran through all levels of American society. Former soldiers volunteered for service in the coming conflict; the Venice, California, Chamber of Commerce offered to form a volunteer torpedo service called the "Rough Riders of the Sea"; and semiliterate citizens wrote government officials reporting the discovery of Japanese spies. A fictitious crisis literature began to emerge—later epitomized by Homer Lea's *The Valor of Ignorance* (1909)—that proclaimed that Japan's emigrants were a military vanguard. Some leaders of public opinion and some government officials took the prospect of war seriously. Alfred Thayer Mahan wrote of the "menacing appearance" of the Japanese question for the future,[16] while Chief of Staff James Franklin Bell warned the President of the rampant war fever in Japan. General Leonard Wood, the commander of the American forces in the Philippines, sent back alarming reports of Japanese espionage. The highest leadership in the American army displayed a remarkable sensitivity to alleged Japanese intelligence activities in Hawaii, the Philippines, and the United States. Secretary of War Taft, although unaffected by the army's nervousness, allowed his subordinates to begin intensive studies of the defense of the Philippines against a Japanese attack.

The American navy seemed much less preoccupied than the army with the Japanese threat. Since 1899, when the acquisition of the Philippines brought new defense responsibilities, naval leaders had desired a foothold on the China coast as well as the development of a major base in the Philippines at Subic Bay, a fine

---

[16]*Ibid.*, p.82.

harbor 30 miles north of Manila. The navy assumed that in the event of war in the Pacific, it would transfer the fleet from the Atlantic. Prior to 1907, however, naval planners had given no serious study to the possibility of a conflict with Japan; they viewed a German attempt to violate the Monroe Doctrine as the main danger to American security and kept the bulk of the American fleet concentrated in the Atlantic. War in the Philippines, they thought, would come as an outgrowth of German aggression in the Western hemisphere. Prodded by Roosevelt, in early 1907 the navy began a more detailed analysis of a war with Japan, an analysis that later in the year grew into war plan Orange (the code name for Japan). But the navy undertook these studies with no sense of urgency. Admiral George Dewey summed up the prevailing sentiment within the service when he wrote that friction with Japan would not "reach a critical stage for a long time to come."[17] The primary concern of naval planners remained the Atlantic and the naval rivalry between Germany and Great Britain.

As the summer of 1907 progressed, the President and Secretary of State leaned more toward the army's than the navy's point of view. Both were clearly disturbed by rumors of Japanese espionage and the reported estimate of British and German naval circles that Japan would win an encounter in the Pacific. Moreover, both were alarmed by the fact that Japanese immigration to the continental United States had increased since the conclusion of the Gentlemen's Agreement. Roosevelt worried about more serious outbreaks in California and rising exclusionist sentiment in Congress; he was also perplexed by the inaction of the Japanese government and angered by what seemed, from his vantage point, the rising chauvinism of the Japanese people. He still did not believe that war could come in the near future, but he did see it as more of a possibility than previously. Root summed up the President's outlook as well as his own when he wrote in early August that "the tendency is towards war—not now but in a few years. But

---

[17] *Ibid.*, p. 99.

much can be done to check or divert the tendency."[18] Japan, once a protégé, was now a potential enemy in the Pacific.

X

In Japan the mood among the civilian oligarchy was much different from that in the United States. Portions of the press and various political activists engaged in noisy criticism of the government's diplomacy, but American leaders took this agitation far too seriously. They simply did not understand the very different relationship in Japan between public opinion and the decision makers. Members of the ruling oligarchy dismissed public opinion. They seldom talked of war with the United States, nor did they think in terms of a fundamental conflict of Japanese and American interests in the Pacific. They found the crisis between the two nations profoundly upsetting and were unable to understand how it had grown so serious. All were willing, if necessary, to direct Japanese expansionism in other directions, although they did not entirely agree on the extent of the concessions they should make in the immigration dispute. Tension with the United States so alarmed Prince Itō Hirobumi that he proposed giving the United States virtually a free hand in regulating Japanese emigration. Foreign Minister Hayashi, however, was more reluctant to tighten emigration restrictions. The Japanese government did so only slowly and in response to mounting pressure from the Roosevelt administration.

Army and navy leaders also avoided serious consideration of war with the United States. The army General Staff remained preoccupied with the Russian threat, and the war plan it drew up in 1906 barely mentioned the United States. In redrafting the army's proposal for final submission to the Emperor, Yamagata Aritomo removed even these few references. The army viewed a Japanese-American conflict as extremely unlikely and ignored the implications of the anti-Japanese agitation in California. The navy was more sensitive to tension with the United States and, because of its insistence, the 1907 war plan listed Japan's possible enemies,

---

[18]*Ibid.*, p. 133.

in their order of importance, as Russia, the United States, and France. But most of the navy's desire to include the United States stemmed from bureaucratic rivalry with the army, which would receive the bulk of defense appropriations unless a major naval power seemed a likely enemy. Naval leaders felt that Japan must and could avoid war with the United States and wished only to balance American naval power in the Pacific. They recognized the inferiority of the Japanese navy and believed that war would bring a major defeat.

The contrasting moods and assumptions among leadership groups in each nation indicate how large a gap had been produced by the crisis beginning in October 1906. Despite the efforts of Japan's oligarchs and America's president, it was virtually impossible to span the vast cultural distance separating the two nations. The more direct contact of the two governments and peoples revealed how superficial the traditional friendship had been and how fragile any diplomatic accommodation would be.

XI

By the late summer of 1907 the President, disturbed by the mounting tension with Japan, decided that William Howard Taft should extend his trip to the Philippines to include a stop in Tokyo. In late September the Secretary of War arrived in Japan, prepared to concede naturalization to Japanese residents in the United States in return for the President's long sought after treaty of reciprocal exclusion. He received an exceptionally warm reception from Japanese officials, but found Foreign Minister Hayashi and Prime Minister Saionji unexpectedly firm on the immigration question. Hayashi insisted that the Japanese people would not permit a formal treaty, but that the government could apply restrictions quietly and informally. Saionji confirmed this position, emphasizing that Japan would sign no agreement that demeaned its national dignity. Nor would Japan conclude a more general treaty proclaiming the friendship of the two nations and the principles to which they would adhere in dealing with China. Ambassador Aoki had suggested such an understanding to a receptive Roosevelt, only to be disavowed by his own government. The Japanese government wished to avoid any formal accord until the tension eased between the two nations. It could, of course, have made greater concessions on the immigration question, but it still underestimated the breadth and depth of anti-Japanese agitation in the United States. Until late in 1907 Hayashi and Saionji failed to grasp Roosevelt's growing sense of urgency. In fact, they unwittingly contributed to it by reinforcing the President's image of a cautious, conservative oligarchy about to be overwhelmed by a chauvinistic public.

The Japanese position impressed Taft, who informed the President that the United States could achieve its objectives through administrative regulations instead of by a formal treaty. Over the past year this course had been suggested by many others, but ignored by the President; he was receptive, however, to the same recommendation coming from a trusted friend with considerable experience in dealing with Asian peoples. He quickly dropped his treaty plan and pressed on Japan a series of administrative measures aimed at cutting off the flow of laborers to the continental United States. Roosevelt and Root warned of exclusionist legislation if Japan did not promptly respond.

At the very end of December Japan largely conceded the American demands; most important, the number of Japanese laborers entering the United States fell sharply for the first time since the conclusion of the Gentlemen's Agreement. The administrative regulations agreed on by the two governments completed the Gentlemen's Agreement and, although Root continued to prod the Japanese government, immigration dropped to a trickle as 1908 progressed. Clearly the most acute phase of the Japanese-American crisis had passed.

In Washington, however, much suspicion remained as the President and Secretary of State anxiously watched the monthly immigration figures. Their suspicion was reflected in one of the stranger diplomatic maneuvers of Roosevelt's presidential years—an attempt to draw Great Britain into the Japanese-American crisis. By early 1908 the President was uncertain that the Japanese government would actually enforce the regulations to which it had just agreed. Japanese immigration, he speculated, might shoot up in the near future, bringing violence in California and perhaps exclusionist legislation from Congress. The public reaction in Japan might sweep that nation's leaders along a path ending in war. Roosevelt and Root vividly remembered the popular frenzy that had forced the McKinley administration into war in 1898. They realized that the rulers of Japan—whom they regarded as wise old men—had serious domestic problems and did not wish to challenge the United States. But how long could these oligarchs hold out against an aroused public and extremists in the army and navy? In a crisis situation, Roosevelt reasoned, an Anglo-American coalition might buttress their position and avert war.

The President decided to approach Great Britain through Canada, for he knew that Prime Minister Wilfrid Laurier faced similar immigration problems. In early 1908 Roosevelt indirectly asked Laurier's young protégé, William Lyon Mackenzie King, Deputy Minister of Labor and Immigration, to visit Washington. Roosevelt wished to send King as an emissary to London, where he would convince British Foreign Secretary Sir Edward Grey to warn Japan of the urgent necessity of honoring its agreements with Canada and the United States. In discussions with King and British Ambassador James Bryce, Roosevelt and Root spoke as if war between Japan and the United States was imminent. King and Bryce were understandably startled, as was Grey, who could not believe that Japan would provoke trouble with the United States by failing to restrict immigration.

Roosevelt's loose and belligerent talk only confirmed the view of British officials that the President was an unstable mixture of shrewdness and impulsiveness. The British Foreign Office believed that Roosevelt might rashly precipitate a far more serious crisis with Japan, and Grey refused to undertake any action that would further strain the Anglo-Japanese Alliance. His talks with King broadened his understanding of the immigration problem and, in this sense, Roosevelt achieved a part of his larger goal, a common attitude toward Japanese immigration among the three governments. But his devious approach and exaggerated rhetoric only increased doubts in London and Ottawa about his reliability and further eroded his effectiveness in dealing with those two governments.

While Roosevelt was reaching across the Atlantic for diplomatic support, he was acutely conscious of American naval and military weakness in the Pacific. He wrote his son Kermit that "I do not believe there will be war with Japan, but I do believe that there is enough chance of war to make it eminently wise to insure against it by building such a navy as to forbid Japan's hoping for success. I happen to know that the Japanese military party is inclined for war with us and is not only confident of success, but confident that they could land a large expeditionary force in California and conquer all of the United States west of the Rockies."[19] He was determined to secure four dreadnoughttype battleships from Congress to improve America's naval position in the Pacific. Aroused by his army advisers, he also struggled to increase appropriations for the nation's Pacific defenses. Army planners had become convinced that it would be impossible to hold either Subic Bay or Manila until the arrival of the Atlantic fleet. They reasoned that American forces could only retreat to fortifications on Corregidor Island. The navy, however, stubbornly refused to give up its plans for a great East Asian base at Subic Bay. The two services failed to agree on a location until November 1909, when they finally concluded that the primary naval base in the Pacific would be at Pearl Harbor.

The army was far more insistent than the navy on keeping the fleet permanently in the Pacific. Chief of Staff Bell believed that in a war with Japan, only a powerful Pacific fleet could maintain America's position in Hawaii and the Philippines. On the Pacific Coast many felt that the fleet ought to remain nearby and, when the 17 battleships visited California's ports in the spring of 1908, they received a tumultuous reception. The President, however, did not believe war with Japan was imminent, nor did he wish to further strain relations by leaving the fleet in Pacific waters. He had originally planned the cruise to whip up popular enthusiasm for larger naval appropriations and only later had decided that a world cruise would impress the Japanese with American naval power. It might also quiet doubts in Europe over America's naval preparedness and, through visits to Australia and New Zealand, symbolize the unity of English-speaking peoples in the Pacific.

---

[19] Morison, *The Letters of Theodore Roosevelt*, VI, p. 1013.

The voyage did have a substantial impact on other nations and also stimulated "big navy" sentiment on the Pacific Coast. It had no effect, however, on the Republican leadership in Congress, which bitterly opposed a four-ship program. Roosevelt won only two, with a guarantee of two more in each succeeding year.

Despite the heated Senate debate, the President refused to exploit popular animosities toward Japan. He wished to leave not only a heritage of naval strength to his successor, but also a restored friendship with Japan.

By the early summer of 1908 it seemed that Roosevelt had largely achieved both of these goals. He had convinced the Congress to resume naval expansion and had persuaded Japan to curtail drastically immigration to the United States. By June more Japanese were leaving than entering the country. Secretary of State Root believed that "everything between us and Japan is moving very smoothly now."[20] The United States had accepted a Japanese invitation for the Great White Fleet to visit its shores, and the President and Secretary of State probably anticipated a public exchange of notes before they left office.

The calmness of these two leaders, however, was not shared by a vocal segment of the public. A group of East Asian activists, led by journalists such as Thomas F. Millard, bitterly attacked Japan's policy in Southern Manchuria and demanded that their government champion the administrative and territorial integrity of China. Some diplomats in China and in the State Department agreed. Roosevelt and Root, who dominated American-East Asian policy, rejected this advice. They did act to uphold American treaty rights in Manchuria, but had no intention of challenging Japan's dominance in the southern portion of that region. Both wished, more urgently than before, to direct Japanese expansionism away from the Pacific toward the continent of Asia.

XII

In July 1908 Japanese policy shifted more decisively in this direction. Although Foreign Minister Hayashi had reduced Japa-

---

[20]Quoted in Neu, *An Uncertain Friendship*, p. 254.

nese emigration to the United States, he was reluctant to relinquish the idea of peaceful expansion throughout the Pacific. In midsummer, however, Saionji's government fell, and Katsura and Komura once again became Prime Minister and Foreign Minister. Both agreed with Roosevelt that Japanese emigrants must not cross the Pacific if they provoked hostility in the United States; they viewed commercial relations with Australia, Canada, and the United States as more important than emigration. In September the cabinet formally decided to focus the nation's expansive energies on Korea and Manchuria. After the Russo-Japanese War continentalism would, in any event, have been a powerful theme in Japanese foreign policy. With expansion across the Pacific blocked, it received an even more prominent place in government policy and popular psychology.

In the years after 1905 Japanese continentalism faced serious problems. Japan was securely lodged only in Korea; in Southern Manchuria its control was much less complete. To develop the region economically, Japan needed foreign capital and large numbers of its own settlers. At first progress was slow, for it was difficult to secure foreign capital on the right terms and to stimulate large-scale emigration. Moreover, the fabled China market, in which Japanese expansionists, like their American counterparts, placed so much hope, proved elusive, and rising Chinese nationalism brought an economic boycott against Japanese goods. By 1908, however, dramatic progress in Manchuria had overshadowed the dim threat of Chinese nationalism. Trade and investment were growing rapidly, and substantial numbers of Japanese were settling there. With the initial obstacles surmounted, the enthusiasm for continentalism reached a new peak.

In late September 1908 Japanese leaders decided to seek an accord with the United States, one that would quiet public opinion in both nations and clarify the understanding between the two governments. Japan staged a carefully prepared welcome for the American battle fleet in Yokohama; it recognized that the fleet's voyage represented a demonstration of American power in the Pacific and wished to prove that the United States had no cause for alarm. Even Japanese navy leaders agreed that no opportunity should be overlooked to remove American suspicion of Japan. In late October negotiations began in Washington between Ambassador Takahira Kogorō and Secretary of State Root for a statement that would affirm the friendship of the two nations. With the exception of some disagreement over the exact phrases referring to China, the talks proceeded smoothly and, on November 30, Root and Takahira exchanged notes in which the two governments agreed to: (1) respect each other's possessions in the Pacific; (2) maintain the status quo in the Pacific area; and (3) affirm "the independence and integrity of China and the principle of equal opportunity for the commerce and industry of all nations in that Empire."[21]

The Root-Takahira Agreement was supplemented by private conversations between Katsura, Komura, and an American journalist, John Callan O'Laughlin. Roosevelt had dispatched his old friend to Japan in order to engage in the sort of frank exchange of views that he did not want to entrust to the normal diplomatic channels. In October O'Laughlin conducted lengthy conversations with the two Japanese leaders. The President's emissary reassured them of America's peaceful intentions toward Japan and they, in turn, revealed that Japan's rulers had never considered war with the United States. Komura promised to shut off all emigration, but warned against insults to the nations's dignity. While Japan would maintain an open door for commerce in Manchuria, he explained that Southern Manchuria was Japan's outer line of defense or sphere of interest and that Japan excluded that region from pledges to respect China's territorial and administrative integrity. Japan was eager, the Foreign Minister concluded, to cooperate with the United States in the Pacific.

Undoubtedly Roosevelt was pleased with the results of these confidential talks, for they confirmed his belief that the vital interests of the two nations need not clash. The United States accepted Japanese expansion on the continent of Asia, while Japan recognized the impossibility of expansion into the white-dominated areas of the Pacific. With this firm understanding in hand, Roosevelt felt that he had left things in good shape for his successor.

---

[21] *Papers Relating to the Foreign Relations of the United States: 1908* (Washington, D.C., 1912), p. 513.

All sections of the American public—including East Asian activists—had hailed the Root-Takahira Agreement, which served as a symbol of restored cordiality while obscuring the real intentions of the American government. The President, however, paid a price for building such a superficial consensus. By refusing to state openly his limited concept of American interests in East Asia, he avoided controversy, but failed to impede the growth of popular myths about the importance of American interests in China. In short, his unwillingness to speak out made an eventual reversal of his policy more likely.

During the final months of his presidency Roosevelt confronted another anti-Japanese outbreak in California. The spread of Japanese settlers into rural areas of the state, along with growing fears about the cohesion of Californian society, stirred up anti-Japanese sentiment. The Republican organization's grip on the legislature was less firm than in 1907, and it was by no means certain that it could block the passage of a variety of discriminatory proposals. Roosevelt intervened, demanding a square deal for the Japanese in California and exerting all his influence to turn back the anti-Oriental tide. In February 1909 he succeeded by a narrow margin.

Roosevelt had weathered over 2 years of serious tension with Japan. Initially he floundered, misjudging both the attitude of the Japanese government and the people of California. Gradually, however, he had elaborated a delicate compromise between domestic and foreign needs, one that, for a time, eased the antagonism between the two nations. The President was never swayed by the vague rhetoric about the vital American stake in China; his vision of limited American interests there cut through contemporary illusions. But he did succumb to one of the potent ideological currents of his era—the belief in a yellow peril. His fears of Japanese militancy gave his policy an exaggerated urgency. In the minds of the President and his advisers the encounter between Japanese and American expansionism seemed ominous—the near future secure, but the more distant future filled with strife.

CHAPTER III

The Triumph of Idealistic Diplomacy

I T SEEMED THAT THEODORE ROOSEVELT HAD LEFT HIS FOREIGN POLICY IN GOOD HANDS, for William Howard Taft had played an important role in its execution. As a former Governor-General of the Philippines and Secretary of War, he had been closely associated with many of the accomplishments of Republican diplomacy and had spoken out often in defense of America's expanding world role. During four trips to Japan he had come to know many of that nation's leaders, and in July 1905 and October 1907, had engaged in significant conversations with Japanese statesmen. Throughout the crisis of 1906 to 1908 Taft was less suspicious of Japan than either Roosevelt or Root. But he never completely shared the President's assumptions about East Asia. His sympathy for China surpassed Roosevelt's, as did his estimate of America's interests there. After visiting China in October 1907, Taft had warned Root that the United States might have to resist firmly Japanese encroachments on the Chinese Empire. Later he had sided with those within the administration who favored keeping the battle fleet in the Pacific. The seeds of a different policy were present well before March 1909.

A variety of forces converged after 1909 to impel the Taft administration toward a new course in East Asia, one that marked a major shift in the history of American-East Asian relations. Instead of continuing Roosevelt's power-oriented diplomacy, with its view of international relations as a controlled state of tension, Taft and his Secretary of State, Philander C. Knox, adopted a benevolent view of international relations, an approach that foreshadowed in many ways the idealism of Woodrow Wilson. Both men felt that the United States was a world power with heavy responsibilities for the advancement of Anglo-Saxon civilization.

As Taft put it, the United States must do its part "in keeping the house of the world in order"[1] and in using its great wealth and power to help weaker, unfortunate nations along the path of progress. The President and his Secretary of State felt an obligation to employ American power for humanity's benefit, particularly in Latin America and East Asia.

Like Roosevelt, their preeminent concern was the maintenance of stability in the Caribbean and Central America; they devoted more attention to this task than to any other foreign policy objective. In contrast to Roosevelt, however, they had an intense interest in East Asia, but had little if any sense of America's role in the preservation of the European balance of power. Their idealistic conception of America's mission in backward areas made it difficult for them to appreciate traditional balance of power politics. Both felt that the old, brutal type of world order was passing away, and they perceived a growing harmony among nations. Knox foresaw an international federation in which the strong would help the weak and corporate righteousness would destroy injustice; Taft argued that the movement toward interdependence would one day lead to a situation in which all powers could submit their disputes to an international arbitral court. In time, a world public opinion would emerge to enforce the decisions of the court.

Both men lacked that disciplined understanding of international realities that might have kept them from acting on these ideas; their good intentions were unmatched by good sense. Soon after taking office Taft and Knox took bold initiatives in East Asia. In May 1909 the administration demanded entry for an American group of financiers into the Hukuang railway loan, organized by British, French, and German interests. In November, before resolving the first issue, it urged that the powers' finance China's purchase of Manchuria's railroads. While China repaid the loan, those nations lending the money would run the lines. The second proposal, striking at the vital center of the Japanese and Russian spheres in Manchuria, was sure to provoke a strong reaction from the powers.

---

[1] Quoted in Charles E. Neu, "1906-1913," in Ernest R. May and James C. Thomson, Jr., eds. *American-East Asian Relations: A Survey* (Cambridge, Mass., 1972), p. 161.

The administration's assertive diplomacy reflected a new assessment of China's relation to the United States. After 1905 reforms there led Americans to believe that China had reached a pivotal point in its history. Taft noted in 1908 that China was finally "rousing itself from its sleep of centuries," and even Theodore Roosevelt, shortly before leaving office, published an article in the *Outlook* on "The Awakening of China."[2] Some Americans argued that, given the traditional friendship of the two nations, the United States had an obligation to guide China's transformation. Without defining the precise nature of American interests there, the President took it for granted that the United States would have a great civilizing role in China as it had in the Philippines. China was obviously an area in which Taft and Knox could practice their new brand of idealistic diplomacy.

This profound concern with China was reflected in the careful consideration given the ministership to Peking. Taft and Knox replaced William W. Rockhill, whom they regarded as passive and pessimistic, with Charles H. Crane, a prominent Chicago businessman and world traveler. When Crane's indiscretions forced his recall, they turned to William J. Calhoun, a Chicago lawyer who had served on the Interstate Commerce Commission and undertaken special diplomatic missions for both McKinley and Roosevelt. The ambassadorship to Japan received far less attention. Thomas J. O'Brien remained in Tokyo until August 1911, when he moved to Rome. As his successor, Taft and Knox chose Charles Page Bryan, a former Illinois legislator who had held ambassadorships to Belgium, Brazil, Portugal, and Switzerland. Bryan stayed only 4 months and, during the remainder of the Taft years, the American representative was Larz Anderson, a Washington, D. C. socialite and philanthropist. Taft and Knox were determined to send a minister to China who would aggressively promote American interests, while they were content to leave the Tokyo embassy in the hands of second-rate career officers and an amateur diplomat.

---

[2]Quoted in Neu, "1906-1913, in May and Thomson, *American-East Asian Relations,* p. 161; "The Awakening of China," *Outlook,* XC (1908), pp. 665-667.

The President and Secretary of State did not turn to China because of any substantial pressure from the business community or American financiers. After 1905 American trade with China—always small—sharply decreased, while trade with Japan substantially increased. In terms of both trade and investment Japan was far more important to the United States than China. Curiously, however, the myth of the China market retained a certain currency, while few spoke of the vast, untapped potential of Japanese-American economic relations. Taft and Knox came into office concerned about big-power economic rivalries and intent on promoting America's commercial supremacy abroad. They expanded the State Department's Bureau of Trade Relations and sought, without success, a ship subsidy bill and the lowering of trade barriers with Canada. The underdeveloped nations of the world, particularly in the Orient, seemed to offer the greatest opportunities for American goods and capital. The promise of the China market impressed both the President and his Secretary of State, who saw economic expansion into China as an important objective that flowed into larger goals—the maintenance of America's standing as an Asian power and the fulfillment of its obligation to a large, backward nation.

Changes within the foreign service also shaped the Taft administration's policy. There a group of energetic young men wanted to make the Open Door policy a reality. They had been drawn to diplomacy primarily because life in America seemed stale and flat in comparison with the opportunities for adventure in exotic lands. They dreaded conventional careers and felt an urgent need to widen their horizons. Led by Francis M. Huntington-Wilson, William Phillips, and Willard Straight, these novices scorned the cautious, skeptical diplomacy of an older generation and conceived bold plans to challenge the status quo in China and Manchuria.

These young diplomats were moved by a variety of considerations—a strong aversion to Japanese culture and policy, a belief in the need for American economic expansion and, at times, an almost mystical faith in the future of China. After spending 9 years in the American legation in Tokyo, Huntinton-Wilson returned to Washington in 1906 and became a leading advocate of State Department reorganization and of a more systematic governmental promotion and regulation of economic activity abroad. Knox made Huntington-Wilson First Assistant Secretary of State, putting him in a powerful position to advance his belief that Japanese ambitions on the mainland of Asia were a threat to American interests there. Willard Straight agreed, but he had an emotional involvement with China that Huntington-Wilson lacked. A lonely, restless youth, he dreamed of great exploits and at Cornell absorbed the poems of Rudyard Kipling and developed a fascination for China. Upon graduation, Straight entered the Chinese Imperial Maritime Customs Service in search of fame. He saw himself as the potential Cecil Rhodes of China, a bearer of civilization and progress. Straight was Consul General at Mukden from 1906 to 1908, returned briefly to the State Department, and then resigned in June 1909 to accept a position with the group of financiers representing the United States in the China Consortium. He continued, however, to have a close connection with the administration's East Asian policy.

Men with this sort of mission were hard to resist, particularly because of a series of organizational changes that influenced the way in which American foreign policy was implemented. After the turn of the century the first signs of professionalism and bureaucratization had appeared in the diplomatic service. These forces had already made a deep impact on other areas of American life; now they began to affect those young men who had chosen to represent their country abroad. Many began to acquire a sense of uniqueness, of professional identity, and to feel that foreign policy should be the preserve of those with expert knowledge and specialized training. These emerging elitists soon saw the need for a more elaborate organization in the State Department and, in 1908, a small but significant change occurred when Root set up the first of the State Department's geographical units, the Division of Far Eastern Affairs. Taft and Knox were more eager than their predecessors to apply scientific, business methods to government. They continued to reform the foreign service and appointed far more career men than had Roosevelt. Within the State Department, Knox instituted in the second half of 1909 an important reorganization that resulted in three more geographical divisions and a substantial expansion of the State Department's staff. Now it was more likely that policy would move upward from lower bureaucratic levels.

Before 1909 subordinates had pressed for a more vigorous East Asian policy, but Roosevelt and Root had resisted because of their own strong alternative vision of American-East Asian relations. The new President and Secretary of State, however, were more vulnerable to initiatives from below. Taft had been a loyal adviser, dazzled by Roosevelt's intellectual range and quickness, who had never comprehended the inner dynamics of his chief's policy. Without much reflection, he had willingly aided in its implementation, glad to be free of the burdens of decision. Knox, a highly successful Pennsylvania lawyer who had served as Roosevelt's Attorney General, had no experience in foreign policy. Both emphasized formal lines of authority and delegated unusual autonomy to subordinates, without effectively coordinating and controlling the activities of those beneath them. The President's lack of confidence and the Secretary of State's lack of knowledge, combined with the growth of a foreign policy bureaucracy, gave career officers much influence in the formulation of East Asian policy.

Taft's sudden reversal of Roosevelt's course in Asia indicated just how episodic American foreign policy was. In the past presidents and secretaries of state generally had little notion of what policies their predecessors had pursued, for the small State Department bureaucracy could not be relied on to transmit policies from one administration to another. Sometimes, as in the transition from McKinley to Roosevelt, a key figure such as John Hay provided a vital thread of continuity. Roosevelt gave a new cohesiveness to policy merely by thinking systematically about America's relation to the world, but the bureaucracy that had begun to expand late in his presidency was initially not very effective. Roosevelt issued executive orders furthering careerism in the diplomatic service and also set a compelling example of public service for wealthy young men. He largely ignored, however, his diplomats in the conduct of policy, preferring to draw on a wide range of personal contacts. He wished to avoid the restraints a sizable foreign policy bureaucracy would place on him. It is not surprising that State Department officials conveyed a misleading impression of Roosevelt's East Asian policy to the new administration. It is astonishing, however, that Taft, so involved in the execution of that policy, could be so misled about Roosevelt's intentions in China. He actually believed that, while continuing the principles of Roosevelt's policy, he had devised more effective means to fulfill them.

The initiatives and rhetoric of the State Department professionals became so intermingled with those of the President and Secretary of State that it is difficult, in retrospect, to untangle them. It was Taft and Knox, however, who publicly justified their policies and left the fullest records of their thoughts. Like their East Asian experts, both men believed the United States must take the initiative in preserving the Open Door in China. They reasoned that the best way to protect China was to promote reforms in its systems of currency, taxation, education, and defense, and encourage the development of communication and transportation facilities. They hoped to foster internal reform, stability, and republican institutions through the use of the only available instrument—American investments. With the penetration of American capital into China on an equal basis with that of the European powers and Japan, the United States could create a base for the expansion of its own trade and, more important, develop material interests that would force the other powers to share political decisions with it. Thus, the United States would have its say in the direction of Chinese reforms. It would seek neither economic nor political supremacy in Manchuria but, instead, an equality and cooperation among the powers. Basically Taft and Knox believed that shared investments would produce interdependence, and that a community of interests would develop that the United States could direct toward idealistic and humanitarian goals. Time and time again they declared their concern with the fate of China and their determination to use American dollars to secure influence there.

This grandiose vision climaxed with the attempt to place Manchuria's railways under the joint supervision of the great powers. Taft and Knox viewed this as a plan for the scientific administration of Manchuria, an effort to systematize and rationalize the development of that chaotic area. If successful, it would take Manchurian development out of East Asian politics, creating a huge commercial zone from which all the powers would benefit. It would lessen tensions, spread the burdens of guiding a wayward nation, and quicken the pace of economic growth. While expecting some resistance from Japan and Russia, they assumed that these two nations would find much of the proposal attractive. Lacking any real knowledge of world politics, they stumbled into an assertion of American power in East Asia.

Ultimately the American government did force its way into the Hukuang loan project but, by early 1910, the Manchurian railway plan had clearly failed. The British government, preoccupied with European affairs, was caught between its need to maintain the alliance with Japan and its desire to promote Anglo-American understanding. In early 1908 Great Britain had rejected Roosevelt's overtures for a coalition against Japanese immigration, a far more modest project than the adventurous diplomacy of the Taft administration in Manchuria. American initiatives irritated and embarrassed the British, who could not possibly risk offending Japan and Russia by undermining their spheres of interest in Manchuria.

The railway scheme aroused the deepest fears of the Japanese government, for the South Manchurian railway was the key to Japan's dominance in that region; internationalization would destroy its special position. Japanese leaders had assumed that Taft would be more friendly than Roosevelt; now they were shocked to discover that he was challenging a status quo in Manchuria that Roosevelt had accepted. Refusing to give way, Japan drew closer to Russia in an attempt to strengthen its Manchurian sphere.

Taft and Knox were unable to pick up much public support for their projects in China. Their policy stirred no great enthusiasm, except among some missionaries and a few businessmen obsessed with the economic potential of China. By 1910 even the widespread faith in the China market had weakened as more and more Americans recognized the absorption of businessmen in domestic opportunities and the insuperable obstacles of trading with China. Most of those concerned with foreign policy reacted apathetically to the government's intervention in Chinese affairs. In part this resulted from the fact that the administration obscured its goals by the means used to achieve them—the intimate collaboration with great American financiers and their institutions. Progressives were inevitably hostile to a policy labeled "Dollar Diplomacy," particularly when it emanated from an administration identified with domestic conservatism. In part, too, the widespread awareness of the awakening of China had not yet crystallized into a demand for specific government action. A more skillful politician than Taft might have convinced the public that his policies could translate their concerns into concrete achievements. By early 1910 his failure to lead the public and to comprehend international realities left his China policy in a shambles.

Nevertheless, the administration continued to pursue its goal in a limited way. Knox believed that British public opinion would eventually force a modification of that government's position. Later, in 1910, the United States took the initiative in a loan to China for currency reform and Manchurian industrial development and approved the formation of a Four Power Consortium; in 1912 the government consented to the expansion of the Consortium to include Japan and Russia. Taft's and Knox's extravagant hopes for the cooperation of the great powers diminished, but remained the basis of their approach to China. They never lost their faith in the value of American participation in the Six Power Consortium.

After the outbreak of the Chinese revolution in October 1911, the administration adopted a cautious neutrality toward the contending factions and hoped that, if intervention was necessary, it would be a cooperative venture. Eventually the American government refused to recognize the government of Yuan Shih-k'ai until the other powers concurred. Like most Americans, Taft and Knox had little understanding of the upheaval in China, and they hesitantly continued a policy dominated by earlier patterns of thought. They left office convinced the United States had accom-

---

[3] *Papers Relating to the Foreign Relations of the United States: 1912* (Washington D. C., 1919), p.xxvii.

plished much in China and had followed a policy that was, in Taft's words, "modern, resourceful, magnanimous, and fittingly expressive of the high ideals of a great nation."[3]

The President and Secretary of State were unable to conceive of the possibility of renouncing America's moral and economic position in China. In 1910 Roosevelt devoted several long letters to an explanation of his East Asian policy, but Taft and Knox seemed not to understand. Knox could not see any connection between the Manchurian and immigration questions. Japan could hardly expect concessions in Manchuria, he felt, for observing its legal obligations to restrict emigration to the United States. But both men—unlike some of their subordinates—sought expanded influence in China without any apparent sense of hostility toward Japan. Taft admired Japan's achievements and had approved of its absorption of Korea. The President and Secretary of State were, to be sure, suspicious of Japanese imperialism, but this never seemed to be a major factor in their decisions. A sense of mission instead of antagonism toward Japan inspired their policy toward China.

Taft and Knox showed no reluctance to protect Japanese interests in the United States. In fact, their attitude toward anti-Japanese agitation in California was identical to Roosevelt's. Despite Japan's rejection of the Manchurian railway proposal, in late 1910 and early 1911 the President and Secretary of State intervened in California politics to prevent the passage of anti-Japanese legislation. They won the support of Governor Hiram Johnson and bargained effectively with various anti-Japanese leaders in California. At the same time, they pondered, then rejected, Roosevelt's advice in renegotiating the Japanese-American Treaty of 1894. After some hesitation, the administration accepted Japan's proposal to omit from the new treaty a clause permitting the United States to exclude Japanese laborers and settled for a Japanese memorandum promising to continue emigration restriction. Roosevelt feared that this concession might bring an outbreak in California or at the very least intensify the specter of a Japanese menace. As it turned out, however, Taft and Knox judged political conditions more accurately than Roosevelt. Realizing that Japan would no longer tolerate a discriminatory clause, they convinced Californians to accept the new treaty and worked patiently with the Senate to insure its quick approval in February 1911.

The President did not succumb to any of the fears that had agitated Roosevelt during the crisis of 1906 to 1908. Then Roosevelt had sought a larger naval program to strengthen the nation's Pacific defenses. Taft thought war was impossible and felt reassured by his acquaintance with important Japanese statesmen. His vigorous advocacy of naval expansion seemed unrelated to his foreign policy, as if he kept diplomacy and strategy in different compartments. Roosevelt's awareness of America's military and naval weakness in the Western Pacific had influenced his diplomacy; Taft lacked his predecessor's ability to see the whole instead of its separate parts. Taft believed American initiatives in China and Manchuria would appeal to the powers despite the nation's lack of military and naval strength in the Pacific.

Taft's calmness could not, of course, quiet the concern of his military and naval advisers over Pacific strategy. In the spring of 1910 the navy began more systematic consideration of war with Japan and, by March 1911, had worked out a detailed Orange plan. The army continued to be even more sensitive to the Japanese menace than did the navy. Its top leaders, assuming a fundamental antagonism between the two nations, studied Japan's war potential and its ability to move troops to the Pacific Coast; they also worried about the activities of Japanese spies and fretted over the vulnerability of the Philippines. In November 1909 the army and navy had largely resolved a long and bitter dispute by deciding to leave only a small repair station at Subic Bay and to locate the nation's chief Pacific base at Pearl Harbor. But the problem of defending American forces in the Philippines against a Japanese attack remained. The navy was reluctant to confront it and uncertain whether Germany or Japan was the nation's most likely enemy. Germany seemed the most formidable, however, and the navy resisted pressure to transfer the fleet to the Pacific. Nor would naval leaders concede, as army planners argued, that a base should be developed at Corregidor that would support the fleet once it reached the Western Pacific. These important strategic issues remained confused and unresolved, partly because Taft presided passively over the evolution of the nation's Pacific strategy.

Important segments of the foreign policy public shared the assumptions of the military. They, too, believed that the encounter of Japanese and American expansionism had produced a fundamental conflict of interests in the Pacific. A prominent Harvard scholar, Archibald C. Coolidge, predicted in his influential *The United States as a World Power (1909)* that tension between the two nations would inevitably increase. In 1911, when a group of Japanese fishermen in California was offered a leasehold on Magdalena Bay in lower California, some American papers claimed that Japan was covertly seeking a naval base in the Western hemisphere. Senator Henry Cabot Lodge took this threat seriously and introduced a resolution stretching the Monroe Doctrine to prohibit the acquisition of any harbor in the hemisphere by foreign interests. There were, to be sure, powerful voices of dissent within the foreign policy public. The American Ambassador in Tokyo, Thomas J. O'Brien, saw no tangible reasons for a conflict, and the prominent journalist George Kennan denied any basic antagonism between the two nations. Men who took this position placed little faith in the China market and were not optimistic about the future of China. In short, they denied that the United States had any moral or economic mission in China and emphasized the importance of friendly relations with Japan.

The shift in American attitudes toward East Asia, so evident after 1909, produced a profound dilemma for Japanese statesmen. They had given up their vision of peaceful expansion across the Pacific and had turned their attention fully toward the continent. No sooner had they done so than the United States suddenly challenged the status quo in Manchuria and proclaimed its own intense concern with the fate of China. Slowly the dominant image in Japan of a peaceful intermingling of the two peoples gave way to the conviction of an inescapable antagonism with the United States. Somehow the growing economic ties counted for little. It was more and more difficult for men on both sides of the Pacific to conceive of a harmonious relationship between their two nations. Instead, the images of conflict and strife so deeply embedded in the American official and popular imagination gradually became embedded in Japan as well.

II

The Wilson years brought to a climax many of the assumptions about international affairs that, for over a decade, had been gathering momentum. Like Taft, Woodrow Wilson believed that America's moral position and political institutions were unique and that both God and destiny compelled the nation to carry its example to other peoples. Wilson hoped "that as the years go on and the world knows more and more of America it will . . . turn to America for those moral inspirations which lie at the basis of all freedom . . . and that America will come into the full light of day when all shall know that she puts human rights above all other rights and that her flag is the flag not only of America but of humanity."[4] He had no doubt that mankind was moving toward a new era of democracy, peace, and human brotherhood and envisioned a world without strife, dominated by men of goodwill. The President's lofty, stern idealism, along with his soaring rhetoric, gave old ideas a new luster and projected progressive assumptions on the world stage with unprecedented clarity and force.

Wilson and his associates failed to perceive the continuity of their foreign policy assumptions with those of the previous administration. They believed that Taft had pursued a selfish and materialistic policy that repressed the democratic aspirations of backward peoples. Taft's collaboration with imperialistic European powers in China and his refusal to recognize the new republican government there had particularly offended the President, who possessed a deep sympathy for China and a belief, shared by Secretary of State William Jennings Bryan, that China's awakening was a momentous event in world history. Wilson's close contact with China missionaries had convinced him that Christianity was at the center of that nation's regeneration.

Soon after taking office Wilson told his cabinet that he felt "so keenly the desire to help China."[5] Acting on this impulse, he quickly withdrew American support from the Six-Power Consortium, declaring that such financial cooperation among the powers

---

[4]Ray S. Baker and William E. Dodd, eds., *The Public Papers of Woodrow Wilson,* 6 vols. (New York, 1925-1927), III, p. 147.
[5]E. David Cronan, ed., *The Cabinet Diaries of Josephus Daniels, 1913-1921* (Lincoln, 1963), p. 17.

infringed the sovereignty of the Chinese Republic. He also broke with the powers in recognizing the new republic. Wilson was determined to pursue an independent policy that would restore America's traditional position as the protector of China's integrity and independence and as the spiritual mentor of that great nation. His arduous search for an eminent minister revealed the importance Wilson assigned to that post. He finally settled on Paul S. Reinsch, a professor of Political Science at the University of Wisconsin and a leading authority on world politics. Reinsch's concept of America's mission in China ran beyond even that of the President or Secretary of State.

Wilson's idealistic China policy, although popular with the American people, met with the disapproval of State Department professionals. Assistant Secretary of State Frances M. Huntington-Wilson issued a bitter protest and resigned. Wilson and Bryan had taken their new initiatives in China without consulting professional diplomats, whom they associated with conservative Republicanism. In foreign policy they relied on their own intuition, along with a meager network of unofficial agents and private friendships. It was a risky process, for the President had given little if any serious thought to foreign affairs and none at all to East Asia. As a scholar, he had been absorbed in Western political theory and institutions; as a politician, he had intended to make his mark by restructuring domestic society. Thus, his initial gestures toward China did not represent any coherent policy toward East Asia; they were, in fact, only the expression of vague, moralistic impulses. Wilson and Bryan seemed to believe that government policy would be less significant in the reconstruction of China than business activity and private philanthropic endeavors, particularly the work of Protestant missionaries. Under their guidance American-East Asian policy remained both undisciplined and episodic. They misread not only the intentions of their predecessor, but the whole course of the American government's encounter with China. Illusions about the present and the past dimmed their sense of reality.

What little attention Wilson devoted to East Asia centered on China, not Japan. Wilson cared so little about Japan that he gave the ambassadorship to George W. Guthrie, a former mayor of

Pittsburgh and an associate of one of Pennsylvania's powerful Democratic leaders, A. Mitchell Palmer. Bryan cared more, for he remembered the warm welcome he had received in Japan in 1905 and was enthusiastic about that nation's progress. Both men, however, were totally unprepared for the Japanese-American crisis that erupted in May 1913.

The tension between the two nations once again grew out of anti-Japanese agitation in California. While the Gentlemen's Agreement had been effective, it could not prevent the natural increase of the Japanese population in California. A larger Japanese community encouraged the growth of racist sentiment, as did the Japanese acquisition of agricultural lands. The very prosperity of many Japanese led one prominent politician, Senator James D. Phelan, to claim that the state would soon be a "Japanese plantation."[6] By 1912 the Japanese question had become a potent issue in California politics, one that California Democrats exploited during the presidential campaign. When the legislature convened in January 1913, a large majority in both houses favored legislation that would bar Japanese residents from holding real estate. Organized farm and labor groups were solidly behind alien land legislation, as was the state's Democratic Party. The political situation gave Governor Hiram Johnson—a progressive Republican—little incentive to restrain anti-Japanese forces in the legislature and save the Wilson administration from embarrassment. He wished to remove the issue from California politics and knew that, in fact, such legislation would not seriously affect the land tenure of Japanese-Americans.

Wilson and Bryan passively observed the developing crisis. They sympathized with the efforts of Californians to protect their society and actually encouraged the passage of a less overtly discriminatory alien land law, which they did not believe would violate the Japanese-American Treaty of 1911. Wilson's respect for states' rights made him reluctant to meddle in California's affairs; in mid-April, when the lower house of the legislature approved an alien land bill, he only suggested a modification of its

---

[6]Quoted in Arthur S. Link, *Wilson: The New Freedom* (Princeton, 1956), p. 289.

language. Later in the month he dispatched Bryan on a mission to Sacramento to urge delay and moderation. Bryan, however, had nothing to offer the legislators in return for concessions and, on May 3, the Webb alien land bill passed the Senate and Assembly. Many Californians felt that the yellow tide had at last been turned back.

The government of Prime Minister Yamamoto Gombei quickly protested. Sensitive to Japan's international prestige, on May 9, 1913 it claimed the legislation violated the Japanese-American Treaty of 1911 and warned that it undermined "the spirit and fundamental principles of amity and good understanding upon which the conventional relations of the two countries depend."[7] This sharp challenge jolted Wilson and Bryan. They had never seriously considered the Japanese point of view and had assumed that friendly words and gestures would be enough to mollify that nation. Japan's bitter protest made it clear that they had erred.

Japan's note precipitated a minor war scare in the United States, one that revealed that the belief in a yellow peril had lost none of its potency among the public and government officials. Army and navy leaders were particularly alarmed. General Leonard Wood, Army Chief of Staff, and Rear Admiral Bradley A. Fiske, aide for operations, believed war was iminent. Fiske warned that the Japanese—a "highly strung proud, sensitive race"—must expand to survive and intended to seize Hawaii and the Philippines.[8] In April the Army and Navy War Colleges began detailed planning for a Japanese-American war and, later in the month, the Navy's General Board recommended the transfer of ships from the China coast to the Philippines. In early May the General Board renewed its request and, several weeks later, the Joint Board pressed the President still a third time and leaked its proposal to the press.

Furious at his military and naval advisers, Wilson suspended further meetings of the Joint Board. Neither the President nor the Secretary of State could believe that war was possible; Wilson

---

[7] *Papers Relating to the Foreign Relations of the United States: 1913* (Washington, D. C., 1920) p. 629

[8] Cronan, ed., *The Cabinet Diaries of Josephus Daniels,* p. 60.

found the very thought preposterous. He seemed free of any animosity toward Japan and, along with Bryan and Secretary of the Navy Josephus Daniels, opposed any troop or ship movements that might excite public opinion. Although the majority of the cabinet agreed, three members strongly supported the Joint Board's recommendations, as did Assistant Secretary of the Navy Franklin D. Roosevelt. Even Daniels, who rejected the advice of his subordinates, shared some of their assumptions. The Secretary of the Navy accepted the prevalent image of an inflamed Japanese public opinion, which was about to overwhelm the government and force the nation into war. He wished the fleet was in the Pacific, but feared that any attempt to move it there would precipitate a Japanese attack on the Philippines. Wilson and Bryan did not, of course, share this line of reasoning, nor had they considered the nation's strategic needs in the Pacific. Their dismissal of alarmist views of Japan helped ease the crisis, but alienated important military and naval advisers. Fiske and Wood doubted the competency of men such as Wilson, Bryan, and Daniels to determine the nation's Pacific strategy.

In the summer of 1913 Japanese-American tension ebbed as the American government sought to conciliate Japan. Wilson and Bryan, however, had nothing to offer but words of friendship, for they did not believe the California statute violated Japan's treaty rights. Japan continued to seek some concessions and, in August, indicated its willingness to accept the alien land law in return for a confirmation of land titles previously acquired by Japanese subjects. Bryan enthusiastically greeted this proposal, but Wilson rejected it. He disliked its infringement of states' rights and feared that a Japanese-American treaty would stir up controversy in the Senate and interfere with domestic reform legislation. In early 1914 Wilson partly yielded—too late—to Japan's entreaties. In April Count Ōkuma Shigenobu became Prime Minister and rejected any compromise. Throughout the rest of the Wilson years the alien land controversy remained unresolved, embittering relations between the two nations.

The outbreak of World War I pushed Japanese-American relations even further down the President's list of priorities. Wilson and Bryan realized that the war would have profound implications for East Asia and were disturbed by Japan's rapid entry and seizure of the German leasehold in Shantung province (acquired in 1898 and including the port of Tsingtao and a neutral zone surrounding it, along with railway and other rights in the interior). But they felt unable to interfere. In November 1914 Robert Lansing, then Counselor of the State Department, summed up their position. The United States, Lansing wrote, while hoping to further China's welfare, realized "that it would be quixotic in the extreme to allow the question of China's territorial integrity to entangle the United States in international difficulties."[9] Soon the American government was absorbed in the ordeal of neutrality, while Japan's attention was monopolized by a radical transformation of the East Asian balance of power.

III

By 1914 important changes had taken place in the governing structure of Japan. The power of the genro, still great during the era of Theodore Roosevelt, had noticeably declined, although Yamagata remained influential until his death in 1922. As their grip on the government loosened so, too, did that of their protégés, who were unable to establish their legitimacy as a second generation of oligarchic leaders. Earlier the genro had used their unique authority to impose unity on the elites competing for dominance; now they found it more and more difficult to discipline these elites and to find protégés who could manage the government. The increased fluidity within the oligarchic structure brought far more power to the political parties, particularly the Seiyūkai under the shrewd leadership of Hara Kei. The parties infiltrated the civilian bureaucracy and became indispensable for the survival of any government well before 1914. In September 1918, with the selection of Hara as Prime Minister and the beginning of more than a decade of party rule, it seemed that their triumph was complete.

The new generation of leaders lacked the genro's prestige and ability to coordinate the policies of the various elites. There was

---

[9] *Papers Relating to the Foreign Relations of the United States: 1914,* 2 vols. (Washington, D. C., 1922-28), II, p. 190.

a dispersion of power and of beliefs that made it difficult to settle disagreements and to create firm support for any particular policy. As policy formation became more volatile, government leaders became more vulnerable to pressures from a poorly informed public opinion and from political activists and patriotic societies.

It was within this context of governmental change that Japanese leaders faced great challenges in China. During the last years of Manchu rule the Chinese government had employed Japanese advisers, and Japanese influence on Chinese students and reformers had been enormous. The Japanese government would have preferred to see the continuance of a reformed but still conservative Manchu state and was unprepared for the revolution of 1911. Uncertain of how to proceed, Japanese leaders observed the decline of their influence with alarm as Yuan Shih-k'ai, President of the new Chinese Republic, turned to Europe for advice and financial assistance. Japan lacked the economic strength to compete with the European powers in China and steadily fell behind in the race for economic concessions there. Even the Japanese spheres in Southern Manchuria and Eastern Inner Mongolia were no longer secure, for the United States seemed unwilling to accept them, and the rights acquired in Southern Manchuria from Russia would soon expire. All segments of the oligarchy believed it was essential for Japan to consolidate its interests on the mainland and achieve a paramount position in the whole of China.

The uncertainty over Japan's position on the continent of Asia intermingled with uneasiness over the nation's standing among the great powers. At the opening of the Taishō Era (1912-1926) a sense of stagnation permeated Japan's ruling elite. The nation seemed far from its goals of preeminence in East Asia and of acceptance as one of the major imperialist powers. Yamagata had become alarmed by the depth of racist feeling in Europe and the United States and foresaw a worldwide racial struggle in which China and Japan would face a united West. While he hoped to avoid such a conflict by strengthening Japan's ties with the West, he also wished to prepare for it by seeking a new relationship with a reconstructed China. Few members of the oligarchy shared Yamagata's frightening vision of a race war, but all shared his desire for closer ties with China and viewed the United States as the major obstacle to the achievement of this goal. The American government seemed determined to obstruct Japan's destiny in East Asia.

The outbreak of the war in Europe created a sense of euphoria in Japan, for the weakening of European influence in East Asia gave Japan new opportunities there. Only the United States could now oppose the fulfillment of Japan's mission, and few believed that the American government would, under the circumstances, actually do so. A cabinet memorandum in August 1914 expressed the widespread feeling that the nation confronted an "opportunity of a thousand years."[10] At last Japan could make its bid for supremacy in East Asia and create a position of strength from which to fend off a possible postwar counteroffensive by the Western powers. The unexpected events in Europe had created the dazzling prospect of achieving in a few years what might otherwise have taken decades.

In the autumn of 1914 the Foreign Office began considering the concessions it would extract from China. Foreign Minister Katō Kōmei had planned to focus on Southern Manchuria and Eastern Inner Mongolia but, as the wishes of the various elites became known, the 21 demands assumed a form that went far beyond the Foreign Minister's original intentions. It was an indication of the Ōkuma Ministry's vulnerability to chauvinistic agitation, as well as the lack of coordination among the elites, that the 21 demands, intended to bring a new closeness between China and Japan, alarmed not only China but also Great Britain and the United States. The first four groups—dealing with Shantung, Fukien, Southern Manchuria, Eastern Inner Mongolia, and the control of iron and coal mines in central China—represented a reasonable effort to consolidate Japan's interests and achieve equality with the European powers in the remainder of China. But the fifth group, with its insistence on the attachment of Japanese advisers to the Chinese government, would have transformed China largely into a Japanese protectorate. Both the extent of these de-

---

[10] Quoted in Sadao Asada, "Japan and the United States, 1915-1925" (Ph.D. dissertation, Yale University, 1963), p. 11.

mands, as well as Japan's devious presentation of them in January 1915, were certain to create a bitter international controversy.

IV

The Chinese government, stunned by the 21 demands, quickly leaked their contents to Western diplomats. Minister Reinsch and Edward T. Williams, chief of the Division of Far Eastern Affairs, informed the President and Secretary of State that Japan had precipitated a great crisis in East Asia. Reinsch had a passionate attachment for China, as did Williams, who had spent years there as a missionary. Both believed that the United States must intervene to preserve its influence and to fulfill its moral and economic mission. China must follow the path of the West, not that of Japan.

Wilson, however, was far more cautious. His previous failure to ponder the nation's interests in China left him uncertain of how to proceed; his experience with foreign policy had taught him the need for patience in dealing with international crises. He wished to be a "prudent friend"[11] of China and feared that American intervention might do more harm than good. Preoccupied with turmoil in Mexico and Germany's new U-boat campaign, the President remained aloof during the first phase of the East Asian crisis and allowed Secretary of State Bryan to dominate American policy.

Bryan admired Japan and trusted its leaders. Although his subordinates, with the exception of Robert Lansing, were bitterly hostile to Japan, Bryan was not alarmed by the 21 demands. The American note of March 13, 1915 reflected his moderation and friendliness. It recognized that "territorial contiguity creates special relations" between Japan and its spheres on the Asian mainland,[12] but objected to those demands, primarily in group five, that menaced China's political independence. The reply of Foreign

---

[11]Quoted in Arthur S. Link, *Wilson: The Struggle for Neutrality, 1914-1915* (Princeton, 1960), p. 278.

[12]*Papers Relating to the Foreign Relations of the United States: 1915,* 2 vols. (Washington, D. C., 1924-1928), I, p. 108.

Minister Katō minimized the differences between the two governments and pleased Bryan, who was inclined to accept the Japanese
explanation of group five. He hoped to mediate the issues remaining between China and Japan and soon sent both a note suggesting
possible compromises.

Upon learning of Bryan's efforts, Minister Reinsch dispatched
a furious protest to Washington, claiming that such an accommodation would be a betrayal of China's independence. By now the
apocalyptic warnings of Reinsch and Williams, along with the
outraged protests of American missionaries in China, were beginning to have an impact on the President, who had, from the start,
been more skeptical of Japan's motives than his trusting Secretary
of State. Even Bryan shifted to a more critical attitude.

In mid-April President Wilson took control of American policy.
He concluded that Japan had deliberately deceived the United
States and was raising a major threat to China's welfare. The
American people, Wilson wrote, must be the "champions of the
sovereign rights of China."[13] It was a measure of his previous
inattention that he seemed unaware of the significant concessions
that the United States had already made. On May 7 the American
government, in a note reflecting the President's mood, affirmed its
support for the Open Door and the political independence and
territorial integrity of China and seemingly revoked its previous
acceptance of Japan's spheres of influence.

This protest came too late to affect the settlement between
China and Japan, one that brought closer economic ties and a
confirmation of Japan's spheres. The United States did not directly
challenge this accord but, in identic notes to Peking and Tokyo,
refused to recognize any agreement impairing its treaty rights in
China or the broad principles of its policy there. Wilson wished
to draw a clear line between Japanese and American policies in
China and to leave no doubt of American opposition to Japanese
expansion. He only partly succeeded, for Bryan, in talking with
the Japanese ambassador, blurred the President's purpose while
Wilson was distracted by the *Lusitania* controversy. Nevertheless,

---

[13]Quoted in Link, *Wilson: The Struggle for Neutrality*, p. 294.

the crisis over the 21 demands had briefly focused the President's attention on East Asia and precipitated a direct confrontation between Japan and the United States. Wilson emerged from it with a greater hostility toward Japan and a fervent faith in China, a nation that, he believed, had been "cried awake by the voice of Christ" and now shared a common republicanism with the United States.[14]

V

Japan's modification of the 21 demands, particularly its withdrawal of group five, stemmed from a stern British protest as well as internal opposition to the China policy of the Ōkuma Ministry. The genro, angered at their exclusion from foreign policy by Foreign Minister Katō, argued that his arrogant and devious diplomacy was the primary cause of the crisis. Along with other powerful groups, they felt Japan's prestige had been badly damaged and insisted that group five be dropped. Despite this concession, Japan strengthened its position in China and, for the remainder of the war, sought to win international recognition of its prerogatives there and to prepare for a possible postwar reaction by the West.

Japanese foreign policy became more defensive and cautious. Foreign Minister Katō felt confident that the Allies would win the war and that the Anglo-Japanese Alliance provided sufficient protection; Yamagata and many army officers, however, respected German power and believed that Germany would triumph. Yamagata feared the disruptions of the postwar period and the renewal of imperialistic rivalries in China. Like the other genro, he wished to supplement the Anglo-Japanese Alliance with a close understanding with Russia. Katō's dismissal as Foreign Minister, along with the chastening experience of the 21 demands, allowed them to pursue these goals more effectively. In mid-1916 Japan and Russia signed a new accord and, through treaties with France and Great Britain, Japan won recognition of its wartime gains in

---

[14]Quoted in Paolo E. Coletta, *William Jennings Bryan: Progressive Politician and Moral Statesman, 1909-1915* (Lincoln, 1969), p. 236.

East Asia and created an impregnable position at the Paris Peace Conference.

During the rest of the war Japan's apprehension of the United States persisted. It seemed axiomatic to many Japanese that after the armistice Japan and the United States would struggle for supremacy in the Western Pacific and on the continent of Asia. Even the navy, which had once hoped to avoid trouble with America, came to feel that a conflict between the two nations was certain. America's growing military and naval strength worried Japanese leaders, as did its economic activity in China and its close wartime collaboration with Great Britain.

Influential groups in Japan, however, resisted the notion of an inevitable clash. As they pondered the China problem and observed the rapid growth in Japanese-American trade and the flow of American capital into Japan, they saw no unbridgeable gap but, on the contrary, felt that some agreement might be reached. These civilian bureaucrats, financial leaders, and party politicians believed that Japan must secure financial cooperation with the United States in China—preferably on its own terms—or run the risk of being overwhelmed by America's economic power. The Foreign Office shared these views. It contemplated a quid pro quo in which Japan would accept the American position on immigration and alien rights in return for American acceptance of Japanese expansion in China. It was a bargain reminiscent of that struck between Japanese statesmen and Theodore Roosevelt less than a decade earlier, except that Japan now sought hegemony over the whole of China, not just the recognition of its South Manchurian sphere. By early 1917 the Japanese government was eager for a settlement with the United States. If Japan waited until the end of the war, the terms of such an accord might be much less favorable.

VI

Japan's aggressive wartime diplomacy fanned the long-standing enmity of many Americans toward that nation. As early as August 1914 Theodore Roosevelt confided to a friend that "there is always the chance of hostility between us and Japan, or Oriental Asia under the lead of Japan,"[15] and Hudson Maxim in *Defenseless America* (1915) argued that Japan could land a quarter of a million men on the Pacific Coast. Congressmen often expressed concern over the Japanese military threat and the strategic implications of Japan's acquisition of Germany's Pacific islands north of the Equator. Journalists portrayed Japan as the Germany of Asia—a brutal, grasping, militaristic nation—while other writers claimed that the intermingling of white and yellow peoples would bring racial degeneration. Substantial opposition did, of course, still exist to this anti-Japanese agitation. Some business leaders, educators, and missionaries attempted to quiet fears and affirm the tradition of Japanese-American friendship. They worked through the Japan Societies of America and particularly through the Federal Council of Churches of Christ in America. The central figure in this campaign was Sidney Lewis Gulick, a missionary with years of experience in Japan who wrote a large number of books and pamphlets on relations between the two nations. These efforts, however, had little impact on deeply embedded national stereotypes.

The views of American military and naval strategists vividly reflected popular anxieties. They assumed that Germany and Japan were the major potential enemies of the United States and, in 1914, the General Board developed a new Orange plan. It concluded that the opening of the Panama Canal would greatly improve American security in the Pacific; Japan could then no longer launch an offensive in the eastern part of that ocean. Army planners were less certain of the safety of Hawaii and began studies of the defense of Oahu against an amphibious assault. The coming of war in Europe heightened fears of both Germany and Japan, for now the possibility emerged of a coalition between a victorious Germany and a vengeful Japan. The prospect of an eventual Black-Orange attack (German-Japanese) obsessed naval planners, who designed the large 3-year building program adopted by Congress in 1916 to meet such a contingency. Naval strategists were so absorbed in yellow peril fantasies, in fact, that they ignored the

---

[15]Elting E. Morison, ed., *The Letters of Theodore Roosevelt,* 8 vols. (Cambridge, Mass., 1951-1954), VII, p. 812.

decline—since 1915—of Japan's naval strength compared to that of the United States. In 1916 Japan's building program was less than one eighth that of America's. The navy, however, was no longer satisfied with a strong defensive position in the Eastern Pacific. In January 1917 the General Board, after an exhaustive survey of conditions in the Pacific, decided that the United States must have a fleet twice the size of Japan's. The navy was now resolved to achieve American supremacy in the Western Pacific.

The American government emerged from the crisis over the 21 demands as the most determined antagonist of Japanese expansion in East Asia. The possibility of a postwar clash with Japan was much on the minds of American policymakers. The State Department, with the exception of Secretary of State Lansing, was solidly anti-Japanese, and even Lansing wrote in mid-1915 that a German victory would bring a coalition of the three chief enemies of democracy—Germany, Japan, and Russia. Colonel Edward M. House wanted a navy that would allow the United States to handle both Germany and Japan. The President was far less worried than his advisers about a future conflict, but he was concerned over Japan's increasing hegemony in China. The problem was how to translate into policy his fierce determination to help China.

By the early months of 1917 even the most anti-Japanese members of the State Department recognized the importance of reducing tensions between the two nations. With the American declaration of war, this became an urgent need. Wilson and his advisers feared that a hostile Japan might defect to the Central Powers and hoped that a modus vivendi would slow Japanese expansion in East Asia and bring more active Japanese participation in the war. There was no consensus, however, on the nature of the understanding that should be reached. Lansing had always disliked the idealism of Wilson's approach to China and had viewed American interests in East Asia in terms of commercial expansion and the security of American possessions. He was prepared to recognize narrowly defined Japanese spheres in Southern Manchuria and Eastern Inner Mongolia in return for Japanese observance of the Open Door and acceptance of the California alien land law. Lansing believed that concessions would strengthen the precarious hold of moderates on the Japanese government and help to direct

Japanese expansionism toward the continent of Asia. Better to conciliate Japan, he reasoned, while the West was divided by war.

Colonel House went beyond Lansing in his willingness to concede a special position to Japan in East Asia. Previously unconcerned about Japan, in late April 1917 the ignorance of Wilson and British Foreign Secretary Arthur J. Balfour startled him, and he decided to learn more about Asian affairs. His efforts were always erratic and superficial, for he was largely absorbed in the relations of the United States with its European allies. Nevertheless, House quickly concluded that China was not worth any American sacrifice, that it was a chaotic and degenerate nation and a menace to civilization. It must be reformed under the guidance of three of the great powers, one of which would have to be Japan. House was uneasy, however, about Japan as well as China. He felt it was "not much more of a democracy than Germany or Austria" and worried about Japan's future hostility toward the United States.[16] In the spring and summer of 1917 he sought unsuccessfully to work out an arrangement in which Great Britain, in return for American concentration on the construction of destroyers and merchantmen, would agree to give the United States an option for the purchase of British battleships at the end of the war.

At the same time, however, he believed that the United States must pay more attention to the needs of Japan, a nation that had been insulted and geographically confined by the West. Japan, House warned Wilson, was at a turning point in its history, one in which it would decide to follow either German or American civilization. By conceding a moderate Japanese predominance in East Asia, that nation could be brought into the new Wilsonian world order. "We cannot," House wrote the President, "meet Japan in her desires as to land and immigration, and unless we make some concessions in regard to her sphere of influence in the East, trouble is sure, sooner or later to come. Japan is barred from all the undeveloped places of the earth, and if her influence in the East is not recognized as in some degree superior to that of the Western powers, there will be a reckoning."[17]

---

[16]House Diary, May 2, 1917, Yale University Library.

[17]House to Wilson, September 18, 1917, House Papers, Yale University Library.

Both Lansing and House, then, placed great importance on the special Japanese mission under Ishii Kikujirō that arrived in Washington in September 1917. They believed that Japan's leaders were in a receptive mood and would respond to American concessions. The President, however, was unmoved by their advice. He wished to avoid a wartime confrontation in the Pacific, but not at the expense of China. His devotion to that nation remained undiminished. He insisted, along with his State Department subordinates, that Japan must renounce its spheres of influence in China as well as its claim to hegemony there. During the talks between Lansing and Ishii, the President had only two interviews with the Japanese emissary, but he followed the negotiations closely and set his own firm stamp on them.

Given the refusal of Wilson and Japan's leaders to compromise their essential positions, an open break could be averted only through ambiguity and the incorporation of contradictory principles into the agreement Lansing and Ishii initialed on November 2, 1917. On the one hand, Japan and the United States affirmed the Open Door and the independence and territorial integrity of China; on the other, they concluded that Japan had "special interests" in China,[18] particularly in those areas contiguous to its possessions. In a secret protocol, they agreed to maintain the status quo in China during the remainder of the war. Lansing realized that the two governments interpreted the term "special interests" differently and remarked to Ishii that its use left "ample room for suitable interpretations on both sides."[19] The Secretary of State failed to report this particular statement to the President, who was probably unaware of the extent of the gap still separating the two nations. He believed the Lansing-Ishii Agreement committed Japan more firmly than ever to the Open Door policy. Whatever its meaning, it served Wilson's immediate purpose by delaying a showdown until the postwar period, when the American government could devote more attention to East Asian affairs.

---

[18] *Papers Relating to the Foreign Relations of the United States: 1917,* 4 vols. (Washington, D.C., 1926-1932), I, p. 264.
[19] Quoted in Asada, "Japan and the United States, 1915-1925," p. 47.

Wilson accepted a vague accommodation more readily than did the Japanese government. Although the Japanese press hailed the agreement as a great diplomatic victory and claimed that the United States had recognized Japan's special position in China, members of the government knew better and had to overcome serious opposition to win approval of the accord. Even those who favored it were unenthusiastic, for they realized that the passage of time would work to the disadvantage of Japan.

While the Lansing-Ishii Agreement smoothed over Japanese-American differences, it did not affect the sources of tension between the two nations. New conflicts were inexorably added to old ones and, by early 1918, the possibility of intervention in Siberia confronted both governments. The withdrawal of Russia from the war created consternation in France and Great Britain and drove those governments into a frenzied search for a way to relieve the pressure on the Western front by renewing the war in the East. Only Japan and the United States had the resources available for such a massive effort.

The Japanese, of course, were concerned with events in Russia, but viewed them in an Asian context. Prior to the Russian Revolution Japan had provided military aid to the tsarist government in return for concessions in Northern Manchuria and Siberia. By 1916 Japan had developed a large economic stake in Asiatic Russia and, with the coming of the civil war, the possibility arose for a further extension of Japanese interests there. But turmoil in Russia brought dangers as well as opportunities, for the Bolsheviks' triumph and the spread of their authority imperiled Japan's special position in Northeast Asia. Clearly the Bolsheviks would not recognize the concessions Japan had extracted from a tottering tsarist regime. These circumstances led to the development of a powerful interventionist movement within the Japanese army and Foreign Office. Interventionists urged that a major military expedition be sent to Eastern Siberia in order to consolidate a conservative puppet government. The army had no intention of ever moving its forces beyond Siberia to aid the Allies in European Russia. Nor did it wish to become entangled in a joint expedition subject to conditions imposed by the Allies and the United States.

The interventionists encountered formidable opposition within the Japanese oligarchy. Both the genro and important party leaders such as Hara Kei opposed any expedition that was not acceptable to the Allies and the United States. They feared American disapproval and possible unilateral action. Already aroused by American economic expansion into Siberia, they foresaw an endless conflict with the Bolsheviks while the United States stood aside and preserved its strength for the postwar period. They also knew that other conditions—such as an agreement with China and the creation of a pliable regime in Siberia—must precede Japanese action. It seemed unlikely that the Japanese government would ever reach a firm consensus for intervention.

American approval, therefore, became the key to a Siberian expedition. During the first half of 1918, as the situation on the Western front deteriorated, Allied pressure on the United States mounted. The President and his advisers resisted tenaciously, but not primarily because of their distrust of Japan. While convinced that Japan would use any intervention as a pretext for expansion into Siberia, they refused to sanction Allied plans because of their belief that a Siberian expedition would draw vital resources away from the Western front, where the war must be won or lost. No Allied force could ever be large enough to recreate a front in Russia, and it would undoubtedly offend the Russian people and drive them into the hands of Germany. Wilson hoped to rally the Russian people to his ideals, not to repress them.

Nevertheless, in the early summer of 1918, his resistance crumbled and, in July, he issued an invitation to Japan to join the United States in a limited intervention. The plight of the Czech forces allegedly attempting to escape from Russia allowed the President to justify this decision, as did his belief that intervention, if properly conducted, might somehow stimulate democractic forces in Russia. Basically, however, Wilson concluded that the issue of the Siberian expedition was seriously jeoparaizing relations with the Allies and that some concessions were imperative. Even so, he gave the Allies little of what they wanted. He proposed an expedition only to protect the Czech forces during their withdrawal and asked that Japan and the United States send no more than 7000 men, respectively.

Wilson's invitation set off violent debates between moderates and militant interventionists within Japanese governing circles. The former, led by Hara, insisted that Japanese-American relations deserved a higher priority than expansion into Northeast Asia. Hara wanted a postwar understanding with the United States and suspected that the army would enlarge any expedition it undertook. He rallied enough support to impose a limited expedition on the military, one that was only slightly larger than that proposed by the United States and that could be expanded only after Japanese-American consultations. Despite Hara's apparent victory, he could not prevent the army from taking over the expedition and enlarging it far beyond the government's original intention. By the end of October Japan had 72,000 men in Siberia and was actively intervening in the Russian civil war. The army's unilateral action violated assurances given to the American government and enraged both Wilson and his advisers. Even more than before, they now believed that Japan could not be trusted. What had begun as an American attempt to appease France and Great Britain became, in the months ahead, a determined effort to prevent Japan from controlling Siberia and the whole of Northeast Asia.

With the end of the World War in November 1918 American policy in East Asia became more active. The American government was convinced that a vigorous diplomacy would strengthen civilian moderates in Japan and allow them to win their struggle with military extremists. So many outstanding issues existed between the two nations that the State Department moved on a variety of fronts. In November the United States issued the first of many protests about the size and activities of Japanese forces in Siberia. It also became involved in prolonged negotiations with Japan over a new China consortium designed by American policymakers to bind Japan to a Western-dominated financial group and restrain its economic activities in China. The negotiations over Siberia and the consortium dragged on for months. The two governments could reach no agreement and, in May 1919, tensions between Japanese and American troops in Siberia reached a dangerous level. The President wanted to pull out, but hesitated to act independently of the Allies. The State Department, in contrast, wished to prolong American intervention and did so until early 1920, when American troops were withdrawn. The question of Japan's presence in Siberia still remained, however, as did the dispute over the scope of the consortium. Ultimately the consortium negotiations ended in a vague and unsatisfactory compromise, while the Siberian question became a major issue during the Washington Conference of 1921 to 1922.

VII

By late 1918 Japanese leaders feared that the United States would turn its attention fully to East Asia. Many military officers intended to pursue continental expansion regardless of American opposition and talked of waging a defensive war in the Western Pacific and on the Asian mainland. In 1919 the navy won approval for a large building program. But powerful civilian politicians and business leaders hoped to ease tension by working out some kind of accommodation. Worried about labor violence and the spread of radical political ideas at home, they also realized that Japan's economic and political dependence on the United States would grow.

Prime Minister Hara agreed with Yamagata that Japan's past policies had excited worldwide hostility and that the nation dare not isolate itself further. With tension between China, Japan, and the United States already dangerously high and, with a hostile revolutionary regime established in Russia, the future, under the best of circumstances, would be precarious. Japanese policy must be more cautious and come to terms, in one way or another, with Wilsonianism, which seemed to represent a new tide of world history. Soon after taking office Hara privately conveyed to the American government his belief that intervention in Siberia had been a mistake and his intention to assert control over the army's General Staff. While reducing Japanese forces, Hara hoped to cooperate with the United States to prevent the spread of Bolshevism into Siberia. News of America's withdrawal destroyed these hopes, but Hara still proceeded to reduce Japan's commitment. Ultimately he was able to defeat the General Staff and bring Japan's Siberian expedition to an end.

Hara's concept of cooperation with the United States involved few other tangible concessions. His China policy was basically only a shift in tactics, a use of more moderate means to achieve traditional ends. Hara had no intention of relinquishing Japan's spheres of interest or its goal of supremacy over the whole of China. Japan should serve as China's mentor and as a point of contact between East and West. At the Paris Peace Conference the Japanese government was determined to win recognition of its wartime gains in Shantung and the Pacific and to insert a racial equality clause in the covenant of the League of Nations. The nation must retain its privileges in Shantung, for they rested on wartime treaties with China that also formed the basis for spheres in Southern Manchuria and Eastern Inner Mongolia. A successful American challenge to the transfer of German rights to Japan would undermine that nation's whole position on the Asiatic mainland.

VIII

Along with most of his advisers, President Wilson regarded Japan as the major obstacle to a just settlement in Asia and to the application there of the principles of the new diplomacy. The President was particularly disturbed by Japan's control of Germany's Pacific islands north of the equator and by the Japanese presence in Shantung. He could do little about Japan's claims to the Pacific islands without challenging those of Australia and New Zealand to islands south of the equator. Shantung, however, assumed a far greater significance in the President's mind. For years he had been preoccupied with the fate of China but had been unable, because of more pressing needs, to help in more than a minor way. Now he had an opportunity to stand up for China and to challenge Japan's attempt to perpetuate the old, imperialistic diplomacy in East Asia.

Most of Wilson's advisers were strongly against any recognition of the Japanese claim. Minister Reinsch believed that the future of China hinged on the Shantung settlement, and even Secretary of State Lansing argued that the time had finally come for the United States to "have it out once and for all with Japan" in order to stop its "Prussian militarism."[20] American public opinion, more hostile

---

[20]Quoted in Asada, "Japan and the United States, 1915-1925," p. 75.

than ever toward Japanese imperialism and aroused by propaganda for China's cause, was sure to protest any concession. As Wilson told the Council of Four, "there was nothing on which the public opinion of the United States of America was firmer than on this question that China should not be oppressed by Japan."[21]

Only Colonel House urged conciliation. Convinced that Wilson was unfair to Japan, he believed that nation might still be led to understand that it could achieve dominance in East Asia only within the framework of Wilson's new world order. Wilson did not share House's sympathy for Japan, although he may have felt some guilt over his failure to support Japan's attempt to insert a racial equality clause in the League Covenant. At any rate, by late April 1919, he agreed with House that Japan, if denied German rights in Shantung, would refuse to join the League of Nations. Already confronted with Italy's withdrawal from the conference over the Fiume issue, Wilson finally conceded, with the understanding that Japan would eventually relinquish sovereignty and retain only economic privileges there.

Wilson's capitulation brought bitter outcries both from his own peace commissioners and from the American public. Minister Reinsch resigned in protest and the American delegates—with the exception of Colonel House—urged Wilson not to "abandon the democracy of China to the domination of the Prussianized militarism of Japan."[22] The Shantung agreement became the most unpopular and vulnerable aspect of the peace settlement in the United States, one that was eagerly seized on by opponents of the Versailles Treaty to whip up popular opposition to the President's postwar plans. Wilson tried to defend his concession, but undoubtedly he harbored a sense of guilt over having failed, once again, to advance the welfare of China. He could only hope that the Shantung settlement, like so many other aspects of the peace, would eventually be set right by the League.

---

[21] *Foreign Relations of the United States: 1919, The Paris Peace Conference,* 13 vols. (Washington, D.C., 1942-1947), V, p. 316.
[22] Quoted In Seth P. Tillman, *Anglo-American Relations at the Paris Peace Conference of 1919* (Princeton, 1961), p. 340.

The Paris Peace Conference left an ugly heritage in Japanese-American relations. Soon the two governments were publicly quarreling over the nature of Japan's verbal assurances on Shantung, the meaning of the Lansing-Ishii Agreement, and the question of whether the island of Yap—an important cable station—was included among Japan's Pacific mandates. In August 1919 Wilson, amid all his worries, wrote that "Japan certainly has China very much in her grasp, and I am eager to concert methods by which China may be extricated and set free."[23] The revulsion against Japan was widespread, both within the government and among the American people. Edward T. Williams summarized this feeling when he wrote that "the spirit of Japan is that of Prussia, whom the Japanese leaders openly admire and whose government they chose for a model."[24] Many Americans anticipated war in the near future and found their fears confirmed in inflammatory literature that described hypothetical naval and air battles stretching across the Pacific. In California another anti-Japanese campaign began in 1919 as exclusionist forces organized to close the loopholes in the alien land law. A new law passed the legislature in 1920, although it was no more effective than the earlier measure. Finally, the collapse of talks on the ambassadorial level aimed at settling the immigration issue further strained relations. Never before had the tension between the two nations been so great.

As always, American naval planners shared the more extreme popular fears. Even after American entry into the war, they had worried about a future conflict with Japan and had agreed only reluctantly to a change in construction priorities from battleships to destroyers. With the end of the war naval strategists shifted their attention to the Pacific, where many believed a Japanese-American war would soon erupt. Both army and navy intelligence concluded that Japan was preparing for a war with the United States and, in June 1919, Secretary of the Navy Daniels announced that the United States would divide the battle fleet equally be-

---

[23]Quoted in Asada, "Japan and the United States, 1915-1925," p. 83.
[24]Quoted in Akira Iriye, *Across the Pacific: An Inner History of American-East Asian Relations* (New York, 1967), p. 140.

tween the Atlantic and the Pacific. With a powerful force in the Pacific, the navy could concentrate on the development of shore support and chart the details of a Western advance that would culminate in an American blockade of the Japanese home islands. The American navy was now thinking in terms of a bold attack that would carry it to the shores of Japan.

As the Wilson era drew to a close, Japan and the United States faced an unprecedented crisis in their relations. Hostility toward Japan pervaded the American government and public and led to the widespread belief in a fundamental conflict of interests in the Pacific and on the Asiatic mainland. The Wilson administration had drifted into this confrontation, dealing with East Asian policy in an episodic, *ad hoc* fashion and succumbing, all too readily, to popular fears and enthusiasms. In Japan, disunity among the elites had produced more aggressive diplomacy and less coherent policy then in earlier years. Hara and other Japanese moderates wished for amity with the United States without sacrificing the substance of their traditional aims in China. Wilson and his advisers wished to befriend China without any systematic commitment of American power in East Asia. The confusion within both governments, the internal contradictions in their policies, and the enormous distance between the two cultures made any real meeting of minds unlikely.

CHAPTER IV

Toward a New Order in the Pacific

WORLD WAR I BROUGHT SWEEPING CHANGES IN INTERNATIONAL POLITICS. In Europe the prewar balance of power disintegrated with the defeat of Germany, the demise of the Austro-Hungarian Empire, the frightening transformation of Russia, and the weakening of France and Great Britain. The eclipse of Europe was an overwhelming reality, one that reverberated around the world. In East Asia the imperialist system seemed imperiled as revolutionary ferment spread in China and as Japan emerged in a more dominant position. In both Europe and East Asia the old order was clearly passing; men wondered what new order would arise to take its place.

President Warren G. Harding and Secretary of State Charles Evans Hughes could not avoid confronting this question. Although the American people had rejected the League of Nations and the extreme aspects of Wilsonianism, the need remained to work out a moderate, alternate approach to foreign affairs. Unresolved postwar issues pressed in relentlessly from all directions. The administration had to reach a separate settlement with the defeated states of Europe, readjust relations with the Caribbean and Latin American nations, and deal with the crisis between Japan and the United States.

The end of America's absorption in war and peacemaking brought all the hostilities aroused by Japan's wartime expansionism into the foreground. Some Americans worried about their government's neglect of China and shared the fears of Senator Henry Cabot Lodge that the Anglo-Japanese Alliance was "the most dangerous element in our relations with the Far East and with the Pacific."[1] Within the Department of State there was a strong residue of anti-Japanese animus left over from the last of the Wilson years; many diplomats felt that the time had finally come for the United States to turn its attention to East Asia. The chief of the Division of Far Eastern Affairs, John V.A. MacMurray, argued that America's primary task was "restoring the equilibrium in the Far East which has been so dangerously upset by Japan's process of aggrandizement."[2] President Harding and Secretary of State Hughes agreed that something must be done. Harding told a reporter that Japan was "the most difficult point diplomatically for the next few years."[3]

The American government seemed determined to curb Japan's hegemony in East Asia. Hughes and his subordinates reasoned that only by turning back Japan's wartime gains could they carry out America's traditional policy of preserving the Open Door and the integrity of China and begin to build a new order based on international cooperation and respect for the rights of weaker nations. One key symbol of the old diplomacy, the Anglo-Japanese Alliance, must be ended. American policymakers felt it gave a British sanction to Japanese imperialism and, in China, aligned Great Britain with Japan. In June 1921 Hughes told the British ambassador that the alliance prevented Anglo-American cooperation in East Asia and was inimical to the interests of the United States in China.

It was, however, the danger of a postwar naval race between Great Britain, Japan, and the United States that dominated the public's attention and provided the immediate impetus for the Washington Conference. The General Board's drive to build a navy second to none alarmed many Americans, who saw no need to overcome Britain's traditional supremacy. The American people and Congress wanted peace and government retrenchment, not

---

[1]Quoted in Sadao Asada, "Japan and the United States, 1915-1925," (Ph.D. dissertation, Yale University, 1963), p. 147.
[2]Quoted in Akira Iriye, *After Imperialism: The Search for a New Order in the Far East, 1921-1931* (Cambridge, Mass., 1965), p. 14.
[3]Quoted in Ernest R. May, unpublished manuscript on the Washington Conference.

huge naval appropriations and a continuance of international tensions. In December 1920 Senator William E. Borah of Idaho introduced a resolution directing the American government to enter into negotiations with Great Britain and Japan to reduce their building programs by 50 percent over the next 5 years; the Borah resolution excited the popular imagination and received overwhelming support from a wide variety of influential Americans. The public saw the limitation of armaments as a key to world peace.

The Borah resolution confronted Harding and Hughes with a difficult challenge. It whipped up enthusiasm for disarmament with a highly simplified formula and, at the same time, represented an effort by some senators to seize the initiative in foreign policy. The President and Secretary of State had to bend before the popular will while elaborating a more complex and workable program for naval limitation. They also had to avert a clash with Congress without sacrificing their control of foreign policy. Both wanted to avoid naval competition, for only through a reduction in the navy's budget could the administration satisfy the popular desire for economy. They needed time, however, to sort out their thoughts and to prepare the groundwork for a conference. After delaying as long as possible, in early July Harding finally accepted the Borah resolution in return for congressional approval of a large naval appropriation bill. Harding calculated that such a bill could be used advantageously in the negotiations at a forthcoming conference.

The popular clamor for naval limitation reinforced the feelings of the President and Secretary of State that, having rejected the League of Nations, they must take some positive initiative in world affairs. Harding wrote Senator Lodge that "I am quite as convinced as the most bitter irreconcilable that the country does not want the Versailles League. I am equally convinced that the country does wish us to do some proper and helpful thing to bring nations more closely together for counsel and advice."[4] Thus, the

---

[4] Quoted in Thomas H. Buckley, *The United States and the Washington Conference, 1921-1922* (Knoxville, 1970), p. 15.

administration moved more rapidly than it otherwise would have toward a Pacific conference. In doing so, however, it greatly expanded the original notion of Borah and other peace enthusiasts. They had thought exclusively in terms of naval reduction, while Harding and Hughes realized that any successful conference would have to deal with a wide range of Pacific and East Asian diplomatic questions.

In Great Britain the government of Prime Minister David Lloyd George had also concluded that a conference was essential. Faced with endless troubles both at home and abroad, Lloyd George found the prospect of serious difficulties with the United States unthinkable. Naval competition would increase the strain on Britain's economy and frustrate domestic demands for budget cutbacks. Worst of all, Anglo-American tension would erode Britain's international prestige further and make any settlement with the Irish nationalists—one of Lloyd George's principal objectives— virtually impossible. The Foreign Office, worried about the vulnerability of British interests and the course of an isolated Japan, hoped to extend the alliance and use it as a restraint. But Lloyd George dominated the government so completely that the wishes of the Foreign Office counted for little. He had never given much attention to East Asian affairs or placed much importance on Britain's position there. Strong opposition from Canada and the United States made the renewal of the alliance too dangerous. He intended to use the possibility of renewal as a bargaining lever, one that would help bring an Anglo-American naval and political accord. Searching for some way to strengthen his fragile hold on British political life, Lloyd George impatiently waited for an American overture. In July 1921 Britain finally urged the United States to call a conference on naval limitation and East Asian diplomatic affairs. Harding and Hughes, concerned with Japanese-American tension and faced with overwhelming domestic pressure, quickly did so.

II

The initiative for calling the Washington Conference lay jointly with Great Britain and the United States. Japan was a nervous bystander, reconciled to the need for a gathering but fearful that it would be used by the Western powers—particularly the United States—to call Japan to account for its wartime excesses in China. Aware of the need to lessen their isolation from the West, Japan's leaders knew they must renounce some of their wartime gains. Soon after taking office in September 1918, Prime Minister Hara had begun this slow and agonizing task. The problem of drawing closer to the West, however, also had an intellectual dimension. Initially, governing circles in Japan had underestimated the importance of the new ideas about international relations and viewed the League of Nations with skepticism, as an attempt by Western powers to block Japan's legitimate aspirations in East Asia. Well before 1921, however, important figures in the various elites had come to realize that Japan must make an accommodation with Wilsonian principles. Professional diplomats were particularly sensitive to the changing currents of international thought. They were convinced that Japan would have to forego traditional diplomacy in China and enter into a new era of cooperation and peaceful expansion. The Foreign Office believed that Japan would benefit from an end to spheres of influence on the mainland of Asia; it could gain more through open competition in China instead of through a concentration of its activities in Northeast Asia.

Much of the public, however, along with army and navy leaders, wanted a less decisive break with the past. While agreeing that Japan should make concessions, they believed it must retain the essence of its special position on the continent of Asia. These groups regarded Southern Manchuria and Eastern Inner Mongolia as vital to the fulfillment of Japan's mission in East Asia. At the same time, however, army and navy leaders feared American power. Old Prince Yamagata retained vivid memories of the western bombardment of Chōshū in 1864, and Admiral Katō Tomosaburō, the Navy Minister, believed that Japan's economic weakness made it imperative to avoid a war with the United States. Somehow relations must be improved, but not at too high a price.

The widespread support for these views confronted Prime Minister Hara and Foreign Minister Uchida Yasuya with the delicate task of appeasing the United States without offending powerful domestic elites. Despite Secretary of State Hughes' assurances of

American friendship and goodwill, they accepted the invitation only on the condition that the conference discuss general principles for the future instead of specific issues such as Japan's wartime treaties with China or its position in Southern Manchuria, Eastern Inner Mongolia, Shantung, and Siberia. The Japanese government hoped to settle the controversial questions of Shantung, Yap, and Siberian withdrawal outside the conference. If the United States did, in fact, use them as part of a major diplomatic offensive against Japan, the Foreign Office intended to raise the explosive issue of an open door in the Pacific region for trade and emigration.

Japan approached the Washington Conference warily, concerned with both its relationship with the West and its special position on the continent of Asia. Whatever the needs of the latter, domestic unrest drove the Hara ministry toward a settlement with the United States. The wartime boom had collapsed, leaving in its wake a depressed economy and considerable popular discontent over domestic inequities and continual naval expansion. Without improved Japanese-American relations, Hara could not cut the naval budget or deal effectively with left-wing agitation. Only through Japanese-American cooperation could the nation enter an era of peaceful economic expansionism and find a secure place in the new international order evolving in East Asia.

III

Within the American government, preconference planning, particularly on naval matters, was elaborate. Charles Evans Hughes was largely responsible for these intensive American preparations. A man of great force and intellect, he had already become the major figure in the Harding cabinet and in the formulation of American foreign policy. Hughes exercised his power with care, closely consulting with the President and relying on his judgment in dealing with the Senate and in devising domestic political strategy. Moreover, his rapid mastery of the issues allowed him to deal effectively with State Department experts. Although sometimes influenced by subordinates, he essentially used the foreign policy bureaucracy to achieve his own larger goals.

Hughes realized that naval limitation hinged on a comprehensive diplomatic settlement in East Asia. He also knew, however, that the public and Congress, although concerned about China's fate, cared more about naval disarmament. He therefore gave the naval situation his highest priority and devoted the bulk of his preconference preparations to working out a concrete program. Aided by Secretary of the Navy Edwin L. Denby and Assistant Secretary Theodore Roosevelt, Jr., along with a handful of naval officers, Hughes elaborated a bold proposal aimed at halting naval expansion and reducing existing tonnage.

Most high-ranking officers vehemently objected to Hughes' plan. The General Board insisted that Japan's vast ambitions imperiled the integrity of China, the Open Door, and the Asiatic exclusion policy. Echoing turn-of-the century fears, the General Board argued that Japan, if successful in controlling China, would turn on the United States and endanger not only American security but the whole of the white race. Only a massive naval preponderance would contain Japanese expansionism until the day when Japan adopted a democratic form of government. Assuming the termination of the Anglo-Japanese Alliance, the General Board would settle for a navy equal to Great Britain's and twice the size of Japan's. This preposterous proposal would have called for a substantial improvement in the relative naval position of the United States. In going to such extremes the General Board ignored public opinion, alienated the civilian secretaries in the Navy Department, and isolated itself within the government bureaucracy. Hughes could safely ignore its proposals and overtures for consultation. The situation was painful for naval planners. At the very time they seemed about to realize their long sought after goal of dominance in the Western Pacific, they found themselves faced with a naval limitation movement that they were unable to control.

It was far more difficult for Hughes to decide on the details of a diplomatic settlement in East Asia, and in this area he entered the Washington Conference with a less precise program. Initially he was uncertain about how he should handle the explosive issues of Shantung and Siberia or the whole question of Japan's special position on the Asian mainland. The Division of Far Eastern Affairs displayed the pro-Chinese orientation that it had held since its inception in 1908. Edward T. Williams, chief of the division under Wilson, had been a China missionary; his successor in 1919, John V. A. MacMurray, had served twice in both China and Japan, but considered himself a China expert, one sympathetic to the aspirations of that nation. The special consultants he employed during the Washington Conference—Tyler Dennett, Stanley K. Hornbeck, and his former superior, Williams—all shared his identification with China. Viewing Japan as a rapacious, imperialist power, MacMurray insisted that the United States should demand the return of Shantung, withdrawal from Siberia, and the elimination of Japan's remaining continental sphere. If necessary, the United States should use a show of force to curb Japan's "dangerously aggressive temper."[5] All of these East Asian experts elevated the Open Door policy into a major tradition of American diplomacy and stressed the unique friendship of America and China. This version of American-East Asian relations was largely a myth, but it did influence Hughes' conception of America's historic role in China.

Other voices within the American government gave Hughes conflicting advice. The Treasury Department and the Bureau of the Budget wished to avoid a costly arms race, while Secretary of Commerce Herbert Hoover, eager for expanded trade and investment in East Asia, believed that China's extreme disorganization justified most of Japan's policies. Hoover represented major business and financial interests that viewed Japan as a promising area for postwar economic development.

This advice strengthened Hughes' own inclination to avert a showdown. Even the Division of Far Eastern Affairs admitted that Japan, if pushed too hard, might resort to war. A special mission to Tokyo by the new Governor General of the Philippines, Leonard Wood, reinforced this warning. In talks with former War Minister Tanaka Giichi, Wood learned that the Japanese government believed that the prosperity of the nation depended on hegemony in Southern Manchuria. While Japan would not close the open door there, it would, if necessary, defend its special

---

[5]Quoted in Asada, "Japan and the United States, 1915-1925," p. 198.

interests with force. Japan's firmness impressed Wood, who felt that the United States "could not expect to be blocking Japanese aspirations in all directions indefinitely, unless we were really prepared for war."[6] A more understanding American policy would strengthen the influence of Japanese moderates, who realized that their nation would surely be defeated in a war with the United States.

Wood's report must have confirmed Hughes' impression that a direct attack on Japan's spheres would wreck the conference. He knew that the internal strains in Japan that were driving the government toward a conference were counterbalanced by fears of humiliation at the hands of the West. It was wiser, he reasoned, to avoid the Siberian issue and to hope that Japan, in separate negotiations with China, would voluntarily surrender its rights in Shantung. He worked to win Japan's cooperation by assuaging suspicions and by emphasizing the friendly spirit with which the United States approached common problems.

While intent on affirming America's traditional China policy, Hughes lacked Woodrow Wilson's fervent desire to help that nation. He hoped that all the powers—particularly Japan—would restrain their selfish impulses and give China time to set its own house in order. But he had no illusions about the use of force to achieve this end and told the American delegation to the Washington Conference that the United States would never go to war over Japanese aggression in China. Hughes' naval limitation proposal tacitly conceded this fact by accepting Japanese superiority in the Western Pacific. American goals could be achieved only by inducing Japan, through diplomatic negotiation and the invocation of world public opinion, to enter into a partnership with Great Britain and the United States in East Asia.

By the opening of the Washington Conference on November 12, 1921, Hughes and his State Department experts calculated that they could extract diplomatic concessions from Japan in return for modifying the American building program. They wanted to end the Anglo-Japanese Alliance, curtail Japan's presence on the Asian

---

[6]*Ibid.*, p. 193.

mainland, and secure a pledge from Japan to respect the territorial and administrative integrity of China and the Open Door. Hughes knew that a vocal sector of the American public expected these principles to be written into the Washington treaties and also expected an American victory on Shantung. This emotional issue, which the Republicans had used against Wilson, had to be re-solved if the administration was to avoid serious trouble in the Senate. Yet Hughes could achieve his primary purpose—naval limitation—only by avoiding an overt challenge to Japan and qui-etly working for a resolution of outstanding problems. In some areas he would have to settle for the sort of ambiguous compro-mise that had in itself become a tradition in Japanese-American relations.

Hughes stunned the delegates and aroused the American people with his dramatic opening address proposing naval limitation based on existing strength and specifying exactly how the tonnage quotas of the major powers should be fulfilled. Determined to give the conference an impetus that would carry it to success, Hughes believed the United States was, in fact, sacrificing little, since the Congress would not vote the funds necessary to complete vessels on the ways. By offering substantial American sacrifices, he hoped to excite public opinion and stimulate the cooperative spirit of the other powers.

The leaders of the Japanese and British delegations, Admiral Katō Tomosaburō and Arthur J. Balfour, responded favorably. Katō had considerable leeway in the naval negotiations, for Prime Minister Hara knew that his approval would be essential for the acceptance of any agreement in Japan. Katō feared a race with the United States and quickly accepted a 5:3 ratio that, he believed, would give Japan dominance in the Western Pacific so long as it was tied to a freeze on insular fortifications west of Hawaii. Naval advisers within the delegation, however, objected, claiming that a 5:3 ratio would imperil Japan's security, and the Diplomatic Advi-sory Council in Tokyo demanded more than Katō thought it wise to seek. Katō's view prevailed, but only after hard, prolonged bargaining with the United States over the details of the limita-tions.

Within the British delegation the Admiralty representatives

found parity with the United States in capital ships unacceptable. Balfour and Lloyd George, however, were determined to achieve an agreement as part of a general Anglo-American rapprochement and moved the delegation toward a more conciliatory position. In February 1922 the naval negotiations culminated in the Five Power Treaty, setting ratios of 5:5:3:1.67:1.67 on capital ships and aircraft carriers for Great Britain, the United States, Japan, France, and Italy, respectively, and prohibiting capital ship construction for 10 years. It also imposed the status quo on most of the insular fortifications of Great Britain, Japan, and the United States in the Pacific.

While the naval negotiations proceeded, the powers sought a diplomatic settlement dealing with the Pacific and East Asia. When Hughes firmly rejected Balfour's offer to expand the Anglo-Japanese Alliance into a tripartite pact, Great Britain, Japan, and the United States turned their attention to some looser form of association to cover the Pacific area. The result was the Four Power Treaty, a consultative pact in which the three nations and France agreed to respect their mutual rights "in relation to their insular possessions and insular dominions in the region of the Pacific Ocean."[7] Hughes had insisted on the inclusion of France to ease possible suspicions in the Senate. He was pleased with the Four Power Treaty that would, he hoped, bring British and American policy closer together in the Pacific and reduce tension with Japan. For the Japanese, the pact averted diplomatic isolation by creating a formal tie with three major Western powers and also raised the possibility of a broader understanding with the United States.

As in the past, China produced the most subtle and complex political accommodation. Hughes intended to implant firmly in international law what he and his East Asian experts conceived to be the traditional China policy of the United States. On the surface the Japanese delegation appeared cooperative. Early in the conference Admiral Katō offered sweeping assurances that Japan wanted a strong China and desired no special privileges there. Both Katō and the most influential civilian member of the delegation, Shidehara Kijūrō, were extremely sensitive to disapproval of the

---

[7] *Foreign Relations of the United States: 1922,* 2 vols. (Washington, D.C., 1938), I, p. 35.

West and pleaded with the cabinet in Tokyo for more flexibility in working out an agreement on China. By February 1922 they had finally won enough leeway to sign the Nine Power Treaty. In it the powers pledged "to respect the sovereignty, the independence, and the territorial and administrative integrity of China," promised to give China the opportunity to develop a stable government, and to respect an open door for commerce and industry. Finally, they agreed not to seek "special rights or privileges" that might impinge on the prerogatives of the citizens of friendly states; nor would they countenance "action inimical to the security" of other nations in China.[8]

It was this final security clause—never explained to the conference—that embodied the inner reservations of the Japanese delegates and government. To Japanese leaders this clause contained a tacit recognition of Japan's special position in Southern Manchuria and Eastern Inner Mongolia; in those areas the nation's security would take precedence over pledges to respect the integrity of China. Japan's retreat from wartime expansionism was so great that its ruling circles had to settle for this oblique reference to traditional privileges in Northeast Asia. In part they did so because Elihu Root assured them that the Nine Power Treaty would not disrupt their position in that area. Still sympathetic to the enlightened, liberal leaders of Japan, Root, who played a key role in drafting the treaty, did not believe it applied to Manchuria or Mongolia or that it voided agreements that Japan and the other powers had negotiated with China over the years. It looked to the future, not to the past. Root reflected the views of a significant segment of American business, financial, and political leaders who wanted the United States to disregard its sentimental attitude toward China and enter into an arrangement with Japan to bring stability to East Asia.

These leaders, however, had seldom spoken out. Since the turn of the century those American statesmen with pro-Japanese beliefs had seemed on the defensive, unwilling to publicize their assumptions and engage in controversy over priorities in East Asia.

---

[8]*Ibid.*, pp. 278–279.

They sensed that, unlike those with a pro-Chinese bias, they had no large reservoir of public affection to tap. As a result, myths about American China policy gained a firmer hold than they otherwise might have. The vague, romantic notions about America's role in China were seldom challenged and eventually came to have a life of their own, influencing the perceptions of those policymakers with little grasp of the realities of East Asian politics.

Hughes was a case in point, at once influenced by the China myth but unwilling to pay the price of transforming it fully into American policy. He had no wish to cut through traditional ambiguities or to expose assumptions and priorities to public debate. Although irritated by the intransigence of the Chinese delegates, Hughes kept his faith in China's future and saw the Nine Power Treaty as a major instrument in the process through which China would "work out her own political salvation."[9] It endowed the principles of the Open Door and the integrity of China with a new vitality. Even the Japanese government now realized that it would have to bend before the tides of world opinion and pursue a more moderate course in China. During the conference Japan had settled its quarrel with the United States over Yap, announced its intention of quickly completing its withdrawal from Siberia and, after Hughes' vigorous intervention, made such substantial concessions on Shantung that a Sino-Japanese accord was finally reached. Japan's willingness to give way had impressed Hughes. It had been part of his larger purpose to evoke such a response. By avoiding a confrontation with Japan he not only brought the Harding administration a major domestic and international success, but also created a spirit of trust that he felt was so essential to the new order in the Pacific and East Asia.

Hughes' assumptions, shared by many Americans, help to explain why he and others believed the Washington treaty system would work. He had always thought that Wilson had attempted to alter world politics too rapidly and had overemphasized the role of force in the settlement of international disputes. Like the bulk of those who had participated in the prewar peace movement, he

---

[9]Quoted in Asada, "Japan and the United States, 1915-1925," p. 268.

adhered to a more gradual international reformism that emphasized the codification of international law and the development of institutions to interpret it. Assuming a natural harmony of interests among nations and the emergence of an enlightened world opinion, he believed that governments would settle their differences more and more through reasoned compromise.

Japan and the United States had just done so. They had cleared away old disputes and embodied the time-tested principles of American China policy in the law of nations. These principles, if observed, would allow China to resume an orderly political evolution that would one day bring a stable, republican government. As China achieved political maturity, the United States and the other powers would gradually relinquish their privileges there. Hughes and his advisers had no premonition of the crisis that Chinese nationalism would soon precipitate in East Asia, nor did they ask what might occur if their assumptions about China proved false. With the end of the conference Hughes proclaimed an "era of good feeling in the Far East," one based on mutual trust and understanding and "a new state of mind."[10] "We are taking," the Secretary of State boasted, "perhaps the greatest forward step in history to establish the reign of peace."[11]

Although Hughes indulged in hyperbole to inflate the success of the Harding administration, the American public also regarded the Washington Conference as a great success, one in which the United States had won naval parity with Great Britain and forced Japan to accept traditional American goals in China. The press overwhelmingly endorsed the Washington treaties, as did peace groups and many other organized segments of public opinion. But naval officers, Irish and German-American spokesmen, and the Hearst press attacked the Washington settlement, while some senators believed Japan would keep none of its obligations and suspected secret entanglements in the Four Power Treaty. Despite Hughes' assertion that it only involved the obligation to confer, the treaty narrowly escaped defeat. The Nine Power Treaty, how-

---

[10]*Ibid.,* p. 356-357.
[11]Quoted in May, unpublished manuscript on the Washington Conference.

ever, received unanimous Senate approval, while only one vote
was cast against the Five Power Treaty. Most Americans shared
the belief of Harding and Hughes that a new era of peace had
dawned in East Asia.

IV

In Japan the Washington Conference brought to a culmination
the realization—growing since the end of World War I—that the
old imperialist policies were outdated and that Japan must abide
by new principles of international conduct. Professional bureaucrats and party politicians had been the first to recognize this fact
but, by the end of the conference, a significant segment of military
and naval leaders accepted it, too. In the years immediately fol-
lowing the Washington Conference Japanese statesmen and intellectuals referred frequently to the "new epoch" in international
relations based on economic interdependence, naval limitation,
and cooperative action in China.

While Japanese leaders intended to maintain the nation's
spheres in Northeast Asia, they gave up any ambition of further
territorial acquisitions and instead emphasized possibilities of
peaceful economic expansion. They hoped to maintain the large
trade with the United States—which took 40 percent of Japan's
exports throughout the 1920s—while lowering barriers in China
and moving into previously neglected areas such as the Middle
East and Southeast Asia. The nation's leaders also wished to export people as well as goods and capital. All shared the widespread
belief that Japan lacked the resources to sustain its increasing
population and could only find relief through large-scale emigration. But continental Asia, the obvious area for much of this over-
flow, no longer seemed promising. Crowded conditions in Korea
and Taiwan and intense competition from Chinese in Manchuria
discouraged Japanese settlers. Any massive emigration would have
to be directed toward Oceania, Southeast Asia, and South
America.

In the first half of the decade it seemed to Japanese leaders that
enough doors would remain open for the nation to escape stagnation. While the great powers rejected racial equality and territorial
expansion, the Washington treaty system offered Japan more hope

than the aggressive policy of the war years, a policy that had clearly failed. If this vision of peaceful cooperation was to endure, however, it was necessary for all the elites and the Japanese people —not just the civilian bureaucrats—to become convinced that it served the nation well. The great powers would have to achieve a collaborative accommodation with Chinese nationalism and maintain a prosperous world economic system. All of this would require sustained effort, but Japanese diplomats, like their American counterparts, initially remained passive, convinced that the Washington Conference inaugurated an era of fruitful international cooperation in East Asia.

V

The Washington Conference brought a startling shift in the American image of Japan. Even East Asian experts—despite a residue of suspicion over Japan's continental ambitions—became cautiously optimistic. Secretary of State Hughes and other government leaders were much less restrained in their view of the future. Like the general public, they were impressed with the steady development of democratic institutions in Japan. During the 1920s party governments remained in power, bringing new social legislation and universal manhood suffrage. The influence of the military had clearly declined, and Japan was pursuing a policy of moderation toward China. Franklin D. Roosevelt exemplified the change in American attitudes. During the crisis of 1913, he had sided with extremists in the Navy Department; by mid-1923, however, he expressed his faith in the Washington treaty system and Japanese-American amity. The two nations, he wrote, "have not a single valid reason, and won't have as far as we can look ahead, for fighting each other."[12]

The severe earthquake that hit Tokyo and Yokohama in September 1923 stimulated a great outpouring of American sympathy and relief aid that seemed to confirm the new era of friendship. Ambassador Cyrus E. Woods reported that "the old suspicion and antagonism is broken down. Everywhere I go I hear the opinion

---

[12]Quoted in Frank Freidel, *Franklin D. Roosevelt: The Ordeal* (Boston, 1954), p. 135.

expressed that our countries at last understand each other, and that we are united in ties of friendship, more strongly than any paper treaty could possibly establish."[13]

American businessmen and financiers also turned toward Japan with new enthusiasm. While trade with China stagnated and political turmoil there discouraged investment, Japan proved to be a rapidly expanding market for American exports and capital. Its rising standard of living, political stability, and friendship with the West provided ideal conditions for closer economic ties. After the great earthquake huge American reconstruction loans poured into Japan with the encouragement of the Department of State. By the end of the decade Americans held 40 percent of Japan's foreign loans, while trade between the two nations had increased far beyond its prewar level.

In part this shift of interest from China to Japan was tied to a growing disillusionment with China that pervaded all segments of American society. Missionaries as well as businessmen found the situation there discouraging and noticed a decline in their support in the United States. Few college students now volunteered for service in China. Within the government the enthusiasm for China, so evident at the beginning of the decade, also diminished. Diplomats in China and officials in Washington were repelled by nationalistic excesses and the frequent attacks on American missionaries and businessmen. Far from fulfilling their earlier expectations, China seemed to be degenerating into chaos.

The American government saw no hope in Sun Yat-sen's Kuomintang and displayed a growing petulance over China's failure to meet its international obligations. Beyond issuing stern warnings and bemoaning conditions in China, however, the State Department remained passive, reluctant to take any action to improve the situation or to rethink its earlier assumptions. When Ambassador Charles B. Warren returned from Tokyo in early 1923, he told President Harding that the United States must reject myths about China and work with Japan. This was, in fact, the

---

[13]*Foreign Relations of the United States: 1923,* 2 vols. (Washington, D.C., 1938), II, pp. 483–484.

tendency of American policy. As hopes in China faded, Hughes and others placed increasing emphasis on Japanese-American economic ties and Japan's stabilizing role in East Asia. By the middle of the decade it seemed that this aspect of the Washington settlement had exceeded their original expectations.

While popular and official suspicions of Japan receded in the early twenties, the American navy remained intensely anti-Japanese. Throughout the decade Japan was the navy's primary enemy, one that seemed to imperil vital American interests. Sometimes naval officers publicly voiced their fears, but generally they were subdued, depressed by the results of the Washington Conference. The navy's quest for superiority in the Western Pacific had failed; now it faced a hostile Congress and an indifferent public. Naval officers were particularly bitter over the freeze on insular fortifications. Nevertheless, they continued to pursue their previous aims in the Pacific and attempted to find new ways to strengthen American naval power in that ocean. They struggled—unsuccessfully—to maintain the navy at treaty strength and tried —within treaty limits—to improve defenses in Hawaii and the Philippines. In 1921 they had concentrated more ships in the Pacific and, in succeeding years, pushed the modernization of battleships and the construction of heavy cruisers designed to operate in the vast distances between Hawaii and the Philippines. Naval planners anticipated that Japan would begin a war with the seizure of Guam and the Philippines and then assume a defensive posture. Worried about the navy's ability to take the offensive in the Western Pacific, they began to consider an island-hopping expeditionary force and the use of carrier-based air power to compensate for the numerical weakness of the American fleet. During this decade of peace and hope the navy retained a fierce determination to carry a war to the home waters of Japan.

Throughout the 1920s State Department professionals continued to give China a disproportionate share of their attention. Hughes temporarily increased the consciousness of Japan among American policymakers, but familiar ways of thinking reasserted themselves after he left office in 1925. The choice of ministers to China and ambassadors to Japan revealed this essentially unchanging priority. Harding sent Jacob Gould Schurman—a former chairman of the first Philippine Commission and long-time president of Cornell University—to Peking and, in 1925, Coolidge transferred him to Berlin, a key European embassy. Schurman was replaced by John V. A. MacMurray, who was followed in 1929 by his successor as chief of the Division of Far Eastern Affairs, Nelson T. Johnson. The chiefs of that division were authorities on China and, when assigned to East Asia, they went to Peking. Within the State Department the China experts formed a small, closely knit group who handed down concepts of American policy from one generation to the next.

No such group of Japan experts existed to insist that the ambassadorship to Japan be taken as seriously as the ministership to China. From 1921 to 1932 six men served in Tokyo. Most were political appointees; none carried the distinguished credentials of Schurman. Only one, William R. Castle, was a professional diplomat, but he was an expert on Western European affairs and stayed less than a year. The others—Charles B. Warren, Cyrus E. Woods, Edgar A. Bancroft, Charles MacVeagh, and W. Cameron Forbes—were lawyers and businessmen. Only Forbes, who had served as Governor General of the Philippines from 1909 to 1913, had had any prior experience in East Asia. Most of these men were prominent lawyers who had become corporate attorneys and civic leaders. Warren was a member of the Republican National Committee and president of the Detroit Chamber of Commerce; Woods achieved legal and political prominence in Pennsylvania; Bancroft served as general counsel of the International Harvester Corporation and was a popular orator at civic ceremonies in Chicago; MacVeagh helped incorporate the United States Steel Corporation and acted as its general solicitor; and Forbes belonged to an old Boston mercantile family. As far as we know, all served competently, but their rapid turnover and sudden immersion in a strange culture prevented them from seeing beneath the surface of events. Inevitably their contacts were limited to Western-oriented Japanese, particularly businessmen and professional diplomats. It is doubtful that any had much influence on his superiors in Washington.

Professional diplomats in the Division of Far Eastern Affairs had somewhat more weight. As the State Department grew bigger and as the geographical divisions enlarged, the power of the Division of Far Eastern Affairs increased. It offered an expert knowledge that no president or secretary of state could take lightly. During the 1920s presidents were not—except in moments of crisis—deeply involved in foreign policy. Harding and Coolidge recognized the domestic implications of American diplomacy, but possessed only a handful of firm convictions about America's relations with the world. Hoover, with more experience and insight, would surely have done more if he had not been distracted by the depression. Generally, however, these presidents left the initiative to their secretaries of state, setting the bounds within which American policy operated.

All three of the secretaries—Hughes, Frank B. Kellogg, and Henry L. Stimson—were strong-minded men who were never overshadowed by State Department professionals. Hughes, by far the ablest, resisted much of the advice of the Division of Far Eastern Affairs and set American policy toward Japan on a different course. With the conclusion of the Washington Conference, however, his interest in East Asia dropped off, and he focused on pressing problems in Europe and Latin America. The influence of the division reasserted itself when a secretary of state turned to other geographical areas or when the predilections of its chief happened to coincide with those of the secretary. The Division of Far Eastern Affairs exerted a powerful impact on American China policy from 1922 to the end of the decade, partly because Nelson T. Johnson and Kellogg agreed on the American approach to revolutionary nationalism there.

Neither the secretaries of state nor the professional diplomats endowed American foreign policy with the coherence that it had traditionally lacked. Hughes made a start with the Washington treaty system, but neither Hughes nor the professionals surrounding him saw any need to expand or perfect the Washington formula. Their optimism and faith in progress encouraged them to rely on general principles and peaceful economic expansion as a solution to foreign difficulties; their failure to view America as an integral part of a world political community encouraged them to conceive of relations in bilateral terms. Hughes tried to fuse relations with China and Japan into a single East Asian policy but, as the decade progressed, policymakers separated the two more and more. Even in Europe, where the United States acted to help solve the debt question and displayed some concern for political stability, American diplomats failed to grasp the full significance of these efforts. Only in the Caribbean and Latin America did the stakes seem high enough to produce a deeper and more sustained commitment.

The lack of coordination extended to economic expansion as well as foreign policy. Secretary of Commerce Hoover shared Hughes' belief that the United States must undertake a limited diplomatic involvement in the world. Along with internationally oriented businessmen and financiers, Hoover had emerged from the war with a sense of America's enormous economic power and with the belief that the United States was the moral and economic leader of the world. Businessmen viewed increased foreign trade and capital investment as essential for national well-being and saw no conflict between the pursuit of economic self-interest and service to humanity. Hoover, however, wished to impose some controls on economic expansion, particularly in the area of foreign loans. He encountered firm opposition from the banking and business communities. Nor could he find much support within the government, for Harding, Coolidge, Hughes, and Kellogg (as well as the Treasury Department) disliked the notion of any comprehensive supervision of foreign loans. These government leaders wished to keep clear of the whole process of foreign economic expansion. The one exception was oil diplomacy, where their fears that diminishing domestic reserves would endanger the national security led them to intervene vigorously to win American entry into major foreign oil concessions. Divided over most issues of economic foreign policy, the business community did not in general see any need for government assistance. In domestic affairs business and government had achieved a large degree of integration, but in the foreign arena their activities remained largely separate.

The passivity of American policymakers toward East Asia came out clearly in 1924, when Congress passed drastic immigration legislation. For years the immigration restriction movement had been gathering momentum and, by the end of World War I,

Americans had given up their hopes of transforming the new immigrants. Faith in the liberal, democratic values that had helped to sustain the promise of assimilation had weakened. Troubled by a lack of unity, Americans sought to recreate a sense of national cohesion through a spurious racism. Now the debate centered over the degree and method of restriction, not its wisdom. In 1921 Congress adopted a temporary quota system that recognized the Gentlemen's Agreement, but the pressure mounted for a permanent solution. By 1924 the support in Congress for a National Origins Act was overwhelming. Despite its miniscule quantity, Japanese immigration was regarded, like the new immigration in general, as a threat to the national character. West Coast racists were determined to attach a Japanese exclusion provision to any general bill.

Secretary of State Hughes was slow to recognize the diplomatic implications of Japanese exclusion. Shortly after the Washington Conference, Ambassador Shidehara had urged a resumption of immigration negotiations, but Hughes had put him off and allowed the question to drift. Not until early 1924, when the congressional exclusion movement was far along, did Hughes finally act. In February he sent a letter to the chairman of the House Committee on Immigration and Naturalization—where anti-Japanese sentiment was strongest—arguing that exclusion legislation was unnecessary and would "largely undo the work of the Washington Conference."[14] The retention of the Gentlemen's Agreement, along with the application of the quota system to Japan, would result in the entry of only 246 Japanese a year.

This letter, however, seemed to have little effect, and Hughes decided to disarm congressional suspicions of the Gentlemen's Agreement by having the Japanese ambassador explain the nature of the accord. On April 10, 1924 Ambassador Hanihara Masanao handed Hughes a letter that did so and that closed by warning of the "grave consequences" that exclusion legislation would bring.[15] Hughes let this phrase slip by and quickly forwarded the

---

[14] Quoted in Merlo J. Pusey, *Charles Evans Hughes,* 2 vols. (New York, 1951), II, p. 512.
[15] *Foreign Relations of the United States: 1924,* 2 vols. (Washington, D.C., 1939), II, p. 373.

letter to Congress. In the Senate Lodge seized on Hanihara's unfortunate phraseology to claim that it represented a "veiled threat" of war and impugned the nation's honor.[16] Despite Hughes' challenge of this strained interpretation, the damage was done. By now the question of Japanese exclusion had become associated with tensions between the executive and Congress, and Lodge's claim offered senators a convenient excuse to adopt an exclusion amendment by a vote of 71 to 4. It is likely that, in any event, the Senate would have done so by a decisive margin. When President Coolidge sought a delay in the implementation of the exclusion clause in order to negotiate a separate agreement with Japan, the Congress refused. It would no longer tolerate a special arrangement with Japan.

Hughes realized the gravity of the congressional action. "It is a sorry business," he wrote a friend, "and I am greatly depressed. It has undone the work of the Washington Conference and implanted the seeds of an antagonism which are sure to bear fruit in the future."[17] Even MacMurray, once the leader of the anti-Japanese faction in the State Department, felt bitter toward the Congress and was convinced that exclusion would gravely damage the new cooperative order emerging in East Asia. American representatives in Peking and Tokyo shared the melancholy mood of the State Department and despaired over a future that only months before had seemed so bright.

In the United States the exclusion controversy brought anti-Japanese hostilities to the surface once more. Rear Admiral Bradley A. Fiske, long since retired, warned that irreconcilable Japanese and American national attitudes made war imminent, and some American newspapers published sensational accounts of Japanese designs on the United States. In Japan ultranationalists organized mass meetings and many editors objected to the American naval maneuvers west of Hawaii scheduled for the spring of 1925. Both Japanese and American officials spoke out sharply against this war talk. President Coolidge reprimanded his own Secretary of the

---

[16]Quoted in Pusey, *Charles Evans Hughes,* II, p. 514.
[17]*Ibid.,* p. 516.

Navy, while Secretary of State Hughes, in warmly welcoming the new Japanese ambassador in late 1924, deplored alarmist statements and claimed that "nothing but a state of mind"[18] could disrupt the traditional friendship between the two nations.

But the flurry of war rumors temporarily affected each government. Hughes declined an informal Japanese overture that the United States cancel the navy's war games, and Foreign Minister Shidehara rejected Hughes' suggestion that the American fleet might visit Japan after completing its Pacific operations. Nevertheless, this mood soon passed, as each government attempted to minimize the significance of the exclusion legislation and maintain the faith of both peoples in the future of Japanese-American amity.

VI

This proved more difficult in Japan than in the United States. There, right-wing groups and much of the press denounced exclusion legislation and the unwillingness of Foreign Minister Shidehara to protest more strongly. Extremists now argued more convincingly that cooperation could not work with racist Western nations and that Japan must fulfill its Asian destiny through a unilateral policy. Although most Japanese leaders did not go this far, exclusion did have an immense psychological impact. It marked the failure of Japan's quest for racial equality and suggested the closing off of opportunities outside of East Asia. It discredited, in short, the civilian bureaucrats and their policy of cooperation with the West.

By the middle of the decade it seemed more clear that the postwar structure in East Asia was not benefiting Japan. The modest growth of the Japanese economy was felt only in urban areas, while in rural areas the standard of living began to decline. Moreover, the promise held out by the Washington treaty system for joint action in China had disappeared. In America Secretary of State Kellogg and Nelson T. Johnson shared none of Hughes' reluctance to depart from a cooperative policy. Both believed that

---

[18] Hugh R. Wilson, *Diplomat Between Wars* (New York, 1941), p. 188.

the American government, in response to mounting Chinese nationalism, must relinquish its special privileges. Imbued with an
idealism toward China that Hughes never felt, they wanted the
United States to take the lead in readjusting China's relations with
the West. It was not until mid-1928, however, that they placed
their faith in the new Nationalist regime and granted tariff autonomy and de facto recognition. The United States was the first
nation to do so.

Independent action by the United States and Great Britain
helped convince Japanese leaders that the policy of collaboration
in China had collapsed. The launching of the Northern Expedition
in 1926 (the Kuomintang's great military campaign, which
brought the nominal unification of China) and the rise of antiforeignism compelled them to give serious attention to the situation in China and to the protection of special rights in Southern
Manchuria. Foreign Minister Shidehara did not wish to use force
in China and urged patience in dealing with the turmoil there. He
did intend, however, to uphold Japan's treaty rights and to impose
through diplomacy Japan's concept of Sino-Japanese cooperation.
With the old system of foreign privileges breaking down, Japan
had to find a new way to defend its interests. Both Shidehara and
Tanaka Giichi, who became Prime Minister and Foreign Minister
in April 1927, searched for moderates within the Kuomintang and
concluded that Chiang Kai-shek best represented them. As the
Nationalists consolidated their power, the Japanese government
was more and more eager to reach a bargain over Manchuria and
to prevent the civil war from spreading into that region. The
Foreign Office wished to preserve Japan's special position by dealing directly with the Nationalist government, but Tanaka chose
instead to deal with the warlord who dominated Manchuria,
Chang Tso-lin. He intended to integrate Manchuria more closely
with Japan while at the same time supporting the Nationalists in
China proper. Chiang Kai-shek, he hoped, would understand.
Tanaka sought to develop these new arrangements in China without considering the position of Great Britain or the United States.
Like his Western counterparts, he did not connect Japanese activities in China with other segments of the nation's foreign policy.

By 1928 these efforts had failed. Chang Tso-lin proved recalcitrant and was assassinated by Kwantung Army officers. In May Chinese and Japanese troops clashed at Tsinan in Shantung province and, as the year progressed, Sino-Japanese relations steadily worsened. The Nationalists' aggressive foreign policy posed a serious threat to Japan's special position in Northeast Asia and dimmed hopes for further advances in the whole of China. The government's China policy was in disarray, as was its policy of economic expansion. The world economic crisis hit Japan with particular severity, bringing a 50 percent decline in exports between 1929 and 1931 and a sharp drop in the real incomes of workers and peasants.

In July 1929, when Shidehara became Foreign Minister again, he realized that Japan's unilateral initiative in China had not succeeded. He planned to revive the policy of collaboration with the Western powers and win their support for Japanese interests in China. Both Shidehara and Prime Minister Hamaguchi Osachi viewed the London Naval Conference of 1930 as a crucial part of this effort to develop closer ties with Great Britain and the United States. They agreed to a settlement there, which aroused the fierce opposition of many naval officers and party politicians. Through clever bureaucratic maneuvering and with the help of some influential navy leaders, Hamaguchi secured the acceptance of this agreement. In doing so, however, he weakened moderate elements within the navy and so aroused fanatical patriots that in November 1930 he was seriously wounded by a rightist assassin.

Shidehara's efforts brought some response from Great Britain and the United States, but neither government seriously considered a tripartite partnership to confront the dilemma presented by Chinese nationalism. The aspirations of civilian bureaucrats for cooperation with the West seemed more and more hollow to the members of the various elites and to the bulk of the people. The attempt to work out an arrangement with Kuomintang leaders had collapsed; trade with China and the United States had fallen off badly; and Japan's economy had seriously deteriorated. On the surface, party rule still appeared strong, as it had throughout the decade. But the parties had always concentrated too exclusively on holding power instead of using it constructively. They had never achieved either real popular legitimacy or a firm dominance over the other elites.

The deepening crisis at the close of the decade turned the masses, the patriotic societies, and the military decisively against the whole pro-Western Japanese establishment—the parties, the civilian bureaucracy, and the great business combines that had, so it seemed, failed the nation. For years the army and navy had viewed the United States as their most likely enemy; now military planners conceived of an autonomous Japanese empire that would provide the base necessary to sustain such a war. To these dissatisfied groups the United States had come to represent the domestic and international conditions against which they were determined to rebel. Convinced that cooperation with the West had endangered the nation, they believed the time had come to redefine Japan's foreign policy and national policy.

VII

The despair of American policymakers over the consequences of exclusion legislation quickly passed. By early 1925 they had recovered their confidence, and Ambassador Edgar A. Bancroft could write a friend that "there are so many graduates of American universities and colleges in positions of power and influence here that it only requires a sympathetic handling of relations between the two nations to make Japan an absolutely devoted and perpetual friend of America."[19] Aside from army and navy officers and a handful of civilian alarmists, few Americans could imagine a war with Japan or any other nation. President Hoover caught this popular mood when he wrote Secretary of State Stimson in September 1929 that "there is the most profound outlook for peace today that we have had at any time in the last half century."[20]

As the decade drew to a close, American popular and official thinking once again focused on China and the prospects of the new Kuomintang regime. The apparent centralization of authority there created modest optimism among some missionaries, bankers, and businessmen. Like Kellogg, Stimson shared this optimism and

[19] Quoted in Akira Iriye, "1922-1931," in Ernest R. May and James C. Thomson, Jr., eds., *American-East Asian Relations: A Survey* (Cambridge, Mass., 1972), p. 239.
[20] Quoted in Robert H. Ferrell, *American Diplomacy in the Great Depression: Hoover-Stimson Foreign Policy, 1929-1933* (New Haven, 1957), p. 19.

viewed the Nationalist government as a progressive force. Accepting the whole cluster of myths about Sino-American relations, he was proud of the important role of unofficial American advisers in Peking. Stimson and his China experts took continuing Japanese-American amity for granted. They ignored Ambassador William R. Castle's report that Japanese leaders believed war could come with the United States only over China. Nelson T. Johnson expressed the prevalent sentiment when he observed that "all of the evidence seems to point to the friendliest of feelings between us and the Japanese which should continue more or less indefinitely."[21]

The complacency of American officials emerged clearly at the London Naval Conference in 1930. Stimson's great concern, from the moment he took office until the end of the conference, was the repair of Anglo-American relations through the conclusion of a naval agreement. Determined to avoid the mistakes made at the disastrous Geneva Naval Conference of 1927, Hoover and Stimson overrode the General Board and spent 6 months in detailed preliminary negotiations with Great Britain. Although Stimson knew in advance that Japan would demand a 10:7 ratio, he dismissed the Japanese position as extreme. Japan, he reasoned, would have no choice but to go along with an Anglo-American accord.

Once the conference opened, Stimson absorbed himself in completing Anglo-American negotiations on cruiser strength and trying to devise some formula to meet the French demand for a consultative pact. He assigned the long and tedious negotiations with Japan to another member of the delegation, Senator David A. Reed. When these talks stalled, Stimson threatened to proceed with a separate Anglo-American agreement if Japan failed to reduce its demands. Apparently he believed that the concessions to Great Britain on cruiser strength had already upset the American navy and that he might arouse substantial opposition in the United States if he made further ones to Japan. Only pressure from

---

[21]Quoted in Akira Iriye, *Across the Pacific: An Inner History of American-East Asian Relations* (New York, 1967), p. 166.

President Hoover and the State Department moderated Stimson's position and led him to accept the Reed-Matsudaira compromise, which granted Japan a 10:7 ratio in light cruisers and destroyers and equality in submarines. Theoretically Japan won only a 10:6 ratio in heavy cruisers, but it actually received a 10:7 ratio during the life of the treaty (which ran until 1936) because of an American promise not to complete three of its ships until 1936, 1937, and 1938.

The American failure to build up to treaty strength during the 1920s conditioned the meaning of the settlement with Japan. In fact, it allowed the American navy far more new construction than the Japanese navy and reduced the margin of superiority in the Western Pacific to which Japan had grown accustomed. Prior to the conference Prime Minister Hamaguchi had announced that Japan must have a ratio of 10:7 in all combat categories and, in Japan, the belief had become widespread that the nation's security depended on such a ratio. Stimson understood the intensity of the Japanese opposition to the London Naval Treaty, but missed its long-run significance; he was impressed with the determination of the Hamaguchi Ministry to cooperate with the West instead of with its tenuous position in Japan's political life.

In 1930 and 1931 officials in Washington, more and more preoccupied with the depression, gave little serious thought to events in East Asia. Stimson spent most of the summer of 1931 in Europe, discussing international financial problems. In September of that year, on the eve of the Manchurian crisis, he surveyed Japanese-American relations with the Japanese ambassador and observed that they were "more tranquil than for many years past."[22] Stimson speculated that in the near future Japanese immigration might be put on a quota basis. Diplomats in the field were no more prescient than the Secretary of State. Minister Johnson in Peking did not believe that Japan would occupy Manchuria or that a Sino-Japanese conflict was imminent. Ambassador Forbes in Tokyo agreed, as he prepared to return to the United States on

---

[22]Henry L. Stimson, *The Far Eastern Crisis: Recollections and Observations* (New York, 1936), p. 3.

leave. American diplomats, along with the general public, were oblivious to the crisis about to burst on East Asia. By 1931 much of the glitter of the 1920s had faded, but old habits of thought died hard, and men could still not conceive of the decade as a brief prelude to a new era of chaos.

CHAPTER V

The Challenge of the 1930s

B Y THE AUTUMN OF 1931 THE SITUATION IN EAST ASIA HAD BECOME EXPLOSIVE. The rise of Chiang Kai-shek, along with the extension of the Chinese Nationalist movement into Manchuria, had put Japan on the defensive in Northeast Asia. In Manchuria the Chinese regime, although only nominally under the sovereignty of Nanking, had undertaken an economic offensive against Japanese interests and encouraged the spread of anti-Japanese sentiment. Deteriorating conditions in Manchuria intensified the conviction among Japanese army officers that the domestic and international status quo was intolerable. Viewing themselves as the guardians of the nation, they felt the army must act to reinvigorate traditional values and to safeguard vital interests abroad. In Mukden staff officers of the Kwantung Army were particularly alarmed by the threats to Japan's Manchurian sphere. They concluded that only through the occupation of Manchuria could Japan create the strategic and economic base essential for a future war. General Staff officers in Tokyo agreed. They approved of the Kwantung Army's plan to fabricate an incident on the South Manchurian Railway near Mukden and use it as a justification for assuming control of all Manchuria.

The Mukden Incident of September 18, 1931 brought a clash between local defenders and Japanese forces and the rapid spread of Japanese troops throughout Southern Manchuria. The Japanese people responded enthusiastically, for most believed that somehow the destiny of their nation was linked to the fate of Manchuria. They felt a sense of relief and exhilaration over the Kwantung Army's bold act. Matsuoka Yōsuke, a Seiyūkai deputy who would achieve fame later in the decade, expressed the mood of his countrymen when he remarked that "we feel suffocated as we observe internal and external situations. . . . We are seeking room that will let us breathe."[1] Pro-Western liberals, party politicians, and members of the nationalistic societies all applauded the use of force in Manchuria and helped to create an overwhelming national consensus that made effective resistance impossible. The Emperor and his advisers and major industrial leaders opposed military action in Manchuria, as did Prime Minister Wakatsuki Reijirō and Foreign Minister Shidehara Kijūrō. But these men were largely immobilized by a sense of impotence, a lack of confidence in their own leadership and a lack of any convincing alternative to the army's policy. For over a decade they had pursued cooperative diplomacy; now its failure was painfully clear. The crisis in Manchuria and in Japan had produced an insistent demand for a new course in both domestic and foreign affairs. Even within the Foreign Ministry many diplomats believed that Japan must take strong measures against China to strengthen its leadership in East Asia.

The Prime Minister and Foreign Minister had little support within the cabinet or nation and the assurances that they quickly gave Western nations—that Japanese forces would soon return to the South Manchurian Railway zone—were meaningless. Wakatsuki and Shidehara could neither control the military nor discover its future plans. Initially, however, they won the partial cooperation of army authorities in Tokyo, who were unwilling to challenge their civilian rulers overtly and who had mixed feelings about the vast ambitions of the Kwantung Army. Army leaders, along with many of their middle-echelon staff officers, were sympathetic with the action of the Kwantung Army in Southern Manchuria, but were unwilling to sanction the occupation of Northern Manchuria or the outright annexation of the whole region. They worried about the excessive independence of the Kwantung Army and the international repercussions of any Northern Manchurian operation. Their caution did, for a time, impose some restraints on the forces in the field and enabled the cabinet to pursue a negotiated settlement. Wakatsuki and Shidehara hoped to reconcile the

---

[1]Quoted in Sadako N. Ogata, *Defiance in Manchuria: The Making of Japanese Foreign Policy, 1931-1932* (Berkeley and Los Angeles, 1964), p. 35.

demands of the military and cooperation with the West by concluding a new treaty with the Nationalist government, one that
would specifically recognize Japan's hegemony in Manchuria. By
the end of 1931, however, they finally concluded that such a
middle course was untenable. Unable to reach an agreement with
the Kuomintang and confronted with the army's growing impatience, the cabinet resigned on December 12.

II

The conflict in Manchuria seemed extraordinarily remote to
American leaders. Overwhelmed by the demands of the world
economic crisis, Hoover and Stimson had little energy left for the
clash between China and Japan in Northeast Asia. Their initial
impulse was to minimize the significance of the conflict and to
doubt that the interwar peace structure would be seriously challenged. Stimson, who dominated the early phases of American
policy, was almost complacent. He believed that his year as Governor-General of the Philippines had given him a special insight into
the "Oriental mind"[2] and felt that the State Department was
well-informed about the situation in Japan and Manchuria. Although he deplored the use of force by the Japanese military, he
realized that Japan had genuine grievances in Manchuria and assumed that the conflict there would not disrupt Japanese-American friendship. Stimson's instincts and information pointed toward a policy of caution. The United States, by avoiding provoca-
tive statements and quietly mobilizing world opinion, could
strengthen moderate leaders in Tokyo and enable them to control
military insubordination in Manchuria. Stimson had great confidence in Foreign Minister Shidehara, whom he knew personally,
and accepted the Foreign Minister's assurances that the army
would pull back as soon as the government secured Japanese rights
in Manchuria. Shidehara urged the powers to stand aside while
China and Japan solved the dispute.

The soothing reassurances of the Japanese government

---

[2]Quoted in Elting E. Morison, *Turmoil and Tradition: A Study of the Life and Times of Henry
L. Stimson* (Boston, 1960), p. 374.

confirmed Stimson in his course, as did the opinions of his State Department advisers and of professional diplomats. Under Secretary of State Castle, who had served for a year as ambassador to Japan, argued that the United States ought to accept Japanese dominance in East Asia. Japan, Castle believed, was "our one useful friend in the Orient."[3] Ambassador Forbes in Tokyo defended Japan, while Minister Johnson in Peking emphasized the smallness of American interests in Manchuria. Both Johnson and Stanley K. Hornbeck, although worried about the implications of the Mukden Incident for the peace system, accepted Stimson's cautious policy. So did President Hoover and the American people. They still viewed Japan in terms of the imagery of the 1920s and felt little sympathy for China, a nation that had failed to fulfill the hopes of the Washington Conference and that seemed doomed to endless chaos. American businessmen and financiers interested in East Asia, impressed by the growth of Japanese-American economic ties, identified more with Japan than China. Some argued that Japanese control of Manchuria would bring economic benefits to the United States, and many drew an analogy between Japan's action in Manchuria and past American intervention in the Caribbean. Initially the reaction of the business community, like that of the foreign policy public, was strongly pro-Japanese.

In late September and early October Stimson grew impatient as the Japanese military extended its control over Southern Manchuria and as he began to see the widening gap between the assurances of the government and the aims of the army. On October 8 the bombing of Chinchow, well down the railway line toward Peking, shocked Stimson and many other Americans and, in the Secretary's mind, released a flood of inner doubts about his earlier assessment of the situation in Japan. Now Stimson and his subordinates began to connect events in Manchuria with the preservation of the world's peace structure and to consider new American initiatives. The immediate result, however, was no change in policy, but only an increased level of concern. In mid-October

---

[3]Quoted in Armin Rappaport, *Henry L. Stimson and Japan, 1931-33* (Chicago, 1963), p. 38.

Stimson allowed the American Consul in Geneva to sit temporarily with the League Council and, in November, he dispatched Ambassador Charles G. Dawes from London to Paris to maintain a channel of communication with the League. Although the United States urged Japan to withdraw its forces to the railway zone, it disapproved of a League resolution setting a time limit for such withdrawal and carefully avoided taking the lead against Japan. With the creation of the Lytton Commission in early December the crisis seemed to enter a new and quieter stage. Hoover and Stimson assumed that conditions in Manchuria would remain static until the commission issued a report.

American statesmen had once again displayed their misunderstanding of the dynamics of Japanese expansionism. The new cabinet of Inukai Tsuyoshi, the leader of the Seiyūkai, was more vulnerable to pressure from the military and, in late December, authorized the Kwantung Army to occupy the remainder of Manchuria. Soon all Chinese resistance north of the Great Wall ceased.

The completion of the Japanese conquest of Manchuria ended illusions in Washington about the ability of civilian moderates to regain control of the Japanese government. Clearly events in Manchuria were not the result of an isolated military rebellion; they represented the determination of the Japanese people to dominate the whole of that province. To Stimson and many other Americans, Japan's seizure of Manchuria represented a momentous challenge to the rule of law and to the peace system that had been so arduously established since the end of World War I. While Stimson had some sense of the anomalous situation in East Asia, he did not intend to ignore Japan's alleged aggression. In early October he had written in his diary that "the peace treaties of modern Europe made out by the Western nations of the world no more fit the three great races of Russia, Japan, and China . . . than . . . a stovepipe hat would fit an African savage. Nevertheless they are parties to these treaties and the whole world looks on to see whether the treaties are good for anything or not, and if we lie down and treat them like scraps of paper nothing will happen, and in the future the peace movement will receive a blow that it will not recover from for a long time."[4] By early January 1932 Stimson was convinced that the United States must act—independently, if necessary—to preserve the stability of the world and ensure the advance of civilization.

The President shared the Secretary of State's conviction that the United States must in some way condemn Japanese aggression in Manchuria. Hoover had entered office hoping to lead the nation out of the "extreme mental and spiritual isolation" of the past and to deepen its involvement in the furtherance of the "moral foundations of international life."[5] Prior to the Manchurian crisis, he had speculated on the use of moral deterrents such as nonrecognition and the withdrawal of embassies as a means of strengthening the Kellogg-Briand Pact. Confronted with Japan's absorption of Manchuria, he wished to use American influence to arouse world opinion and to curb Japanese excesses in East Asia.

The differences between the President and his Secretary of State were small, more differences of temperament and perspective than of belief. Stimson's extreme legalism and his faith in world opinion combined with an intense combativeness and an uneven recognition of the domestic limits on foreign policy. He applied to international relations the gentlemanly values of his own life and restlessly sought some means of vindicating them. Yet Stimson never advocated more than mild threats of possible military and economic action by the United States. In November and December 1931 he toyed with the idea of sanctions and consulted his State Department advisers, some of whom were for a time attracted to the idea. The Secretary of State, however, was uncertain, worried about their possible ramifications and apparently convinced, along with many in the State Department, that Japan's economic weakness would in any event soon force a pullback in Manchuria. He also knew that Hoover's firm opposition to economic sanctions and the strong sympathy for Japan within the cabinet made the whole discussion theoretical.

[4]Henry L. Stimson, *On Active Service in Peace and War* (New York, 1957), p. 233.
[5]Herbert Hoover, *The Memoirs of Herbert Hoover,* 3 vols. (New York, 1951-52), II, pp. 365, 378.

The President had no doubt that economic sanctions against Japan, or any other power, would bring war. He had no desire to go about "sticking pins in tigers"[6] or to weaken the nation that played a major stabilizing role in Asia. Mirroring the feelings of the Congress and people, he was only willing to register American disapproval of Japanese expansionism. The nonrecognition note drawn up by Stimson and his staff and dispatched to Tokyo on January 7, 1932 fitted his needs perfectly. It warned that the American government would not recognize any agreement or situation that impaired its treaty rights in China or that was brought about by means contrary to the Kellogg-Briand Pact.

The American public, upset by the scope of Japanese ambitions in Manchuria, generally supported Stimson's position, although some influential foreign policy analysts worried over the consequences of nonrecognition. In late January, public concern deepened when bitter fighting broke out between Chinese and Japanese forces in Shanghai. The concentration of Western interests and citizens there was far greater than in the whole of Manchuria and, inevitably, the public came to view Japanese expansionism in more ominous terms. The powerful banker Thomas W. Lamont, while remaining pro-Japanese, warned his Japanese friends to curb the excesses of their government. Peace groups formed two organizations, the American Committee on the Far East Crisis and the American Boycott Association. The first, led by A. Lawrence Lowell, president of Harvard University and Newton D. Baker, secretary of war under Woodrow Wilson, circulated a petition urging the American government to join with the League in sanctions against Japan; the second advocated a private boycott of Japanese goods. The very existence of both movements indicated that a portion of the foreign policy public had adopted a much harsher view of Japan. Neither, however, gained broad public support; most Americans feared a policy that might bring economic disruptions or political complications. The public was in no mood for new crusades in East Asia.

The Japanese navy's reckless invasion of Shanghai angered

---

[6]Quoted in Morison, *Turmoil and Tradition*, p. 382.

Secretary of State Stimson and convinced him of the need for some
further American response. He wished to transfer the small
American Asiatic fleet from Manila to Shanghai both to protect
American citizens and property and to intimidate Japan. "We had
a right," he informed the President, "to rely upon the unconscious
elements of our great size and military strength . . . Japan was
afraid of that, and I was willing to let her be afraid of that without
telling her that we were not going to use it against her."[7] Stimson's
imagination raced ahead of events as he contemplated a Japanese-
American conflict and urged a high level of naval preparedness.
Others within the Hoover administration, however, did not share
his enthusiasm for such a move. The Secretary of the Navy and
the Chief of Naval Operations opposed the shift of the Asiatic
fleet, as did most of Stimson's State Department advisers. To these
men it seemed an overreaction to events in Shanghai, a transparent
bluff that might provoke a dangerous incident with Japan.

The President, however, sided with his Secretary of State. He
approved the dispatch of the Asiatic fleet to Shanghai along with
an increase in the American garrison there. Hoover also wished to
express American indignation over Japan's most recent violation
of the rules of international conduct. As Stimson phrased it, the
fighting in Shanghai made it imperative "to put the situation mor-
ally in its right place."[8]

Stimson sought British support before he acted. The British
government hoped to sustain the League and cooperate with the
United States but, most of all, it hoped to safeguard its interests
in China by avoiding unnecessary friction with Japan. British
leaders were in a defensive mood, insecure at home and skeptical
of America's reliability. Thus, they rejected the American overture
for a new démarche. Nevertheless Stimson, with Hoover's approval, decided to proceed unilaterally and, on February 23, wrote
a letter to Senator William E. Borah, chairman of the Foreign
Relations Committee. In it Stimson reviewed the grand tradition
of American China policy and suggested the interdependence of

---

[7]Stimson, *On Active Service,* p. 245.
[8]Quoted in Morison, *Turmoil and Tradition,* p. 390.

the whole Washington treaty system. In other words, he implied that Japan's violation of China's political independence and territorial integrity might free the United States from the restrictions of the Five Power Treaty. The Borah letter, Stimson believed, would clarify the issues for the American public, further arouse world opinion, and put the Japanese government on notice. It completed his legal and historical indictment of Japan.

The endorsement of the nonrecognition doctrine by the League in March left little for Stimson to do. He had entrapped Japan in a web of historic precedents and fine legal distinctions. He had pointed out the significance of Japan's aggression in Manchuria and laid the basis for a worldwide condemnation of it. Neither the public nor the President would let him go further. Economic sanctions were out of the question. In mid-May Stimson wrote Walter Lippmann that he agreed with the essence of Hoover's position and recognized "all the evils of a boycott; the danger of its leading to war blindly and unwisely."[9] Stimson did what he could, however, to keep the lines of American policy firmly drawn. After the completion of the navy's annual war games in the Pacific in May 1932, he convinced the President to hold the Atlantic scouting force on the West Coast. He also replaced Ambassador Forbes, who openly dissented from his policy, with Joseph C. Grew, a distinguished career diplomat who had served in the 1920s as ambassador to Turkey and as Undersecretary of State. Presumably Grew shared Stimson's perspective on recent events in East Asia. But Stimson could not prevent the emergence of disagreements with President Hoover. At the very time Stimson wished to intimidate Japan, Hoover called for a substantial reduction in the naval strength of the great powers. And, in May 1932, while Stimson was in Europe, Undersecretary of State Castle, at Hoover's suggestion, told the public that the American government would not go beyond moral indictments of Japan.

Nor could Stimson prevent a spreading disillusionment with the efficacy of American policy. In March the Manchurian independ-

---

[9]Quoted in Joan Hoff Wilson, *American Business and Foreign Policy, 1920-1933* (Lexington, 1971), p. 229.

ence movement, sponsored by the Kwantung Army, resulted in the creation of Manchukuo; 2 months later a group of young army and navy officers assassinated Prime Minister Inukai. The new cabinet, while wishing to avoid additional friction with the West, finally succumbed to pressure from the military and, in September, extended recognition. Stimson's warnings and moral censure seemed only to be pushing Japan toward a defiant nationalism and a severance of its ties with the West. Reports reaching Washington described the enormous animosity that American policy had aroused. Ambassador Grew, arriving early in the summer of 1932, was struck by the widespread war psychology and the bitter hostility of formerly Western-oriented figures such as Ishii Kikujirō and Kaneko Kentarō. Convinced that excitable young army officers controlled the government, Grew concluded that American policy had strengthened their hand and delayed the return of moderates to power. The ambassador's assessment confirmed the conviction of government officials that the United States had gone too far in antagonizing Japan and in staking out a position in advance of that of the other powers and the League of Nations. Influential figures outside the government agreed and urged Stimson to stop inflaming public opinion in both nations.

For a time Stimson rejected this advice and continued his campaign to perfect the indictment of Japan. In a well-publicized speech before the Council on Foreign Relations on August 8, 1932, he discounted traditional American neutrality, proclaimed the power of public opinion, and attempted to link the United States with the League enforcement machinery through the Kellogg-Briand Pact. But the resistance of the President, his State Department advisers, and the bulk of the foreign policy public gradually forced Stimson to accept a more passive policy. As his term of office neared an end, his faith occasionally faltered, for all the words and gestures directed at Japan seemed to have had no effect on that nation's policy. These moments of uncertainty, however, did not become dominant; Stimson never altered his convictions about Japan. He sought to commit Franklin D. Roosevelt to the Republican policy in Manchuria and, in a long private talk, seemed to succeed. Stimson left office with a sense of vindication, with a feeling that he had expressed the highest ideals of the nation and helped to preserve the principles on which world peace depended.

III

The new administration was not inclined to continue Stimson's rhetorical belligerence. The outcome of the Mukden Incident had disenchanted American diplomats and eroded their confidence in the interwar peace system. Events in Manchuria—removed from this broader context—lost much of their significance, for American interests there and in North China seemed far too small to justify further provocation of Japan. Minister Johnson concluded that the Manchurian episode had reduced the world's peace machinery to "ashes" and that only force would halt Japan.[10] Ambassador Grew agreed, as did Stanley K. Hornbeck, chief of the Division of Far Eastern Affairs, who felt that the United States must adopt an aloof attitude toward Japanese aggression. "Given time," he speculated, "the flood tide of her invasion will reach its height and the ebb will follow."[11] One of the President's chief foreign policy advisers, Norman H. Davis, retained his faith in international cooperation, but doubted its effectiveness outside of Europe.

These attitudes were an expression of that sense of isolation enveloping most Americans as they experienced the physical and psychological ordeal of the depression. The nation was absorbed in a crisis of domestic reconstruction, one that eroded men's confidence in the promise of America and in its ability to provide leadership in world affairs. Liberals worried that foreign entanglements might bring a war that would destroy their hope for domestic reform; conservatives feared that foreign conflict would create a centralized state and further expand the President's already swollen powers. Most shared an oppressive sense of futility about America's involvement in World War I and were determined to heed the apparent lessons of that futile crusade. Conceding much justice to the claims of the "have not" nations, Americans strug-

---

[10]Quoted in Dorothy Borg, *The United States and the Far Eastern Crisis of 1933-1938: From the Manchurian Incident Through the Initial Stage of the Undeclared Sino-Japanese War* (Cambridge, Mass., 1964), p. 31.

[11]*Ibid.*, p. 35.

gled to avoid the turmoil that the assertive diplomacy of Germany, Italy, and Japan produced.

The President shared much of this isolationist mood and the psychology of appeasement that it engendered. Like his diplomatic advisers, he had become skeptical of the effectiveness in preventing war of American cooperation with other nations, and he feared that private economic interests, if unrestrained, would severely limit his options. Parts of the Wilsonian heritage, however, still lingered in Roosevelt's mind. He occasionally made internationalist gestures, such as his advocacy in 1935 of American membership in the World Court or his wish for more flexible neutrality legislation. But the President had little energy with which to resolve the contradictions in his own thoughts and seemed uncertain of where he stood, drifting somewhere between the extremes of the decade. His foreign policy leadership was weak, influenced more by domestic currents—particularly the clamor of doctrinaire isolationists—than any coherent set of beliefs. Absorbed in the evolution of the New Deal, he attempted to avoid foreign policy controversies that might disrupt his reform coalition.

The period from 1933 to 1937 was a quiet one in East Asia. In February 1933 Japan made its symbolic break with the West by walking out of the League of Nations and, in subsequent years, continued to display a fierce determination to pursue its national mission free from Western restraints. The Japanese government became ever more assertive in its claims for a unique position in China, while the Kwantung Army steadily undermined Kuomintang authority in the northern portion of that nation. In Asia and in Europe the relations of the great powers were confused as old beliefs and structures faded and new ones had yet to emerge. But it was in Europe, not Asia, that eye-catching events occurred. In October 1935 the Italo-Ethiopian War erupted, in early 1936 Germany reoccupied the Rhineland and, in July 1936, the Spanish Civil War began. The attention of the American government and people focused on the activities of Nazi Germany and fascist Italy instead of on the quiet Japanese subversion of China's autonomy. Concern over East Asia reached a low ebb; Japan's activities there drew the sustained attention of only a handful of Americans with special interests in that area.

The American government reacted passively to the simmering Asian crisis. American diplomats tended to minimize their nation's involvement in that region and to accept calmly the possibility of a Japanese conquest of the whole of China. The prospects for unity under the Kuomintang were so bleak that Japanese expansion in China seemed inevitable. Instead of considering ways in which to aid China, the State Department sought to reduce tension with Japan. Reports from Ambassador Grew emphasized the ambitiousness and recklessness of Japanese leaders and, by early 1935, stressed the powerful national consensus for continental expansion. Secretary of State Cordell Hull and his advisers reasoned that American interests in East Asia did not justify the use of force and that, in any event, the United States lacked the necessary naval power for offensive action in the Western Pacific. Sharp complaints would only goad Japan to further extremes. The American government found safety in inaction and solace in occasional notes of mild protest. Although confronted with rumors about Japan's fortification of its mandated islands, the United States did not press for visits by American naval vessels. Nor did it give any thought to the fortification of its own Pacific islands after the expiration in December 1936 of the Five Power Treaty, or imitate various European governments in encouraging trade with China. In fact, the State Department discouraged the efforts of American business groups to increase economic ties with China and opposed any government financial assistance to the Nanking regime.

The American government did, however, draw a fine line between a refusal to challenge Japan's actions and a willingness either to sanction them or to relinquish American rights. It never renounced Stimson's indictment of Japan or conveyed any approval of that nation's policy. Hull and his subordinates wanted to keep the record clear. When Ambassador Grew, in early 1936, suggested a series of limited agreements in which the United States would recognize a portion of the new order in East Asia, the State Department firmly rejected his advice. A strong consensus existed on what not to do in East Asia. At a White House meeting in September 1934, the President, the Secretary of State, Norman H. Davis, and the Chief of Naval Operations agreed "that in no circumstances should we indicate any intention either to weaken ourselves in the Orient, to indicate an unwillingness to join issue under certain circumstances or a willingness to allow Japan to continue pressing forward without protest on our part."[12]

Policymakers agreed that the United States must not go too far in appeasing Japan or in changing traditional American China policy, as it had in the Lansing-Ishii Agreement. Any piecemeal settlement would imply an acceptance of Japan's abrogation of the Washington treaty system; an accord between the two nations must embody all the principles agreed on at that conference. Hull took a highly moralistic view of international relations, one that focused on the pacific influence of international trade. The verbosity of his diplomacy and his endless reiteration of principles reflected the belief that he could educate world opinion and reshape national behavior. In the case of Japan, he hoped to induce that nation to resume its place as one of the leaders of the civilized world. This task could be accomplished only through moral exhortation, not through the abandonment of vital principles.

The passivity of the American government was, to some extent, deceptive, as were the many statements of American diplomats deemphasizing the nation's stake in China. Experienced bureaucrats such as Johnson and Hornbeck knew the mood of the President and people and quietly accepted it. In private letters Johnson displayed far more concern over the situation in China than in official dispatches and, by mid-1936, he was convinced that "the idealism that inspired the Kellogg Pact cannot prevail unless those who hold those ideals are prepared to go and shoot it out with the drunk [Japan] who now confuses our thoughts."[13] For these men American policy was more a tactical adjustment to current realities than an expression of any change of convictions about the situation in East Asia.

Beneath the muffled protests lay a hardness toward Japan and a tough inner adherence to the traditions of American China

---

[12] Quoted in Waldo H. Heinrichs, Jr., "The Role of the United States Navy," in Dorothy Borg and Shumpei Okamoto, eds., *Pearl Harbor As History: Japanese-American Relations, 1931-1941* (New York, 1973), p. 210.

[13] Quoted in Russell D. Buhite, *Nelson T. Johnson and American Policy Toward China, 1925-1941* (East Lansing, 1968), p. 103.

policy. While these traditions could not, for the moment, be advanced, this fact did not alter the belief of East Asian specialists that the United States must remain a power in that region. They were biding their time, aware of a fundamental cleavage between Japan and the United States and convinced that one day a confrontation would come. In the meantime, they were determined to maintain American naval superiority over Japan out of a conviction, as Hornbeck put it, that "the Japanese speak and understand the language of force,"[14] and were quick to object to what seemed excessive concessions to Japan. In 1935 the Division of Far Eastern Affairs so doggedly resisted the President's suggestion for the neutralization of Japanese and American possessions in the Pacific that it aroused his ire. But East Asian experts felt a weighty obligation to police that fine line separating quiet accommodation from the abandonment of sacred principles.

Of all these East Asian experts, Stanley K. Hornbeck was the most influential. He presided over the Division of Far Eastern Affairs from 1928 to 1937 and, although in that year he resigned to become an adviser on political relations to the Secretary of State, he remained in effective control of the division through 1941. The son of a Methodist minister, Hornbeck had gone from the University of Colorado to Oxford as a Rhodes Scholar and had then returned to the United States to take a doctorate in Political Science at the University of Wisconsin under the direction of Paul S. Reinsch. He spent 5 years in China and Manchuria, served as an adviser to the American delegations at the Paris Peace Conference and the Washington Conference and, in the 1920s, taught at Wisconsin and Harvard. When Nelson T. Johnson became minister to China, he recommended his friend Hornbeck as his successor. Throughout the 1930s Hornbeck dominated the division and confirmed its traditional pro-Chinese bias. His two chief assistants —Maxwell M. Hamilton and Joseph W. Ballantine—generally followed his lead. Hamilton was a Chinese language officer who became Hornbeck's nominal successor in 1937; Ballantine, the son

---

[14]*Foreign Relations of the United States: 1934,* 5 vols. (Washington, D.C., 1951-1952), III, p. 193.

of a missionary, had spent years in Japan. As war approached, both men became somewhat more conciliatory toward Japan than their chief, but neither ever challenged his pro-Chinese orientation.

Hornbeck was a wily bureaucratic leader, jealous of the powers of his division and highly conscious of its historic mission to preserve the principles of American East Asian policy. Under Stimson, Hornbeck found it difficult to assert his influence, for the Secretary of State brought in outside advisers with a background similar to his own. In the new Democratic administration, however, the lines of authority within the State Department greatly changed. Hull lacked experience and confidence in foreign affairs and proved ineffective in governmental politics. He became heavily dependent on his advisers and actually encouraged contact between them and the President. Hornbeck and his staff won the Secretary of State's respect both for their expert knowledge and for their moral and legalistic view of America's relations with the world. It was hardly surprising that after 1933 the influence of the Division of Far Eastern Affairs grew. Hornbeck's incessant memoranda not only influenced the Secretary of State, but often found their way to the desk of the President. Over the years, Hornbeck's advice had a cumulative impact, hardening American policy and discouraging any serious effort to rethink its fundamental principles.

The navy, along with the State Department, was a center of resistance to innovations in policy. Having suffered under the economies imposed by Hoover, its officers were eager to exploit President Roosevelt's more receptive attitude and reduce the 10:8 ratio that Japan had won by 1934. Roosevelt wished to achieve decisive superiority over Japan and, at the same time, use naval expansion as one more means of combating the depression. But he moved cautiously. Aware of strong antinavy sentiment in Congress and of the public's yearning for disarmament, in 1934 he rejected the advice of East Asian experts to end the limitation system and launch a naval race with Japan. Instead, he insisted that the United States enter the Second London Naval Conference, which met in December 1935, with a proposal for a 20 percent cutback in naval forces. While Roosevelt was not willing to concede Tokyo's demand for full parity, he was determined that the onus for ending the Five Power Treaty should fall on Japan instead of on the United States.

After Japan's withdrawal from the conference, the President continued to adhere to his moderate naval policy, and the United States proceeded slowly toward the goal, adopted by Congress in 1934, of bringing the navy up to treaty strength by 1942. These efforts were not enough, however, to match Japan's expansion, and the gap between the two navies steadily diminished. Confident of America's material superiority over Japan, Roosevelt refused to take decisive action and precipitate a major domestic controversy. He was content to let the passage of time awaken the Congress and the people to the need for massive naval appropriations.

Naval leaders had little choice but to accept the President's policy, despite their concern over the nation's vulnerability in the Pacific. They sought to increase appropriations by pointing out the impact of naval growth on the domestic economy and by arguing, as they had for nearly 25 years, that Japan, more than any other nation, threatened America's vital national interests. This argument reflected a mixture of service needs and ideological convictions. A great navy could only be justified if the United States had a major enemy outside of the Western hemisphere, and Japan, as in the past, was the most probable foe. Officers found their traditional assumptions reinforced by recent events there. Internal developments, as well as the Japanese seizure of Manchuria, convinced most navy leaders that a fanatical military clique ruled Japan and had united the nation behind an aggressively expansionist policy. Japan's plans for the dominance of East Asia were fixed; the only questions involved the timing and direction of its moves. War with Japan was virtually inevitable if the United States remained a great Asian power and continued to defend China's integrity. Thus, the Orange Plan remained central to American naval thinking. Planners still visualized the American fleet gathering at Pearl Harbor and steaming across the central Pacific to recapture the Philippines, destroy the Japanese fleet, and blockade the home islands. Despite the obvious inability of the American navy to carry out this mission, its strategy remained static until 1937. A succession of weak civilian chiefs made no effort to force a reconsideration of old assumptions. And the admirals tenaciously resisted the army's efforts to withdraw from the Western Pacific. Set on an established course, they were unwilling to explore new directions in Japanese-American relations.

During the first half of the 1930s two powerful departments within the American government continued to rely on old patterns of thought. The State Department would not forsake its concept of American principles in East Asia; the navy would not abandon the nation's role as a great power in the Western Pacific. At a time when the situation in that region retained some fluidity, these two bureaucracies resisted new American initiatives. Neither sought accommodation or confrontation with Japan; neither would make any effort to control the drift of events. It is unlikely, of course, that President Roosevelt would, in any event, have sanctioned any significant conciliatory moves, or that they would have had more than the faintest possibility of success. But the leaders of the American government were not endowed with the clarity of hindsight. They fatalistically succumbed to the larger historical currents of their time.

IV

Throughout the decade Japan pursued an illusory national destiny in East Asia. Determined to supplant the old imperialist order with one of its own making, Japan viewed the creation of Manchukuo as only the first step in the development of an autonomous empire based on the dominance of Manchuria and China and the existence of a powerful military force capable of neutralizing potential foes. A sense of crisis pervaded Japanese society and, with it, an urge to return to partly submerged traditions of the past. The depression, the rise of Chinese nationalism, and the example of European totalitarian nations had all combined to erode the faith in Western institutions. Even in the West, parliamentary democracy, economic liberalism, and individualism were on the defensive, and in Japan, where these concepts were less deeply rooted, they crumbled with astonishing rapidity. In the early 1930s the whole tone of the society began to change as party cabinets and Western ideals gave way to a new emphasis on spiritual solidarity, the virtues of Imperial rule, and the need for a Pan-Asian foreign policy. The tolerance for left-wing or even liberal political thought decreased as men concluded that the salvation of the nation lay in social harmony.

What had, in fact, occurred was a shift in the balance of power among the ruling elites, one that had momentous consequences for the direction of Japanese society. The shift was away from the political parties, court circles, and large business interests toward the great government bureaucracies, particularly those of the army and navy. Beginning with the first whole-nation cabinet in May 1933, the role of the political parties swiftly declined, while the real power of government became concentrated in the middle echelons of the various bureaucracies. Policy was now formally made by the Inner Cabinet, consisting of the prime minister and the war, navy, foreign, and finance ministers.

The political parties offered little resistance to this new style of government. Many party politicians, particularly in the Seiyūkai, had helped to undermine party rule and the moderate foreign and domestic policies with which it was associated. Those who wished to preserve those policies were reluctant to speak out. The terrorization of the civilian establishment by fanatical young army and navy officers made objections risky and, in any event, moderate party leaders had no convincing alternatives. They feared provoking the military and precipitating a decisive confrontation with the government. Invariably the Diet approved the government's budgets and, for the most part, supported its policies. Occasionally party members attacked official policies and, in 1936, the Diet resisted the cabinet's attempt to impose comprehensive economic planning. But these efforts collapsed after the outbreak of the Sino-Japanese War. Despite their continual triumphs at the polls, the parties were too distant from the center of power to affect the main course of events.

In the 1930s the army became the most dynamic and influential elite within the Japanese ruling structure. During the previous decade its officers had acquired an extreme distaste for the directors of the nation's foreign and domestic policies and had, in 1931, initiated the action in Manchuria that had brought dramatic changes in Japan. The army provided the chief impetus for continental expansion and took the lead in defining Japan's new order both at home and abroad. This ascendancy did not, however, quiet the complex factional struggles taking place within the Japanese military establishment. It was crisscrossed by numerous cliques based on personal or clan loyalties, special organizational perspectives, and ideological differences. Remnants of Chōshū influence remained in the officer corp, while officers were also differentiated by their attendance at either the Army War College or officers' training school. The former constituted an elite that controlled the higher ranks of the army; the latter developed more extreme views and gravitated toward the patriotic societies. Moreover, officers attached to the General Staff, the War Ministry, and the armies in the field all viewed events from a different vantage point. Most of these officers suffered from the narrowness of their training, which isolated them from society and encouraged excessive self-confidence. Convinced of the army's unique mission, they had difficulty reaching beyond that service's special concerns and perspectives.

Perhaps the most serious cleavage was ideological. A majority of the senior officers wished to modernize the army and organize Japan's economy, society, and government for total war. They emphasized mechanization and centralized planning and the avoidance of any conflict that would delay the fulfillment of these goals. Others believed that the army's ultimate strength depended on spiritual instead of material forces and contended that the nation, in the near future, must confront the Soviet Union. These officers encouraged army extremists, whose dissatisfaction culminated in an attempted coup in February 1936. Rebellious troops held the center of Tokyo for 3 days before admitting defeat, in what was the most serious revolt in the history of the Imperial Army. With its suppression army leaders confirmed their intention to work through established constitutional forms and to end regional and personal cliques within the service. They tightened discipline and suppressed factionalism, but the possibility of future disorders—if the army did not have its way—gave further momentum to its program.

The Tokyo rebellion tipped the balance of internal forces further toward the army. Previous cabinets had given the military much of what it wanted, but the new cabinet of Hirota Kōki threw its full weight behind army plans for a national defense state. Hirota tightened domestic controls, increased the military budget, and called for the nationalization of key industries. The rhetoric of government officials became more nationalistic, while their sensitivity to the West diminished. Key civilian leaders came to share the domestic and continental aspirations of the army. In the Foreign Ministry those oriented toward the West had been overwhelmed early in the decade. The dominant faction, led by Arita Hachirō, saw no need for concessions to the West and was determined to achieve Japanese hegemony over China. This group reasoned that, once Japan had won ascendancy there, the Western nations would accept it. Arita and his followers believed that Japan's destiny could be fulfilled through diplomatic maneuvers instead of through war. They rejected the views of extremists, who urged an alliance with Germany and Italy and proclaimed the inevitability of war with the Soviet Union.

In the early 1930s the power of the moderates also had been decisively broken in the Japanese navy, the most Western oriented of the major bureaucratic units. Traditionally naval officers had strong ties with Great Britain and the United States and a sharp awareness of the limits of Japan's power. It was these naval moderates who had accepted the treaty ratios of the Washington Conference and the extension of those ratios at the London Naval Conference of 1930 and who, throughout the 1930s, took a realistic view of American power. As one of their leaders, Admiral Yamamoto Isoroku, remarked, "anyone who has seen the auto factories in Detroit and the oil fields in Texas knows that Japan lacks the national power for a naval race with America."[15] Even in the 1920s, however, this acceptance of naval inferiority aroused the bitter resentment of younger staff officers. Festering throughout the decade, it erupted with great fury in 1930, unleashing unprecedented internal dissension in a service that had been noted for its unity and harmony.

Japan's acceptance of the London Naval Treaty was the last

---

[15] Quoted in Sadao Asada, "The Japanese Navy and the United States," in Borg and Okamoto, *Pearl Harbor As History*, p. 237.

victory of the naval moderates. A growing number of middle-echelon officers, led by Katō Kanji, embraced extreme, emotional attitudes, and turned to Germany instead of Great Britain or the United States for inspiration. In contrast to the older generation, they believed that the clash of Japanese and American national interests in East Asia made war inevitable and found the international order imposed by the Washington Conference intolerable. They worked to overthrow the whole of that oppressive structure and to undermine the power of those groups at home that sought to preserve it. By the middle of the decade naval extremists had purged the moderate naval officers and captured the service. Now they could end the humiliating treaties with the West, achieve parity with Great Britain and the United States, and break out of the constricting ring that they felt the American government was tightening around Japan. They were convinced that the development of new and better weapons, along with superior morale and tactics, would enable Japan to compete successfully in a naval race and to defend the Western Pacific.

In 1934 the navy's new leadership, brushing aside the objections of the War Ministry and most other members of the cabinet, threatened to provoke an internal crisis unless the government issued the necessary 2-year notice for the abrogation of the Five Power Treaty. The navy's belligerence represented both deeply held convictions and grandiose ambitions. Dominant middle-echelon officers intended to end the navy's traditional abstention from national politics and its inferior position vis-a-vis the army. They pursued an opportunistic course, seeking to define national strategy in terms of the navy's needs. Thus, they transformed the popular notion of a national mission throughout Asia into a rationale for a southward advance to gain valuable raw materials, commercial advantages, and strategic bases. This sweeping vision gave the navy a mission comparable to that of the army in China and provided it with a justification for enormous budgetary increases.

The army and navy could reach no agreement on strategic priorities, nor could the Inner Cabinet reconcile their conflicting objectives. Each service went its own way. The army sought predominance over the Soviet Union and political control of North

China, along with the integration of Manchuria into a centrally planned Japanese economy. The navy wished to avoid further involvement in Northeast Asia and sought naval supremacy in the Western Pacific and a fleet capable of operating in the Southeast Pacific. These conflicting strategies remained unresolved, adding one more layer of confusion to Japan's national policy.

Since the end of the Manchurian crisis the army had worked to expand Japanese influence in Northeast Asia. Army planners prized the resources of North China and believed that control of that region was essential for the defense of Manchukuo. By the spring of 1933 Japan had absorbed the province of Jehol and had created a demilitarized zone to the north and east of Peking. Contemptuous of the Kuomintang and convinced that Chiang Kai-shek was only another warlord, the army greatly reduced his authority in North China. In doing so it undermined the Foreign Ministry's efforts to achieve Japan's aims through a political settlement with Nanking. By early 1936, however, the Nanking regime seemed more vigorous than ever and the army's aggressive policies in North China had nearly precipitated an unwanted war. Disturbed by the army's failure to achieve its major continental goals, the General Staff went so far as to argue that Japan must be prepared to accept the inevitable unification of China under Chiang. Even more disturbing was the buildup of military power in Russia's Far Eastern provinces that, by 1936, exceeded that of Japan in Manchuria. Moreover, the Soviet government had denounced Japan as a fascist state and concluded a defense pact with Outer Mongolia.

This challenge turned the army's energies away from further encroachments in China and toward intensive preparations for an eventual war with Russia. In 1936 the army and navy agreed to pursue a more moderate China policy, one that consisted of economic subversion in North China and the negotiation of a series of limited Sino-Japanese agreements. The Kwantung Army continued to urge aggressive action in China, but central army authorities curbed its authority and, in June 1937, specifically ordered the field armies in China to avoid incidents with Nationalist troops. The Foreign Ministry assumed the task of convincing the Nanking regime to recognize the special relationship between Japan and North China. The government hoped to restrain the Soviet Union with the Anti-Comintern Pact, which it signed with Germany in September 1936. It began to rely more and more on diplomatic means to achieve its continental goals. The army's urgent concern with accelerating its program of industrial and military expansion was shared by Konoe Fumimaro, who became Prime Minister in June 1937. Konoe intended to create a centrally planned economy, integrate Manchukuo into the home industrial base, and complete the exclusion of the Kuomintang from North China.

In early July the clash between Chinese and Japanese troops near the Marco Polo Bridge west of Peking came as a surprise both to the government in Tokyo and to Japanese forces in the field. Accepting the advice of the General Staff, Chinese and Japanese generals quickly concluded a local settlement. But Chiang Kai-shek objected. During the very period when Japanese policy had been moving toward an accommodation with China, a wave of nationalist feeling swept over that nation, forcing Chiang into collaboration with the communists to turn back the tide of Japanese expansion. Fearful that this incident represented one more Japanese attempt to detach North China from Nanking's rule, he dispatched divisions northward and insisted on direct negotiations with Tokyo. The Konoe cabinet, determined to eliminate Kuomintang influence in North China, refused to deal with Chiang. The diplomatic stalemate brought a deterioration of the situation near Peking and, by late July, intense fighting had broken out between Chinese and Japanese troops.

Konoe and Foreign Minister Hirota complacently observed the outbreak of war with China. They were confident, along with the Kwantung Army, that Japan would bring Chiang Kai-shek to terms through a series of rapid military successes. The army's General Staff warned that a long war would drain the resources of the nation and carry it even further from its primary goal of meeting the Soviet menace. Konoe and the cabinet, however, rejected this warning and formulated far-reaching political demands that made a negotiated settlement impossible. Pressures from navy and army units in the field extended the fighting to Central and South China and, in January 1938, the government decided on an all-out offensive and the creation of a new central government. The war had become a great national crusade that the Japanese people believed would somehow fulfill the nation's mission in East Asia. Konoe won huge budget increases from the Diet and a mobilization bill conferring sweeping economic controls on the government. War with China moved Japan decisively toward a militaristic state.

The government stumbled into the conflict in a thoughtless way, without coordinating its military action and foreign policy. Nor did Japan grasp the impact that a Sino-Japanese war would have on its relations with the United States. Konoe and his associates assumed, as did the army, that the United States would not go beyond diplomatic protests and that, whatever the contents of its notes, it would grudgingly acquiesce in Japan's control of China. Absorbed in pursuing Japan's destiny on the Asian continent, the limited horizons of the nation's leaders precluded any serious consideration of war with America.

V

It was difficult for the American government and its ambassador, Joseph C. Grew, to understand the policy-making process in Japan. Grew, who served in Japan from 1932 to 1942, gave the ambassadorship the continuity and significance it had long deserved. He was, however, ill-prepared to bridge the chasm separating the two cultures and political systems. He suffered from the 5 years that he had spent in Istanbul, a diplomatic experience that had isolated him from the swift current of world events. His optimism and belief in progress, his emphasis on the human dimension of international relations, left him unable to cope with the violence and disintegration of the 1930s and unable to analyze the deeper social, political, and economic forces that shaped the course of Japan.

As the decade progressed Grew's confidence gave way to perplexity. There seemed no firm ground on which to stand. Accustomed to contact with those at the top of the governmental and social pyramid, he established lines of communication with Western-oriented businessmen, naval officers, and members of the Imperial court, men who often spoke English and had some acquaintance with the West. While they possessed considerable prestige, their real power had slipped away rapidly and, as tensions mounted, even these contacts diminished. Grew had no way of reaching—even if he had perceived the importance of doing so—the middle levels of the great bureaucracies where many of the most important policies originated. The American ambassador could not penetrate the obscure struggles within and between the Foreign Ministry and the navy and army; nor could he comprehend the diffusion of power or the growing distance between the formal structure of government and the actual centers of authority. The danger was to rely on Western terms and analogies, on the superficial similarities between Japan and the West, which had always been misleading and were even more so in the 1930s. At first Grew drew a crucial distinction between moderates and extremists and argued that the moderates, temporarily eclipsed, would soon regain dominance. Slowly he came to realize that this was a false dichotomy, that the moderates possessed no influence, and that a powerful expansionist urge gripped the nation. There was always, however, a degree of uncertainty in his analysis. At times he would emphasize the unity of the army and nation, at other times he would dwell on diversity, on the differences among various groups and the possibility of an accommodation between Japan and the United States.

Grew was an influential ambassador whose reports carried weight and whose diary circulated among some high-level friends in the State Department. With the outbreak of the Sino-Japanese War he urged the continuation of an aloof and passive policy and warned that the Japanese people were united in their determination to wage war against China. Initially this advice fitted the cautious mood in Washington. The President's attention was focused on Europe, not East Asia, and Secretary Hull, while he realized the seriousness of the Sino-Japanese War, continued a conciliatory policy toward both China and Japan and repeatedly rejected British overtures for joint action. The American government refused to invoke the neutrality law, a gesture of sympathy toward China, but hedged by prohibiting the shipment of arms or war implements in government vessels. American leaders seemed to be straddling the issues raised by the war.

The appearance of continuity in America's East Asian policy, however, was misleading, for events in Europe and Asia had exerted a cumulative impact on the nation's policymakers. The spreading war in China connected Germany, Italy, and Japan more firmly than ever before and deepened concern about the growing totalitarian menace. A Treasury Department memorandum of September 1937 noted that "the peace of the world is tied up with China's ability to win or to prolong its resistance to Japanese aggression."[16] Within the State Department sensitive bureaucrats such as Hornbeck began to advocate more forceful measures against Japan. Hornbeck argued that Japan, if not stopped in China, would eventually move on to the Philippines and to British and Dutch possessions in Southeast Asia. He felt the time had come to go beyond moral pressure and that the United States must combine coercive measures with a new settlement in East Asia on the scale of the Washington Conference. Ambassador Johnson still wished to remain aloof from the crisis, but was upset by the prospect of the Japanese conquest of China. In 1937 his identification with China had gradually deepened as the Chinese people seemed to coalesce behind Chiang Kai-shek. Throughout the American government, Chiang's improved position strengthened the latent sympathy for China's cause.

Roosevelt and Hull sensed the moral outrage of segments of the public and the hardening of sentiment against Japan. Internationalists, Protestant religious groups, and organized labor demanded action. In September 1937 the American government began to protest sharply Japanese depredations in China. Hull wrote Ambassador Grew that "Japan is destroying the world's good will and laying up for herself among the peoples of the world a liability of suspicion, distrust, popular antipathy and potential ostracism which it would take many, many years of benevolent endeavor on her part to liquidate."[17] In October, when the League assembly condemned Japan, Hull publicly approved. Hull and Norman H.

---

[16] Quoted in Akira Iriye, *Across the Pacific: An Inner History of American-East Asian Relations* (New York, 1967), p. 197.

[17] *Foreign Relations of the United States: 1937,* 5 vols. (Washington, D. C., 1954), III, p. 508.

Davis urged the President to express American revulsion over events in China and to assert that governments must cooperate to uphold the moral and legal foundations of international life. On October 5 the President, in his famous Quarantine Speech, denounced the "epidemic of world lawlessness" sweeping the globe and stated that the United States could not remain unconcerned.[18] Roosevelt, however, had no specific plan in mind; neither he nor his advisers believed the time had come for action in either Europe or East Asia. In early November, when the signatories of the Nine Power Treaty met in Brussels, Roosevelt and Hull refused, like other Western leaders, to consider economic sanctions, and would only agree to a confirmation of the League's condemnation of Japan.

In late 1937 the President and Secretary of State were still unwilling to break decisively with past policy. The unprovoked Japanese sinking of the American gunboat *Panay* on December 12 produced a flash of anger in Washington, but no retaliation against Japan. Hull believed that "wild, runaway, half-insane Army and Navy officials" were responsible for the attack,[19] while Roosevelt considered a wide variety of measures, including the seizure of Japanese assets and naval moves in the Pacific. Japan's prompt apology and indemnification quickly ended the crisis. But American officials felt, more strongly than ever before, that the international situation was tense and explosive. They feared that a reckless and brutal Japan, if successful in China, would move on to new conquests in collaboration with the Axis powers.

---

[18]Samuel I. Rosenman, ed., *The Public Papers and Addresses of Franklin D. Roosevelt*, 13 vols. (New York, 1938-1950), VI, p. 410.

[19]*Foreign Relations of the United States: Japan, 1931-1941*, 2 vols. (Washington, D.C. 1943), I, p. 530.

CHAPTER VI

The Unwanted War

THROUGHOUT 1938 THE UNITED STATES REMAINED ON THE SIDELINES OF THE DEEPENING WORLD CRISIS, inactive but anxiously watching events in Europe and East Asia. Japan's campaign against Chinese nationalism brought unprecedented friction with Western interests there and a growing stream of American protests. One dispute followed another as the backlog of unresolved cases and unanswered notes accumulated. Gradually the faint outlines of a new policy emerged. In June 1938 the American government asked for an embargo on the shipment of bombers to areas where they might be used against civilians, a move obviously aimed at Japan and, in October, Hull dispatched a stern protest against Japan's closing of the Open Door in China.

Within the administration China experts intensified their agitation for more aggressive measures against Japan. Ambassador Johnson confided to his friend Hornbeck that "we will never realize America's heritage as the hope of a warweary world unless we are prepared to stand at Armageddon with the powers of righteousness and the rule of law against the gangsterdom that is raising the banner of might, force and international bad faith."[1] Hornbeck had already reached this conclusion and, by the autumn of 1938, advocated systematic economic warfare against Japan. He was impressed with Japan's weakness, not its strength, and contended that the tide of Japanese aggression would recede before a determined American stand. The new chief of the Division of Far Eastern Affairs, Maxwell M. Hamilton, was more cautious, but Secretary of the Interior Harold L. Ickes and Secretary of the

---

[1]Quoted in Russell D. Buhite, *Nelson T. Johnson and American Policy Toward China, 1925-1941* (East Lansing, 1968), p. 137.

Treasury Henry Morgenthau, Jr. shared Hornbeck's sense of crisis and urged Roosevelt to take the lead against both Germany and Japan. They were, however, a minority within the administration. Under Secretary of State Sumner Welles and other influential State Department officials continued to remain oriented toward the Western hemisphere or Europe. Even Ambassador Grew believed that the United States had no major interests in China. Although indignant at Japan, the President and Secretary of State were still not prepared to act decisively.

The changing mood of the American public made inaction more and more difficult to justify. Traditionally most Americans had been indifferent to China and, in 1938, events in Europe concerned the bulk of the foreign policy public more than those in Asia. But a small, articulate sector of that public had long sympathized with the aspirations of the Chinese people and believed in a special relationship between China and the United States. In the late 1930s this vague identification with China's cause grew as Americans confronted the ugly realities of the Sino-Japanese war and tried to fit China into their emerging global perspective. They were far more receptive to China than to Japan. Pearl Buck's *The Good Earth*—with its romanticization of the Chinese peasantry—found a large audience both as a book and as a movie, but favorable images of Japan, always fragile, disintegrated as stereotypes of brutal and treacherous little yellow men became popular. Public opinion polls charted the mounting hostility toward Japan and, in May 1939, revealed that 72 percent of those polled wished to forbid the sale of war materials to that nation. As early as 1937, prominent figures such as Henry L. Stimson and Frank Knox, the Republican vice-presidential candidate in 1936, called for strong anti-Japanese measures and, in October 1937, Senator Key Pittman, chairman of the Foreign Relations Committee, urged an economic quarantine.

The animosity against Japan in the Congress blurred the normal distinctions between internationalists and isolationists and weakened the latter's opposition to involvement in the East Asian crisis. Even Senator Gerald P. Nye warned that some American exports to Japan might one day be used against American citizens. American missionaries in China—inspired by Chiang Kai-shek's conversion to Christianity and by various Kuomintang reforms—sought to awaken the American public to the evils of Japanese aggression. The missionaries had often personally experienced the brutalities of the Japanese occupying forces and burned with the humiliation inflicted on Westerners. Seeking to convey to officials in Washington and to the American public a vivid sense of China's plight, they campaigned relentlessly and, in December 1938, organized the American Committee for Non-Participation in Japanese Aggression. The chairman of the new committee was Roger S. Greene, the son of a famous American missionary in Japan. Although born and raised in Japan, Greene had spent years in China and now employed a formidable array of connections to harden American policy toward the nation his father had served so long and devotedly.

The China missionaries did not, of course, sweep all before them. Mission boards and most Protestant clergymen, determined to avoid involvement in the Sino-Japanese conflict, resisted their efforts and, as late as May 1940, a prominent group of Protestant ministers refused to take sides in the East Asian crisis. Nevertheless, the powerful anti-Japanese tide gathered force and was noticeable even among businessmen and financiers. Thomas W. Lamont of J. P. Morgan and Company had originally defended Japanese expansion into Manchuria but, by 1938, Lamont's admiration for Japan had faded, and he identified American interests with those of China. Most businessmen did not undergo Lamont's dramatic transformation, although their enthusiasm for Japan diminished. They remained sensitive, however, to the fact that from 1932 to 1939 Japan ranked as America's third largest export market, behind only Great Britain and Canada. American exports to Japan peaked in 1937 and remained high until 1941 as American oil and oil products, raw cotton, metal goods, and machinery flowed across the Pacific. As in the past, the two economies were largely complementary and relations among business groups good. American exporters fought efforts to restrict Japanese imports and were, by and large, successful, for the administration wished to expand American commerce and valued the sizable trade with Japan. American exporters also opposed the movement for economic sanctions, although they made no attempt to defend Japan's war against China and eventually gave way before the mounting anti-Japanese sentiment. Flourishing trade seemed to have little effect on the growing estrangement between the two nations.

When Ambassador Grew reached Washington on leave in June 1939, the intensely anti-Japanese mood in both official and nonofficial circles stunned him. Grew had arrived in an optimistic frame of mind; now he quickly concluded that he had been out of touch and that, on his return to Tokyo, he would have to convey the feelings of the American government and people to Japan's leaders. Clearly, Roosevelt and Hull were not inclined toward conciliation. In late 1938 the United States had refused to accept Konoe's new order in East Asia and, by the early summer of 1939, the administration decided that in order to avoid an eruption in the Congress, it would have to abrogate the commercial treaty of 1911. On July 26 the American government notified Japan of its intention; in 6 months the way would be open for trade restrictions. Leading Senate isolationists, along with the general public, endorsed the administration's action and seemed prepared to support even sterner measures. Assistant Secretary of State Adolph A. Berle, Jr. noted in his diary that "it is a curious fact that the United States, which bolts like a frightened rabbit from even remote contact with Europe, will enthusiastically take a step which might very well be a material day's march on the road to a Far Eastern War."[2]

While Roosevelt and Hull did not wish to provoke Japan, they felt that the time had come to warn Tokyo of growing anger in the United States and to strengthen the morale of China and Great Britain. Roosevelt seemed confident that he could, in one way or another, handle Japan. In October 1939, when confronted with Grew's misgivings about American policy, he spoke of intercepting the Japanese fleet as it moved south and of reinforcing Manila and Pearl Harbor. His widely shared confidence in America's overwhelming material and military superiority had an important influence on American policy until the outbreak of war.

---

[2]Beatrice Bishop Berle and Travis Beal Jacobs, eds., *Navigating the Rapids, 1917-1971: From the Papers of Adolf A. Berle* (New York, 1973), pp. 231-232.

II

As 1938 progressed the China Incident became a vehicle through which Japan's leaders intended to transform both their own society and the international order in East Asia. For several years Japan's lack of a clear national purpose had concerned Prime Minister Konoe; now, with the aid of prominent intellectuals and government officials, he articulated a vision of a new order in East Asia, one based on the fusion of China and Japan. The China war had become a positive good, the progenitor of a purified Japanese society and of an Asian renaissance. Apprehension existed among some businessmen and members of the Imperial household about the widening scope of the war, but this was more than offset by the many bureaucrats, intellectuals, and politicians who shared the military's dissatisfaction with the status quo and its determination to create new spiritual and military strength. Swept along by events, these civilians provided the organizational skills essential for the achievement of the army's domestic and foreign goals.

The China war, however, did not end, nor did the Western nations display any inclination to accept Japan's new order. Mired in China and defeated in a major border clash with the Soviet Union in July 1938, Japan's leaders turned to diplomacy as a way to achieve their national goals. Germany's dynamism and apparent invincibility convinced them that an alliance would provide security against the Soviet Union, restrain the democracies, and ultimately lead to triumph in China. The army, preoccupied with the continent and the traditional Russian menace, sought an alliance so ardently that it accepted German terms to achieve an agreement. Both Konoe and his successor in January 1939, Hiranuma Kiichirō, had no reservations about an alliance directed against Britain and France as well as the Soviet Union. Powerful middle-echelon naval officers also wished to include these two Western powers. Such a pact would support the navy's strategy of a southern advance and strengthen its claim to scarce national resources, while an alliance aimed exclusively at the Soviet Union would confirm the army's predominance and reinforce the priority of continental concerns. The Naval Minister, Admiral Yonai Mitsumasa, along with other older, Western-oriented officers, feared such a sweeping commitment to Germany and, aided by Foreign Minister Arita, he maneuvered to avoid any agreement that would bring about automatic Japanese involvement in a European war. As lengthy deliberations proceeded within the Inner Cabinet, the pro-German forces gained ground and, by August, had forced their opponents largely to give way. The last, faint reservation to which Japan clung concerned only the timing of its entry into a European war. As Yonai remarked in retrospect, "our opposition to the Alliance was like paddling against the rapids only a few hundred yards upstream from Niagara Falls."[3]

Hitler was not, however, satisfied with these major Japanese concessions. He viewed an alliance with Japan as a diplomatic device that would neutralize Britain and France while he solved his problems in the East. Needing a full, unqualified commitment in order to intimidate the Western democracies, he became impatient with Japan's procrastination and turned to the Soviet Union for an agreement that would free him to march against Poland. The conclusion of the Nazi-Soviet Pact on August 23, 1939 stunned Japan's leaders and brought the fall of the Hiranuma cabinet. With Hitler's luster temporarily dimmed, the new government of Prime Minister Abe Nobuyuki resolved to stay aloof from the war in Europe and lessen its isolation by drawing closer to Great Britain and the United States. Ambassador Grew concluded that Abe and Foreign Minister Nomura Kichisaburō would make substantial concessions to Western interests in China and urged Washington to open negotiations for a treaty of commerce. While Grew accurately sensed a new moderation on the part of the Prime Minister and Foreign Minister, the Japanese army and its civilian collaborators, momentarily confused by Hitler's abrupt maneuvers, were hardly prepared to abridge Japan's position in China.

Grew's claim that the pendulum of Japanese politics was swinging toward moderation made no impression on Washington,

---

[3]Quoted in Sadao Asada, "The Japanese Navy and the United States," in Dorothy Borg and Shumpei Okamoto, eds., *Pearl Harbor As History: Japanese-American Relations, 1931-1941* (New York, 1973), p. 248.

where concessions to Japan did not interest Roosevelt and Hull. Skeptical of cabinet changes in Tokyo, they had decided to encourage anxiety in Japan over the future of commercial relations with the United States. Hull and his advisers wanted no crisis, but neither did they want any infringement of American rights or any recognition of Japan's special position in China. From their perspective Japan was weak and isolated, deadlocked in China, and unlikely to proceed farther while France and Great Britain remained so strong. Still optimistic about their prospects, Roosevelt and Hull believed that time was on the side of the United States. They were content to wait.

In Japan, too, government leaders waited for a decisive turn in the European war. Germany's spring victories, capped by the fall of France in June 1940, confirmed their hopes and convinced most that a great moment in Japan's history had arrived. The Asian colonies of France and the Netherlands were dangling unprotected, soon to be joined, so it seemed, by those of Great Britain. Japan's strategists argued that the time had come to expand southward and secure a national self-sufficiency far beyond what could be achieved through the control of China and Manchukuo. In the spring and early summer of 1940 Japan intensified its pressure on Britain and France to remove their garrisons from all international settlements in China and to close supply routes to the Kuomintang through Burma and Indochina. It also asserted more forcefully its special interest in the economic resources of the Netherlands East Indies.

Japan did not move decisively until July 1940, when Konoe returned to power. He was euphoric over the course of events and confident of his ability to unite the nation and lead it to the fulfillment of its historic destiny. Drawing on widespread support from all factions, Konoe brought into office men determined to act. Foreign Minister Matsuoka Yōsuke felt that Japan must win hegemony over the whole of Asia, while War Minister Tōjō Hideki sought more unity within the army and an alliance with

---

[4]Quoted in Robert J. C. Butow, *Tojo and the Coming of the War* (Princeton, 1961), p. 148.

Germany and Italy. In July the new cabinet approved a document outlining "the main Principles of Japan's Basic National Policy" and swiftly began to implement it.[4] The government tightened internal discipline by strengthening its grip on mass communications and by dissolving the political parties into an Imperial Rule Assistance Association. Its aim was a one-party state, the creation of a mass movement that would bind the nation firmly together.

The cabinet also took steps to complete Japan's New Order in East Asia, now transformed into the Greater East Asia Co-Prosperity Sphere. Civilian politicians and bureaucrats shared the desire of army and navy officers to liberate Asia from the West and to create a harmonious confederation of Asian nations dominated by Japan. The German blitzkrieg particularly dazzled middle-echelon naval planners, who were obsessed with Southeast Asia and its promise of imperial self-sufficiency. They urged the seizure of the whole of Indochina and the Netherlands East Indies and were prepared to accept the conflict with Great Britain and the United States that such a policy might bring. Senior naval officers and army leaders, however, were more cautious and confined their immediate ambitions to Northern Indochina. A Japanese presence there would further isolate Chiang Kai-shek and put Japan's forces in a key strategic position. In early August Japan began a series of demands on the Vichy government that culminated on September 22 in an agreement allowing the movement of Japanese troops into Northern Indochina.

By expanding to the south and threatening the colonial possessions of three European nations, Japan crossed a fateful watershed, for the goal of hegemony in Southeast Asia entangled Japan directly with Britain and the Netherlands and ultimately with the United States. This was not, of course, clear in the summer and autumn of 1940, when the scope of Japan's empire in Southeast Asia and the timing of its acquisition were vague and ill-defined, dependent on future events.

The conclusion of an alliance with Germany and Italy constituted the third goal of the Konoe cabinet. Southward expansion required German recognition of the Greater East Asia Co-Prosperity Sphere as well as the neutralization of the Soviet Union. Japanese leaders hoped that a Tripartite Pact would bring a rapprochement with the Soviet Union and, at the very least, immobilize the United States. Matsuoka, who had spent 9 years in America as a youth, had firm ideas about how to handle that nation. He contended that bold diplomacy would intimidate the American government and force its gradual acquiescence in Japan's new empire. He often remarked that "one cannot obtain a tiger's cub unless he braves the tiger's den."[5]

By the summer of 1940 Hitler was once more eager for an alliance with Japan. Determined to destroy Russian power, he reasoned that Japan could tie down Britain in Asia and help to distract the United States while he invaded the Soviet Union and ultimately turned on Britain for a final reckoning. Thus on September 22, 1940 Germany, Italy, and Japan signed the Tripartite Pact, an agreement in which they pledged to aid one another if attacked by a nation not currently involved in the European war. Since the pact specifically excluded the Soviet Union, the American government could not misinterpret its meaning. Few of Japan's leaders questioned the wisdom of the new alliance. For the navy, it opened a path to the south and strengthened its position in the contest for scarce material. For the army, it held the promise of an end to the China Incident and marked a milestone in the quest for national autonomy. For Konoe and Matsuoka the pact, with its vague assistance provisions, suggested a way to achieve the nation's objectives without experiencing the ordeal of war.

III

The fall of France shocked Americans, shattering their complacency about an Allied victory and focusing their attention on the fate of Britain. On June 10, 1940 President Roosevelt, speaking at Charlottesville, Virginia, promised aid for the opponents of force and proclaimed that the United States could not retain its democratic values in a world dominated by totalitarian powers. Recog-

---

[5]Quoted in Chihiro Hosoya, "Retrogression in Japan's Foreign Policy Decision-Making Process," in James William Morley, ed., *Dilemmas of Growth in Prewar Japan* (Princeton, 1971), p. 92.

nizing the nation's increased vulnerability, Roosevelt finally won congressional approval of a two-ocean navy and pondered ways to assist Britain, while his military advisers worried over the protection of the Western hemisphere. The deteriorating situation in Europe produced a new level of anxiety within the American government.

The attention of the President and most American policymakers centered on Europe, not Asia, but Britain's isolation linked these two areas in a new and critical way. Part of Britain's strength lay in its empire—in Burma, Malaya, and the Commonwealth nations in the Pacific. So long as Britain and France were predominant in Europe, that empire seemed secure; now that Britain lay weak and exposed, its empire, along with that of the Netherlands, became an object of vital concern. As early as April, Hull publicly urged the maintenance of the status quo in the Netherlands East Indies and, as the spring progressed, he and the President feared more and more that Japan might attack the British and Dutch possessions. The President and Secretary of State searched for ways to deter Japan and possibly alter its aggressive behavior. In May Roosevelt ordered the American fleet, after the completion of its maneuvers, to stay at Pearl Harbor instead of return to the Pacific Coast, and Hull initiated talks between Ambassador Grew and Foreign Minister Arita. Maintaining close control from Washington, Hull warned Japan about illusions of a German victory and suggested that peaceful cooperation between Japan and the United States would bring far richer rewards than a policy of force. Most of all he stressed the fundamental principles of international conduct on which American policy had rested during the interwar years. Arita indulged in similar abstractions and, as a result, the talks involved no serious give and take, only a clarification and elaboration of ideological positions that revealed the vast distance separating the two nations.

The American government offered no concessions to Japan; Roosevelt and Hull still retained their confidence in American power and their belief that ultimately Japan would retreat in the face of it. The State Department convinced the President, over the objections of his army and navy advisers, to keep the bulk of the fleet in the Pacific instead of transferring it to the Atlantic. Many wished to go far beyond the State Department's policy of cautious deterrence and invoke economic sanctions against Japan. Congressmen frequently called for a tougher policy and so, too, did more and more members of the administration. Those concerned with defense production worried over inadequate supplies of scrap iron and of strategic raw materials and noted that, in the first half of 1940, the export of refined oil to Japan leaped upward. In June the addition of two influential Republicans, Henry L. Stimson and Frank Knox, to the cabinet intensified the debate over sanctions. Both men brought firm, well-known opinions on Japan into the inner councils of the administration and joined Ickes and Morgenthau in contending that American half-measures and passivity had encouraged Japanese aggression. Invoking the lessons of history, Stimson argued that the Japanese were "notorious bluffers" who had invariably backed down when directly challenged by the United States.[6] He believed that the history of the Siberian intervention, the Washington Conference, and the Manchurian crisis supported this generalization. By the summer of 1940 all of these men were contemptuous of Japanese power and impatiently advocating a total economic embargo. Secretary of the Treasury Morgenthau expressed their feelings when he confided to his diary that "the State Department just drives me crazy."[7]

One prominent State Department official, Stanley K. Hornbeck, agreed that the United States must now defend the eternal verities of its China policy. "The Far Eastern policy of the United States," he wrote Under Secretary of State Sumner Welles, "will undergo neither a rapid nor a gradual 'reorientation' *unless and until* . . . the whole world becomes an *utterly different* world from that which it has been ever since the Pilgrims landed at Plymouth and the Cavaliers at Jamestown." Hornbeck tirelessly advanced his belief that "nothing short of or less than the language of force, either military or economic or both, will exercise effectively restraining

---

[6]Harold L. Ickes, *The Secret Diary of Harold L. Ickes,* 3 vols. (New York, 1953-1954), III, p. 346.

[7]Quoted in John Morton Blum, *From the Morgenthau Diaries,* 3 vols. (Boston, 1959-1967), II, p. 351.

influence upon Japan's present leadership."[8] Japan's traditional failure to keep international commitments made an agreement useless; only an uncompromising firmness would force that nation to back down.

Within the State Department Hornbeck found himself in a minority. Hull and Welles feared that a total embargo would drive Japan toward the Netherlands East Indies. They took Grew's warnings of precipitant Japanese action seriously and still retained a slender faith in his recurrent idea that moderates might somehow regain power. Both men regarded limited sanctions as a compromise, one that would uphold American principles and possibly discourage Japanese extremists without risking a showdown.

Distracted by the crisis in Europe, the President wavered between the alternatives offered by his advisers. In July 1940 he signed an order prepared by Morgenthau and Stimson embargoing all oil and scrap metal exports to Japan, apparently under the illusion that the State Department had approved this policy. Acting Secretary of State Welles, along with the Division of Far Eastern Affairs, vehemently objected, arguing that such an extensive embargo would encourage Japan to join the Axis and attack British and Dutch possessions. On July 26 Morgenthau and Welles clashed before the cabinet, and the State Department's view prevailed. The new regulations included only aviation gasoline and lubricants and number one heavy melting iron and scrap steel (which amounted to 15 percent of Japan's scrap purchases).

Activists within the administration were vexed, particularly when it became apparent that Japan could easily evade the restrictions on aviation gasoline. In September further Japanese pressure on French Indochina and news that negotiations between Germany, Italy, and Japan were nearing completion increased their leverage, as did Ambassador Grew's "green light" telegram. Japan, Grew wrote, was a "predatory Power" like Germany, Italy, and the Soviet Union, suppressing "all moral and ethical sense . . . frankly and unashamedly opportunist, seeking at every turn to

---

[8] Quoted in James C. Thomson, Jr., "The Role of the Department of State," in Borg and Okamoto, *Pearl Harbor As History,* pp. 81, 100.

profit by the weakness of others."[9] He believed that only a gradually enlarged embargo would deter Japan and now accepted the possibility of war in Asia, in order to defend the interests of Western civilization. Roosevelt and Hull agreed on the need for further steps and, on September 26, extended the embargo to cover all grades of iron and steel scrap.

The Tripartite Pact, announced to the world on September 27, removed any lingering doubts about the unity of the crises in Asia and Europe and reduced to a flicker hopes for a reconciliation between Japan and the United States. All the constructive work between the two nations, Grew wrote the President, had been "swept away as if by a typhoon."[10] In response, the American government took a number of small but significant actions that indicated its determination to persevere in existing policies. It announced a new loan to China, warned American citizens there to return, and secretly agreed to formal staff talks with Great Britain.

Public opinion surveys indicated solid support for a policy of firmness. Ninety-six percent of those polled approved Roosevelt's decision to forbid the shipment of scrap iron to Japan, while 60 percent viewed an increase of Japanese power in Asia as a serious threat to the United States. Not all groups, of course, shared this consensus. Forty percent of the business executives polled wished to appease Japan; 35 percent wished to let nature take its course; and only 19 percent wished to engage in an embargo or threats of force. Protestant leaders and religious organizations also refused to join in the call for action against Japan. And the polls revealed a reluctance among the people to confront directly the question of war or peace. Nevertheless, nearly every source used to gauge the public's temper indicated a rising current of anti-Japanese feeling.

The President listened and waited, beset by sharp internal rifts within his administration. Activists were dissatisfied, convinced that the United States had done too little too late, while the State

---

[9]*Foreign Relations of the United States: 1940,* 5 vols. (Washington, D. C., 1959-1961), IV, p. 602.

[10]Joseph C. Grew, *Ten Years in Japan* (New York, 1944), p. 359.

Department remained divided. Hornbeck urged the dispatch of American vessels to Singapore, a bastion he considered vital to Britain's security, and argued that Japan and the United States were, in a sense, already at war. Maxwell M. Hamilton, however, still hoped that Japan and the United States could find a way out of their impasse. Nor had Hull altered his conviction that a confrontation must be delayed. He wanted to slow up the tide of Japanese aggression, to conduct "a rear guard diplomatic action" that would allow the passage of time to work to America's advantage.[11] The President agreed, convinced that he must maintain a delicate balance between firmness and provocation.

The advice of navy officers reinforced the President's caution. For decades the navy had viewed Japan as its major antagonist, and throughout the 1930s had taken an alarmist view of that nation's intentions. The metamorphosis of the navy's position began in late 1937, when the deteriorating international situation raised more complex possibilities for future conflict and encouraged naval planners to break with old patterns of strategic thought. The traditional Orange Plan, with its concept of the fleet moving westward to engage Japanese forces and liberate the Philippines, became less and less viable as the navy's concentration on the Pacific faltered. By the spring of 1939 the navy assumed a more defensive posture in the Pacific and elaborated a military version of the popular notion that Japan could be defeated or at least contained through an economic blockade.

The fall of France quickened the geographical reorientation of naval planners. Plan Orange and the advance to the Western Pacific had always been a part of their budgetary strategy; now the navy had a real, ominous enemy in the Atlantic and no longer needed an imaginary one in the Pacific. The German threat to American security overshadowed previous ideas about America's stake in East Asia. On November 4, 1940 Chief of Naval Operations Harold R. Stark formalized the navy's thinking in "Plan Dog," which portrayed Germany as the nation's major enemy and

---

[11] Quoted in William L. Langer and S. Everett Gleason, *The Undeclared War: 1940-1941* (New York, 1953), p. 308.

the preservation of Britain and its empire as its chief concern. Plan Dog speculated that Japan might not attack while the United States concentrated on the Atlantic; if it did, the United States could deal with Japan through economic blockade and possibly a limited war in the Pacific. The latter, however, would be dangerous, since it might assume a life of its own. Stark advocated the avoidance of war with Japan, aggressively opposed an oil embargo, and urged the movement of naval units from the Pacific to the Atlantic.

Roosevelt listened carefully to his naval advisers, with whom he had a special rapport. In contrast, the army's advisers were not close to the President and were less assertive in advancing their views. Throughout the 1930s the army was inwardlooking, intimidated by changes in American society and bound by its traditional deference to civilian policymakers. Its historic interests centered more in the Western hemisphere and Europe than in East Asia, and it wished to withdraw from the commitment to defend the Philippines, where defeat seemed so certain. Army planners preferred to base the nation's Pacific defense on a triangle formed by Alaska, Hawaii, and Panama. By 1940 they regarded Hitler as the real challenge and sought to preserve the army's meager resources—in September 1939 it had only 190,000 men—to meet the German threat. Chief of Staff George C. Marshall worried over war production, the defense of the Western hemisphere, and the training of the burgeoning American army. Marshall and other army officers had less influence on East Asian policy than did the navy but, in 1940, they developed better lines of communication with the President and began to convey their ideas to him more forcefully. Marshall urged caution in dealing with Japan and opposed any further naval buildup in the Pacific. Strongly supporting Plan Dog, he emphasized the need for time to remedy the appalling weaknesses in America's military organization.

The President shared the preoccupation of his military advisers with Europe, along with the conviction of Secretary of State Hull that much would be gained by delaying a showdown with Japan. In October 1940 his mind played with various schemes of deterrence, such as naval patrols in the Western Pacific and the assignment of a portion of the fleet to Singapore or the Philippines. But the President did not seem seriously tempted by any of these plans. When Stimson suggested that the dispatch of a flying squadron could block Japan's seizure of the Netherlands East Indies, Roosevelt promised only to study the maps. When the Secretary of the Treasury again urged decisive action, Roosevelt sharply reminded Morgenthau that he and Hull were "handling foreign affairs."[12] In early December the President informed his cabinet that any enlargement of the embargo would unleash new expansionist energies in Japan. No doubt Roosevelt and Hull found it difficult at times to suppress their pent-up antagonism toward Japan. In late 1940, when Morgenthau proposed a farfetched plan to enable China to bomb Tokyo, he found Hull "just a bundle of fervor and vitality on this thing."[13] Unlike Hornbeck, Ickes, Morgenthau, and Stimson, however, Hull and the President retained their perspective and self-discipline. They swallowed hard and remained in touch with reality.

In the early months of 1941 the President and his advisers continued to focus their attention on the situation in Europe. Britain's deteriorating position in the Atlantic and North Africa raised the possibility that Hitler might close off the Mediterranean and launch a massive assault against the British Isles. In March, soon after Congress passed the Lend Lease Act, Roosevelt faced intense pressure to escort convoys across the Atlantic. Rejecting this proposal, he did take other steps—such as the acquisition of bases in Greenland, the extension of naval patrols in the Atlantic, and the declaration of an unlimited national emergency—to make clear the nation's determination to aid Britain. In June the German invasion of Russia provided a breathing spell for Britain and the United States. Although the question of aid remained acute, the President now had more time to move the nation from nonbelligerency to undeclared war.

The severity of the crisis in the Atlantic did not, however, allow the United States to escape from the problems in East Asia. The American government continued to aid China, to expand the em-

---

[12] Blum, *From the Morgenthau Diaries,* II, p. 362.
[13] *Ibid.,* p. 367.

bargo in a piecemeal fashion, and to strengthen its Pacific defenses. It urged the Dutch to resist Japanese demands for huge quantities of oil and other resources from the East Indies and worked to coordinate Pacific defenses with Australia, Britain, and the Netherlands. The constant, seemingly endless tension with Japan largely had ended the hope for a settlement and dulled the sensitivity of Hull and his advisers to the risks of a full embargo. Within the State Department, the reluctance to provoke Japan was weakening. In February 1941 Counselor of Embassy Eugene H. Dooman delivered a stern American warning to the Japanese government, and Hull himself advocated the dispatch of naval vessels to the Western Pacific. Roosevelt liked the idea of having American ships "popping up here and there and keep the Japs guessing," but gave way before the heated objections of Admiral Stark.[14] Instead of exacerbating relations with Japan, Stark and naval planners pressed Roosevelt to transfer part of the Pacific fleet to the Atlantic, where the navy's commitments were already heavy and rapidly increasing. In early 1941 Anglo-American staff talks had confirmed the Europe-first strategy and the unwillingness of the United States to commit itself to the defense of Singapore or the Western Pacific. Neither the clarity of these priorities nor the advice of Knox, Marshall, Stark, and Stimson persuaded Roosevelt and Hull to shift more than one fourth of the Pacific fleet to the Atlantic in May 1941. Convinced that the fleet's presence deterred Japan, they were unwilling to relinquish a vital ingredient of American policy.

While Washington stiffened its position toward Japan, it also decided that diplomatic negotiations—however faint the possibility of success—would serve its purpose of delay. The impetus came from two Catholic missionaries, Bishop James E. Walsh and Father James M. Drought who, in the autumn of 1940, traveled to Japan and convinced Konoe and other influential Japanese that they were close to high American officials. Both men were ambitious intermediaries whose vague understanding of the issues was matched by a strong desire for peace, a combination that led them

---

[14]Quoted in Langer and Gleason, *The Undeclared War,* p. 471.

to tell each government what it wanted to hear. In Tokyo they suggested to Japanese officials that the United States would make major concessions; in Washington, where the intervention of Postmaster General Frank C. Walker brought a meeting with Roosevelt and Hull, they gave the opposite impression. Although Hull and his advisers disliked these private initiatives and were skeptical of the reliability of Drought and Walsh, they encouraged them to continue their efforts and to reduce Japan's proposals to writing.

The chief outgrowth of this flurry of unofficial activity came in March 1941, when Hull and Ambassador Nomura began conversations that continued until late July. Meeting mostly in the evenings, the two men explored in wearisome detail the conflicting positions of their respective governments. Hull sought to commit Japan to withdraw from China, to renounce forceful expansion in Southeast Asia and, in effect, to abrogate the Tripartite Pact. As was his custom, he formulated the American case in terms of four principles or points. Hull insisted that Japan agree: (1) to respect the territorial integrity and sovereignity of other nations; (2) to avoid interference in the internal affairs of other nations; (3) to respect the principle of equality, particularly the equality of commercial opportunity; and (4) to effect only peaceful changes in the status quo in the Pacific. Japanese leaders had no inclination to discuss abstract principles. They wanted recognition of Japan's special position in East Asia and an end to both America's aid to China and its economic embargo. Any other course would mean the repudiation of the policies of a decade.

Ultimately the Hull-Nomura conversations did more harm than good. Like so many Japanese diplomats abroad, Nomura placed the advancement of his own concept of Japan's policies ahead of the accurate expression of his government's position. Believing that Japan must achieve a reconciliation with the United States, he sought to convince Tokyo of American flexibility and to create the proper climate for negotiations. Nomura did pass on Hull's four principles, but indicated that he had successfully put them aside and failed to report the Secretary of State's full remarks. Not until September would the Japanese government learn of their great importance.

In early April 1941 the efforts of Drought and Nomura converged. With the aid of a young army officer dispatched from Tokyo, Drought produced a draft understanding highly favorable to Japan. Hull and his advisers accepted it as a basis for negotiation, although they had no intention of agreeing to its terms. But Nomura deliberately misrepresented the State Department's position and informed Tokyo that the draft understanding was an American plan. Most members of the Japanese government—including the Emperor—were surprised and delighted and, throughout the rest of the year, they regarded the draft understanding as a yardstick against which to measure all subsequent American proposals. Naturally these were found wanting, and it seemed as if the United States was backing away from its earlier, more generous attitude. By the spring of 1941 the impasse between the two governments was greater than either really knew.

IV

In the winter of 1940 to 1941 Japan's leaders pondered the nation's imperial destiny, puzzled by the failure of the Tripartite Pact and Matsuoka's aggressive diplomacy to bring results. The Soviet Union continued to menace Japan; the United States remained hostile; Britain not only endured but reopened the Burma Road; and, finally, negotiations with the Dutch over the East Indies broke down. With the advance into Southeast Asia stalled, Japan's leaders seemed uncertain of how to exploit the world crisis. Some concluded that a Russo-Japanese accord would increase the nation's diplomatic leverage and, in April 1941, Matsuoka negotiated a neutrality pact with Stalin. Others, encouraged by the draft understanding forwarded from Washington, wanted to explore the possibility of American assistance in concluding the Sino-Japanese conflict. Matsuoka, however, wished to dominate negotiations with the United States and believed that concessions would only be taken as a sign of weakness. He delayed a reply to the apparent American offer and insisted, with some success, on stiffening the demands made on the United States.

By the end of June an American note destroyed the illusion that the United States could be used to end the Sino-Japanese war, and the German invasion of Russia added a new dimension to the world scene. Although Japanese leaders had some warning of Hitler's intention, the actual attack shocked them and upset their strategic calculations. Matsuoka wished to join with Germany and turn north instead of continue south, but only a minority of army planners supported him. Konoe regarded Hitler's act as a betrayal of the Tripartite Pact, and army officers in the War Ministry and naval officers in both the General Staff and Navy Ministry opposed collaboration with Germany against Russia. Aside from the difficulty of relocating its troops, the army was reluctant to take on powerful Soviet forces in Siberia, an area that contained neither oil nor vital raw materials. Most army officers preferred to move into Southern Indochina and to develop closer ties with Thailand before launching a northern drive. By the midsummer of 1941 both Konoe and army leaders were exasperated with Matsuoka, who had infringed on military prerogatives, contested their strategic designs, and interfered with the efforts to avoid war with the United States. In July Konoe reorganized his cabinet and dropped his Foreign Minister, preparing the way for an advance to the south.

Civilian leaders had consistently avoided calculating the probable costs of expansion into Southeast Asia and had clung to the possibility of averting a Japanese-American war. Middle-echelon naval officers were the first group to confront this grim prospect. Since June 1940, these officers, mesmerized by Germany's victories, realized that Britain and the United States could not be separated and that Japan's quest for an autonomous empire would inevitably bring conflict with America. More specifically, they foresaw that the occupation of Southern Indochina would provoke a full American oil embargo. They formed a potent collective leadership that more and more dominated the less decisive senior officers and that led the navy, by late 1940, to seize the initiative within the government and demand preparations for war. By the spring of 1941 the navy called for a drive into Southern Indochina, irrespective of the reactions of Britain and the United States.

The army was slower than the navy to accept the probability of war with the United States. Its main concerns were China and Russia and, for several years after the outbreak of the Sino-Japanese war, the army did not believe expansion into China would disrupt relations with America. As the war in Europe extended the army's horizons, the possibility arose of involvement in the struggle against Great Britain. But the army envisaged the United States on the periphery of such a conflict and calculated that the Tripartite Pact would help keep it there. Not until the spring of 1941 did army leaders finally realize that a southern advance might well bring a Japanese-American war. By midsummer they also saw the United States as a major obstacle to the conclusion of the China Incident. Although less fatalistic than the navy and still hopeful of avoiding a clash, the army fully supported the cabinet's decision in July to demand that Vichy France allow Japanese bases and troops in Southern Indochina. Japan would then be in a position to fulfill its far-reaching aims in the south should Hitler, as expected, triumph in Russia.

V

By the early summer of 1941 tension within the Roosevelt administration over policy toward Japan had reached the breaking point. Ickes thought of resignation, bridling at what he termed the administration's policy of appeasement. Stimson deplored the President's lack of vigorous leadership and longed for Theodore Roosevelt, who, he was convinced, would have led boldly, confident that men would follow. Preoccupied with Europe, Stimson reasoned that Japan would not dare attack southward as long as Britain and the United States remained undefeated.

So, too, did most of the American people, who regarded Japan as a second-class power, one that could be easily disposed of while the United States directed the bulk of its strength against Germany. Organized groups agitating for or against American involvement in the European war had paid little attention to the Asian crisis before 1941; nor did their attitude change much in that year. In late 1940 Roger S. Greene dissolved the Committee for Non-Participation in Japanese Aggression into the Committee to Defend America by Aiding the Allies and convinced its leaders that sterner measures against Japan would aid Britain. Other interventionist organizations found Japan's behavior repugnant but easy to ignore. Many of those with more knowledge of Japan also discounted its strength and doubted its willingness to fight. In June

1941 Thomas W. Lamont—once Japan's ardent defender—wrote State Department officials that he felt "more severe economic sanctions could be imposed upon Japan without undue risk." Japan, Lamont argued, would "curl up."[15] No significant domestic forces opposed a full embargo against Japan. Businessmen had become reconciled to deteriorating relations and were ready to follow where the administration led; some scholars warned against pushing Japan too far, but their voices were submerged in the clamor for a policy that would end American complicity in Japanese aggression.

For a time Roosevelt refused to move. In early June 1941 Morgenthau returned to the attack, suggesting the elevation of Hull to the Supreme Court and the appointment of Stimson as Secretary of State. Roosevelt disliked the idea and surprised Morgenthau by pointing out that "he was not at all sure that Stimson was right in the Manchurian incident and that Hull's tactics might have been better at that time."[16] Seeking to pacify Ickes, he informed him on July 1 that "the Japs are having a real drag-down and knock-out fight among themselves and have been for the past week—trying to decide which way they are going to jump—attack Russia, attack the South Seas . . . or whether they will sit on the fence and be more friendly with us. No one knows what the decision will be but . . . it is terribly important for the control of the Atlantic for us to help to keep peace in the Pacific. I simply have not got enough Navy to go around."[17]

Within a few days, however, evidence of an impending Japanese advance into Southern Indochina brought the agitation for a full embargo to a peak. The Division of Far Eastern Affairs still resisted, as did Stark and naval planners, who warned that Japan would go to war to get oil. But by now the balance within the administration had shifted decisively for further economic sanctions, although confusion persisted over how far the United States

---

[15]Quoted in Mira Wilkins, "The Role of U.S. Business," in Borg and Okamoto, *Pearl Harbor As History,* p. 358.

[16]Blum, *From the Morgenthau Diaries, II, p. 375.*

[17]Quoted in Herbert Feis, *The Road to Pearl Harbor: The Coming of the War Between the United States and Japan* (Princeton, 1950), p. 206

should go. Roosevelt seemed indecisive, while Hull, ill and absent from Washington, accepted tighter controls but remained fearful of their consequences. On July 24 the President and cabinet finally agreed to freeze Japanese assets, but neither Roosevelt nor Acting Secretary of State Welles intended to sever all economic ties. The President preferred "to slip the noose around Japan's neck and give it a jerk now and then."[18]

Whatever the President's preferences, the public's reaction to the freezing order left no room for maneuver. Both the press and the Congress overwhelmingly approved what they interpreted as a decision to end all trade with Japan. In July 1941 51 percent of those polled said that the United States should take steps—even at the risk of war—to keep Japan from becoming more powerful; in August that figure rose to 70 percent. Moreover, 52 percent believed the United States should go to war to prevent Japan from seizing Singapore and the Netherlands East Indies. The American people would have viewed anything less than a full embargo as appeasement of Japan. In August Roosevelt gradually ended the uncertainty and made it clear that trade would not be resumed— even at a much reduced level.

The British and Dutch governments joined the United States in breaking off trade. They had long sought a firm American commitment against Japanese expansionism and were now eager to consolidate a common front. Roosevelt continued to avoid any concrete promises, but he did warn Ambassador Nomura that the seizure of the East Indies would bring war with Great Britain and the Netherlands and create an "exceedingly serious situation" with the United States. Through Harry Hopkins he told Prime Minister Winston Churchill that "our concurrent action in regard to Japan is, I think, bearing fruit. I hear their Government [is] much upset and no conclusive future policy has been determined on."[19] There was an element of complacency in the President's position, a feeling that somehow deterrence would work and that events would unfold as he hoped. Neither Churchill nor Roosevelt

---

[18]Ickes, *Secret Diary,* III, p. 588.
[19]Quoted in Feis, *Road to Pearl Harbor,* pp. 238-239.

believed that Japan would move beyond Southern Indochina and fight both Britain and the United States.

The army's shifting views on Pacific strategy tended to confirm this line of thought. Since the early 1930s, the army had wished to withdraw from the Western Pacific because of the exposed position of American forces there. By late 1940, however, it had begun to change its attitude toward the Philippines. Former Chief of Staff Douglas MacArthur, who had left the army in 1935 to become the commander of a new Filipino force of citizen-soldiers, exuded optimism, predicting in 1941 that his forces could defend the entire archipelago. Most significant, increasing defense production finally gave army planners the means they needed to hold this distant outpost. Air power enthusiasts convinced Marshall and Stimson that a sizable force of B-17 bombers stationed in the Philippines could not only protect the islands, but could also thwart any Japanese fleet advancing into Southeast Asia. Although Marshall continued to adhere to the Europe-first strategy and to emphasize the army's desperate need for time, he offered no objections to the freezing order and, on July 31, told his staff that the United States could retain the Philippines. In August he began the rapid shipment of men and equipment to the Philippines, which by November possessed one half of all the heavy bombers and one sixth of all the pursuit planes stationed abroad. The United States, so it seemed, had a good chance of defending the islands, and military planners doubted that Japan would move south as long as American troops in the Philippines remained undefeated. The army gave Roosevelt one more reason to believe that he could restrain Japan and avoid war in the Pacific.

VI

The freezing order came as a shock to most Japanese leaders, who had not expected such a severe American response to the occupation of Southern Indochina. It forced them to confront, sooner than they wished, the most basic questions of national destiny, to decide whether to go forward or to retreat in humiliation. Few within ruling circles favored the latter course and, if they did, dared not speak out in the strained and emotional atmosphere of the last half of 1941. China was the army's base of power and the core of the Greater East Asia Co-Prosperity Sphere. To relinquish dominance there would erode Japan's prestige throughout Asia and bring a major shift in authority within Japanese society. The army and navy were impatient, intent on diplomatic victory or war, while Prime Minister Konoe, more out of desperation than logic, turned to the idea of a meeting with President Roosevelt as a way out of the impasse. He hoped to retain the substance of Japan's position in Asia while conceding the shadow.

Ambassador Grew urged the President to attend a summit conference. Even the ordeal of 9 years in Japan had not destroyed his faith in personal diplomacy, and he interpreted Konoe's proposal as proof that the embargo had worked, that the pendulum was now swinging toward moderation. He believed that Konoe, once at the bargaining table, would make major concessions and that the conference would set in motion a gradual process of accommodation. Grew was understandably vague about the terms of this accommodation, for the romantic vision of a leaders' meeting had distorted his judgment of the contours of Japanese politics.

While Grew overestimated the power of Japanese moderates, the Secretary of State underestimated the flux within ruling circles in Tokyo. After the freezing order he fatalistically assumed that Japan would plunge ahead. "Nothing will stop them," he told Welles, "except force. . . . The point is how long we can maneuver the situation until the military matter in Europe is brought to a conclusion."[20] Hull and his advisers distrusted Konoe, doubted his authority, and intensely disliked the whole idea of a leaders' conference. The Division of Far Eastern Affairs warned that such a meeting would seem to be a betrayal of China and that Japan would evade any agreement reached. Hornbeck saw no reason to make concessions, for he believed Japan was bluffing and would not in the end fight. All of these men remembered that, since early 1941, a leaders' meeting had been promoted by Father Drought and that it had been a key part of the draft understanding presented to the American government in April. Then State Department officials found the idea unappealing, but agreed to retain it

---

[20]Quoted in Langer and Gleason, *The Undeclared War*, p. 659.

as a basis for negotiations. It was the Japanese government that displayed a lack of interest and eliminated a leaders' conference from its response. In August the proposal was stale, tarnished by Japan's earlier rejection and by its association with the dubious efforts of Drought and Walsh.

To the Secretary of State and his advisers, the risks seemed too great and the chances of success too small. They had little difficulty convincing the President of the dangers of Konoe's plan. Roosevelt knew that it would have offended the American public if—soon after meeting with Winston Churchill off the coast of Newfoundland—he had flown to Hawaii to meet with the Prime Minister of a nation allied with Nazi Germany. Many would have accused the administration of seeking an East Asian Munich. Roosevelt may also have feared that a conference, if it failed, would aggravate tensions and actually quicken a showdown. Hoping to delay a confrontation with Japan, he did not appreciate the desperate sense of urgency in Tokyo.

While not openly rejecting Konoe's proposal, Hull insisted that Japan and the United States reach an agreement on a whole series of unresolved issues before a leaders' meeting could take place. For a time Konoe tried to satisfy Hull while avoiding a full discussion of Japan's terms but, on September 25, he finally sent a comprehensive proposal to Washington. The Japanese government offered certain concessions, agreeing to a virtual nullification of the Tripartite Pact and the neutralization of Southeast Asia, so long as Japan had access to resources there. But it insisted on the restoration of normal trade relations—including an immense amount of oil—and American good offices to bring peace in China. During the peace talks, aid to China must end. Japan contemplated a coalition regime of Wang Ching-wei, the leader of its puppet government, and Chiang Kai-shek, one that would permit Japanese troops and naval units to remain in certain areas and grant Japan a special economic position in China. Only after the conclusion of a Sino-Japanese peace would Japan withdraw from Indochina.

There was no hope for a comprehensive settlement along these lines. It would have meant American recognition of Manchukuo and Japanese hegemony in China. Only through an abandonment of Chiang Kai-shek could the United States halt the Japanese advance into Southeast Asia. But Japan would have remained powerful, capable of striking deeper into that region when the opportunity beckoned. The linkage of the Asian crisis with the global struggle to preserve democracy made concessions on this scale unthinkable. By mid-October 1941 Hull believed that "the area of difference between us was wider than at the start of the discussions."[21]

In Tokyo, too, there was a hardening of wills. More and more preoccupied with operational considerations, the army and navy were gripped by a sense of time running out, oppressed by the knowledge that 12,000 tons of oil were vanishing each day. In the last half of August the general staffs of the army and navy—the dynamic elements in the decision-making process—had decided that war preparations should run parallel to negotiations and that Japan, failing to achieve a diplomatic victory, would have to go to war in the near future. On September 6 an Imperial Conference confirmed this decision. Both the army and the navy believed Japan must fight in order to retain its position in Asia. "The stationing of troops in China," War Minister Tōjō said, "is the heart of the matter. . . . To make concession after concession and to yield on this question is like piercing the heart and tantamount to surrender."[22] In a striking metaphor, the Chief of the Naval General Staff, Nagano Osami, compared Japan with a seriously ill patient who, if spared surgery, was sure to waste away. Only through a drastic operation could he find "a way to life out of a seemingly fatal situation."[23] For the army and navy the struggle with China and advance to the south had blended into war with the United States as part of one great effort to free Asia from the tyranny of the West.

Prime Minister Konoe, along with the Emperor and court circles, did not share the military's conviction that war with the United

---

[21] Cordell Hull, *The Memoirs of Cordell Hull,* 2 vols. (New York, 1948), II, p. 1035.

[22] Quoted in Akira Iriye, "The Failure of Military Expansionism," in Morley, *Dilemmas of Growth,* p. 135.

[23] Quoted in Asada, "The Japanese Navy and the United States," in Borg and Okamoto, *Pearl Harbor As History,* p. 255.

States provided the only solution to Japan's dilemma. More patient and flexible, they drew back from the consequences of their own policies and pleaded for time. The risks of doing so were high in the charged atmosphere in Tokyo, where news of Konoe's conference proposal fanned ultranationalist unrest and endangered his life. These civilians delayed but could not prevent the final decision for war. In late September the army and navy concluded that diplomacy had failed and pressed for an end to negotiations on October 15 and war by early November. Konoe still hesitated. He wished to make some concessions on the question of Japanese troops in China and warned that a war with the United States would become part of a global conflict. Tōjō, however, was determined to force the issue. "Sometimes a man has to jump," he told the Prime Minister, "with his eyes closed, from the veranda of Kiyomizu Temple."[24] Confronted with this desperate faith, Konoe faltered. He had no convincing alternative to war and, instead of leading the nation into conflict with the United States, resigned the premiership on October 16.

With Konoe's resignation, no civilian leader remained who could curb the impatience of the ultranationalists and middle-echelon military and naval groups. The Emperor and his advisers concluded that, in order to avert a major political crisis, they would have to confer the premiership on Tōjō. In doing so, however, the Emperor directed him to ignore the decision of the Imperial Conference on September 6 and to begin over again, with a "clean slate."[25] Tōjō felt a profound obligation to obey the imperial mandate and, at the same time, to end previous procrastination by achieving either a diplomatic triumph or a decision for war. In the second half of October he led an intensive reassessment of Japan's diplomatic position, holding off the demands of the army and navy chiefs of staff for immediate war. Both services finally agreed to more negotiations, with the understanding that diplomatic efforts would end on December 1. On November 5 the Imperial

---

[24]Quoted in Hosoya, "Retrogression in Japan's Foreign Policy Decision-Making Process," in Morley, *Dilemmas of Growth,* p. 93.
[25]Quoted in Butow, *Tojo,* pp. 301-302.

Conference recognized the consensus reached under Tōjō's leadership; unless the United States accepted a diplomatic settlement, war would begin in early December,

The decision for further negotiations resulted in two plans, A and B, which Japanese diplomats presented to the American government in November. Plan A consisted of a comprehensive settlement that had no chance of success; plan B, in contrast, provided for a modus vivendi. In it Japan agreed to withdraw from Southern Indochina upon the conclusion of the modus and from the whole of Indochina upon the conclusion of peace between China and Japan. Japan asked for an assurance of raw materials from the East Indies and the restoration of commercial relations with the United States. Plan B did not mention the Tripartite Pact or make more than a vague reference to America's role in the settlement of the Sino-Japanese War. But the American government knew, through the interception of Japan's diplomatic messages, that Tokyo had not significantly altered the terms of its late September proposal. In effect, Japan offered to halt its advance into Southeast Asia and to stand aside while the United States concentrated on the war in Europe, so long as the American government sanctioned a settlement favorable to Japan in China and resumed substantial shipments of oil. These terms reflected the belief of Tōjō and others that the United States did not really want war with Japan and would pay a large price to avoid it. They also reflected Japan's deteriorating international position. The German offensive in Russia had stalled, Great Britain remained undefeated, and the United States was on the brink of intervention in the European war. With Germany's victory less certain, Japan's leaders temporarily curtailed their imperial program.

Army and navy leaders were, however, far less interested in diplomacy than in operational and strategic imperatives. Their thoughts revolved around the diminishing supply of oil, weather conditions in the Northern Pacific, and the plans for a series of bold and intricately timed offensives that would give Japan a far-flung defense perimeter in the Pacific. Short-term planning was precise and clear; long-term planning was vague and ill-defined. Tōjō and others knew that American productive capacity was seven or eight times that of Japan, but both services avoided any realistic consideration of the feasibility of a long war. The army's ignorance of America encouraged illusions, as did its belief that a Pacific war was essentially the navy's responsibility. Naval planners, more knowledgeable about America, calculated that Japan, by launching a major building program in 1937, had won a 3-year lead over the United States. By the autumn of 1941 Japan had achieved equality in the Pacific with American, British, and Dutch naval forces, but its position would begin to deteriorate in 1942. Thus middle-echelon officers assured their superiors that Japan could seize and defend a large area of Southeast Asia that would provide oil and other raw materials essential for the nation's war effort.

In doing so, however, naval planners were victims of their own wishful thinking, underestimating many of the problems an extended conflict would bring. They ignored the navy's lack of transports to carry oil to Japan, ships for convoy duty, or experience in protecting vital sea lanes in time of war. Nor did they consider the scanty fortifications of the Japanese islands in the South Pacific or the lack of air power to defend them. Naval staff officers had become numb to the perils of war with America. The commander-in-chief of the combined fleet and the originator of the Pearl Harbor attack, Admiral Yamamato, warned Chief of Staff Nagano of the futility of war, but failed to convince him. Army and navy planners calculated that a German victory over Britain and Russia, combined with the staggering defeats Japan would inflict on the United States in the early phases of the Pacific war, would destroy America's will to fight and lead to a negotiated peace. The prospect was so farfetched, however, that not even Japanese strategists could visualize in concrete terms what new equilibrium would emerge.

By late 1941 the mood within Japan's ruling circle was somber. Prior to the freezing order Japan seemed to be riding the crest of a wave; now the nation was on the defensive, clinging to the essence of its new order in East Asia. Euphoria had given away to a sense of despair, to a now or never psychology. Many had moved beyond the realm of rational calculation and concluded that Japan must strike immediately or abandon its national objectives and lose its status as the dominant power in Asia. The humiliation and moral collapse of peace outweighed the risks of war. As Admiral Nagano observed, "if there is a war, the country may be ruined. Nevertheless, a nation which does not fight in this plight has lost its spirit and is already a doomed country. Only if we fight to the last soldier will it be possible to find a way out of this fatal situation."[26] Japan's leaders transcended the realties of power and sought solace and inspiration in certain national traditions. These traditions told them that death was preferable to surrender, that spiritual strength would triumph over material might, and that God would help Japan in its moment of crisis. There was also the comforting memory—still vivid—of the war against Russia from 1904 to 1905 and the victory over seemingly insuperable odds. As the last days of peace slipped by, Japan's rulers accepted the inevitability of war and felt that they could only yield to the great historical currents carrying their nation toward an obscure fate.

VII

In the autumn of 1941 American officials also realized that time was running out. The majority of the cabinet believed Japan would fight, but minimized the seriousness of a conflict and acted as if, in a sense, the two nations were already at war. General Marshall and Admiral Stark, however, were unwilling to abandon all hope. Twice during November they appealed to the President for time and reminded him of the nation's commitment to a Europe-first strategy. Both wanted more diplomatic flexibility so long as it did not imperil British and Dutch possessions in the Pacific, which they regarded as vital to the security of the United States. Roosevelt and Hull were sensitive to the needs of the military and genuinely reluctant for a showdown. In early November their thoughts, like those of Japanese leaders, turned to the idea of a modus vivendi. Initially Roosevelt pondered a truce in which there would be no movement or armament in the Pacific for 6 months, while officers of the Division of Far Eastern Affairs discussed the suspension of aid to China during its negotiations with Japan.

---

[26]Quoted in James B. Crowley, "A New Deal for Japan and Asia: One Road to Pearl Harbor," in James B. Crowley, ed., *Modern East Asia: Essays in Interpretation* (New York, 1970), p. 261.

On November 20, in the midst of these deliberations, Japan presented plan B. Angered by the proposal's one-sidedness, Hull recalled in his *Memoirs* that it asked for "virtually a surrender,"[27] one that would have involved the betrayal of China and the acceptance of Japanese aggression in East Asia. Nevertheless, the Japanese plan gave a certain impetus to the efforts of the President and Secretary of State to define an American modus vivendi. But the price that the American government contemplated paying for a military standstill in Southeast Asia was small, indeed, by Japanese standards. The United States would allow a trickle of oil to Japan and encourage negotiations between Chungking and Tokyo, but would neither abandon China nor discontinue aid during discussions. Moreover, Japan would have to abrogate the Tripartite Pact and agree to certain general principles of international conduct.

On the face of it, an American modus vivendi seemed attractive. Even if it failed it would keep the record straight; if it should, by chance, succeed, it would delay a confrontation until the tide against Germany had turned and forced Japan to retreat further. Certainly the American government had every reason to avoid a two-front war. As the Secretary of State pursued the plan, however, serious difficulties appeared. The Australian, British, and Dutch governments were all cool to the idea, although they did not reject it outright. The British wanted stiffer terms, and Prime Minister Churchill feared the impact of a temporary settlement on China. The Chinese government violently objected and warned of the collapse of its war effort. Hull was shaken by Chiang Kai-shek's protests. He shared the widespread concern over China and did not relish the bitter charges of appeasement that an American modus vivendi was certain to evoke. Public opinion polls revealed little inclination among the American people to compromise with Japan. In late November 48 percent of those polled believed a war with Japan would be comparatively easy; in early December 69 percent felt the United States should risk war to prevent Japan from growing more powerful. Negotiations with Japan over a

---

[27] Hull, *Memoirs*, II, p. 1069.

modus vivendi—whatever its terms—would bring profound confusion over the course of the nation's foreign policy.

Finally, the President and Secretary of State turned away from negotiations because of their pervasive distrust of Japan. They knew that Japanese troop transports were off the coast of Taiwan and realized, through diplomatic intercepts, that the Japanese government would not negotiate beyond November 29. Thus, an American counterproposal, while it would damage the morale of America's allies and divide the American people, would neither buy time nor bring diplomatic success. On November 25 Hull decided not to offer an American modus vivendi; the next day the President approved his decision. He had long allowed Hull to dominate negotiations with Japan and now saw no reason to quarrel with his conclusion. Tired and weary, Hull believed that negotiations were no longer worth the abuse he would receive from America's allies and from critics within the American government. He succumbed to his desire to end the bickering and uncertainty, "to kick the whole thing over" and let events take their course.[28] On November 27 he told Stimson that "I have washed my hands of it, and it [the situation] is now in the hands of . . . the Army and Navy."[29]

There was probably never any chance that the Tōjō ministry—obsessed with time and determined to keep the Japanese army in China—would have accepted the American modus vivendi. The two governments remained so far apart—even on the terms of a temporary settlement—that it is most unlikely Tokyo would have extended its deadline for the completion of the negotiations. Hull's abrupt decision, however, left an element of doubt that would later tantalize historians. The 10-point reply that he dispatched to Tokyo rigidly reaffirmed American principles of international behavior and ended any prospect for disrupting Japan's timetable. It convinced Japan's leaders that the United States would settle for nothing less than a return to the situation in East Asia prior to 1931.

---

[28] Quoted in Langer and Gleason, *The Undeclared War,* p. 892.
[29] Quoted in Feis, *Road to Pearl Harbor,* p. 321.

Roosevelt and most of his advisers, absorbed with events in Europe, now fatalistically waited, hoping for a delay but realizing that Japan would not permit one. A curious passivity settled on the American government. Alerting the public to the critical nature of the crisis with Japan, it concentrated on the domestic political dilemma arising out of an anticipated Japanese move against British and Dutch possessions. The cabinet believed the American people would support the defense of Singapore and the East Indies, but the question remained of how to justify such a policy. The President hesitated, pondering both a message to the Emperor and an address to Congress. As usual, Hull counseled delay, and it was not until December 6 that Roosevelt decided to appeal to the Emperor and to go before the Congress a few days later to explain America's position. In the meantime, the President finally gave the British and the Dutch the promise of support that they had sought for so long. Assuming that Japan would bypass the Philippines in its drive south, he may have envisaged an undeclared naval war in the Pacific similar to that against Germany in the Atlantic, one that would force Japan to respond with an overt act of war.

Throughout the final months of negotiations American attitudes toward Japan were interlaced, as they had always been, with complacency and condescension. Growing defense production, along with the endurance of Britain and Russia, confirmed the disinclination to make concessions. Japan seemed a manageable, second-rate power, far less of a menace to American security than Nazi Germany. Secretaries Ickes, Knox, Morgenthau, and Stimson had long minimized Japanese strength and attacked appeasers within the administration who would make unnecessary concessions. Ickes enjoyed seeing Japan on "the anxious seat" and predicted that the United States and its allies "could probably crush her within a few months."[30] Stimson believed the Japanese were "rattled and scared"[31] and, within the State Department, Hornbeck still argued that Japan would not fight. "Tell me of one case

---

[30]Ickes, *Secret Diary*, III, p. 592.
[31]Quoted in Langer and Gleason, *The Undeclared War*, p. 720.

in history," he taunted his opponents, "when a nation went to war out of desperation."[32] As the final weeks of peace passed, he felt a sense of buoyancy and exhilaration. Ten days before Pearl Harbor he offered five to one odds that Japan and the United States would not be at war by December 15, three to one odds against war by January 15, and even money against war by March 1.

Army officers encouraged this tendency to discount Japan as a military power. Unlike the navy, which regarded Japan as a tough, professional foe, the army characterized Japanese military thinking as rigid and imitative and held a low opinion of Japan's performance in China. General Joseph W. Stilwell, who had observed the Sino-Japanese war at first hand, boasted that with two American divisions and a well-prepared Chinese army he could run the Japanese out of China in 6 months. An American newspaper correspondent in Manila caught the general feeling when he wrote that "when the Japs come down here, they'll be playing in the Big League for the first time in their lives."[33]

Army and navy officers too often forgot that the American military establishment was in a process of transition, suffering from shortages of material and of trained men, as well as from lingering peacetime inadequacies in its organizational structure. At Pearl Harbor the paucity of long-range patrol planes prevented proper reconnaissance around the islands; the lack of a unified command interferred with coordination between the army and the navy; and the perspective of local commanders was far different from that of their superiors in Washington. Admiral Husband E. Kimmel and Lieutenant General Walter C. Short misinterpreted alert messages and assumed that internal subversion, not external attack, was the major threat. Chief of Staff Marshall seemed unaware of these deficiencies, for he regarded Pearl Harbor as the best equipped and most heavily defended American base abroad and in the second half of 1941 concentrated on the Philippines, the real

---

[32] Quoted in Thomson, "The Role of the Department of State," in Borg and Okamoto, *Pearl Harbor As History,* p. 101.
[33] Quoted in D. Clayton James, *The Years of MacArthur: Volume I, 1880-1941* (Boston, 1970), p. 616.

danger point in the Pacific. Like civilian authorities, American army and naval officers assumed that the Japanese planned to move into Southeast Asia without an attack on any American possession. They reasoned that a powerful deterrent in the Philippines might prevent such an advance or, at the very least, seriously complicate it. They could not conceive that the Japanese army and navy had the capability to execute a wide-ranging offensive in the Pacific. The information gathered through the cracking of the Japanese diplomatic code (which occurred in August 1940) provided no clear indication of Japan's military intentions. It further dulled the sensitivity of American policymakers by giving them the illusion of more knowledge than they actually possessed.

The first news of the Pearl Harbor attack on December 7 brought a feeling of relief, almost of calm, to American leaders. Now the months of waiting and anxiety were over, and the President's political problems greatly simplified by the direct assault on an American possession. Initially some, such as Stimson, assumed that the Japanese raid would result in a major American victory. Once the details filtered in they were appalled by the extent of the loss and of American unreadiness. As Morgenthau remarked, "they will never be able to explain it."[34]

VIII

The coming of war in the Pacific still evokes an overwhelming sense of sadness that two nations whose economies and cultures were so intertwined could find no peaceful escape from the impasse they had reached. Neither government wanted war, but neither could, in the end, conceive of a way to achieve its aims without one. Perhaps they could have done so if Japanese-American relations had not been caught up in the European crisis and transformed by it. Without World War II the Sino-Japanese conflict would never have become a pressing concern of American policymakers. Without that war Japan would never have sought to expand its empire south. Once Americans had identified China with the cause of the European democracies and committed them-

---

[34]Blum, *From the Morgenthau Diaries*, III, p. 1.

selves to the defense of Britain and its empire, and once Japan had enlarged its concept of national destiny to include Southeast Asia, there was no turning back. The gap was so wide that leaders in both nations were reluctant to confront it, let alone attempt to lessen it. Even in 1941 American officials never gave the Asian crisis the attention it deserved. Earlier, when the lines were less rigidly drawn, American policymakers were passive and uninterested; later, when the lines were taut, they engaged in wishful thinking and haphazard decision making. Distracted and indecisive, the President was pushed toward a harsher policy by officials who were ignorant of Japan and guided by intuition instead of reasoned calculation. For a long time Hull and some of his advisers, along with army and navy leaders, held these activists in check, but even Hull's approach to Japan's terrible dilemma was inflexible and hostile. Nor was the situation any better in Japan, where civilian and military leaders convinced themselves—despite the impressive economic growth of the decade—that the nation must expand or perish. As they plunged on, their goal of domestic harmony edged toward tyranny and their quest for a great empire in Asia merged into the global struggle. Both nations, in the 4 years of fighting that lay ahead, were to reap the harvest of years of complacency and shortsightedness toward one another.

CHAPTER VII

The Great Transformation

F OR DECADES A PACIFIC WAR HAD EXCITED THE IMAGINATIONS OF SOME JAPANESE AND SOME AMERICANS. Now it was a reality, and the fantasies of prewar years paled before the scale and complexity of the struggle, the huge naval armadas, and the dense, bitter combat on small Pacific islands. Accustomed to underestimating Japanese power and determination, Americans confronted an astonishing series of Japanese successes and began to realize that they were locked in combat with a dangerous foe. By November 1942 56 percent of the American people regarded Japan as the nation's chief enemy, while only 28 percent put Germany in that category. Animosity toward Japan reached new levels of intensity as Americans came to view that nation as a savage and treacherous enemy. Instead of minimizing Japanese power, they now exaggerated it and, in the early months of 1942, talk of a Japanese attack on the continental United States became rampant, particularly in California. Many Americans, including high officials in Washington, believed that Japanese spies in Hawaii had played a crucial role in the success of the Pearl Harbor attack and detected similar espionage activity on the Pacific Coast. Amid the confusion and uncertainty of the war, it was easy to succumb to this anxious mood.

The atmosphere in the army's Western Defense Command reflected these acute fears. General John L. DeWitt and his subordinates responded to the incessant rumors of an imminent attack in a panicky and amateurish way. Worried about the security of vital defense installations, they proposed a variety of plans to deal with the large number of Japanese residents allegedly threatening them. West Coast political leaders on all levels, led by Senator Hiram W. Johnson of California, pressured army and government officials to take drastic action. The mass evacuation of Japanese-Americans appealed to a variety of traditional anti-Japanese groups, who sensed an opportunity to achieve their long sought after goals.

In Washington the army's Provost Marshal General, Allen W. Gullion, took the lead in formulating plans to remove Japanese residents and place them under army control. He encountered little resistance at the highest levels of government. Chief of Staff George C. Marshall and his staff discounted the danger from Japanese-Americans, but were preoccupied with the staggering burdens of the war; they acquiesced in the program so long as it did not tie up a large number of troops. Secretary of War Henry L. Stimson was reluctant to accept such an extreme measure and hoped that the removal of Japanese from certain limited security zones would suffice. But Assistant Secretary of War John J. McCloy finally convinced Stimson that half-way measures would not do and that only mass evacuation would prevent anti-Japanese sentiment from getting out of hand.

Some New Dealers resisted the decision, but none was willing to throw his full weight against it. The President, doubtful of the loyalty of Japanese-Americans, chose, without any visible anguish, the most expedient path. In fact, if the army had acquiesced, he would have gone a step further and interned Hawaiian Japanese-Americans as well. On February 19, 1942 the President signed an executive order authorizing the evacuation of nearly 120,000 Japanese-Americans from California and the western halves of Oregon and Washington. In the most glaring domestic injustice of the war, Japanese-Americans were forced into barren camps under the aegis of a newly created War Relocation Authority. Most stayed until January 1945, when the administration, with the presidential election safely past, finally abolished its wartime concentration camps.

The relocation of Japanese-Americans was a peripheral issue for American policymakers, who were absorbed in the vast array of problems brought by total war. Although committed to a Europe-first strategy and to the rapid concentration of forces for a cross-channel assault, American planners had to halt the Japanese advance in the Pacific and to seize the initiative there. Public opinion demanded action, and American strategists knew the limitations of a static defense. What they did not anticipate, however, was the momentum that American forces in the Pacific would generate nor the resources that they would consume. By the end of 1942 the number of troops in that theater almost equaled the number sent to Great Britain and North Africa. With the completion of the North African campaign, the invasion of Italy, and the approach of OVERLORD, the balance tipped decisively toward Europe, but the Pacific war continued to require large American naval and military resources.

The depth of the enmity between the two nations and the distance between the aspirations of their ruling elites made compromise impossible. At the Casablanca Conference in January 1943, President Roosevelt, proclaiming the doctrine of unconditional surrender, expressed the American determination to impose total defeat upon Japan. Less than a year later, in the Cairo Declaration of December 1, 1943, China, Great Britain, and the United States left no doubt that victory would bring the destruction of Japan's Asian empire. On both the official and popular level Americans and Japanese developed extreme stereotypes of one another and, in the field, brutality became a commonplace. The behavior of American soldiers appalled Charles A. Lindbergh, who in 1944 toured the Southwest Pacific front. "They have no respect," he recorded in his journal, "for death, the courage of an enemy soldier, or many of the ordinary decencies of life."[1] Lindbergh sadly concluded that the conduct of American troops was not much better than that of the Japanese.

As the unprecedented character of the Pacific war unfolded, navy and army leaders differed over how to defeat Japan. The former wished to advance across the Central Pacific, bypassing the Philippines; the latter wished to climb up the islands of the South Pacific toward the Philippines, which they believed must be captured prior to an assault on Japan. In fact, both strategies were largely pursued and, by the spring of 1945, the American government had to settle on a plan for the final defeat of Japan. Naval and air force officers argued that naval blockade and air bombardment would force Japan's surrender, while Marshall and army planners contended that a major American force would have to

---

[1]Charles A. Lindbergh, *The Wartime Journals of Charles A. Lindbergh* (New York, 1970), p. 859.

strike at the heartland of Japan. President Harry S. Truman and his political advisers, impatient to end the strains and sacrifices of war, agreed that a strategy of attrition would be too slow and uncertain. They accepted the army's concept of an invasion and also hoped, as American leaders had since December 1941, for Soviet entry into the war. Enthusiasm for Soviet participation had, to be sure, diminished, and some within the American government suggested a reexamination of agreements with Stalin on East Asia. But the growing anxiety over Soviet postwar aims did not alter the conviction that Russia's entry would reduce American casualties and hasten Japan's surrender. After seeking assistance for so long, the United States could hardly reverse its position without creating great mistrust; nor could it, in any event, prevent the Soviet Union from entering the Pacific war at a time of its own choosing.

In late May 1945 Undersecretary of State Joseph C. Grew first raised the possibility of clarifying the unconditional surrender formula. Along with others in the State Department who were familiar with Japan, Grew wished to encourage Japan's moderates and to avoid destroying the entire fabric of Japanese society. On May 8 President Truman had taken one small step in this direction by assuring the Japanese people that unconditional surrender did not mean "extermination or enslavement."[2] But in the early summer neither the President nor his key advisers were willing to proceed further. The Joint Chiefs of Staff wished to avoid political concessions until Japan was further weakened; the Secretary of State wanted to wait until the Allies could act together; and the Secretary of War sought to delay a declaration until an atomic bomb could quickly follow a Japanese rejection. Not until July 2, on the eve of Truman's departure for Potsdam, did Stimson take the lead in expressing the emerging consensus within the American government. He urged the President to remember that Japan contained many liberal leaders and that the United States ought to avoid driving that nation into a last, desperate stand. Japan should receive a warning of massive destruction if it continued to resist, along with the promise of an enlightened peace if it laid

---

[2]Harry S. Truman, *Memoirs,* 2 vols. (New York, 1955-1956), I, p. 207.

down its arms. Most important, Stimson wished to assure the Japanese that they could, if they so desired, retain a constitutional monarchy.

President Truman and Secretary of State James F. Byrnes had no quarrel with the thrust of this advice; they were not, however, willing to risk the domestic outcry that a guarantee of the imperial institution would bring. A June 29 Gallup Poll revealed that 70 percent of those polled favored either the execution of Hirohito or some other harsh punishment, while only 7 percent would leave his position largely unchanged. Upon learning of Stimson's memorandum, former Secretary of State Hull objected to concessions on the Emperor and pointed out that, if such a policy should be adopted and fail, there would be "terrible political repercussions."[3] On July 26, when China, Great Britain, and the United States issued the Potsdam Declaration, they left the future of the Emperor unsettled and proclaimed their intention of stripping Japan of its empire and of punishing the militarists who had led the nation to disaster. They also held out the hope that with the establishment of a new democratic order in Japan, the occupation would end and Japan could reenter international life. A refusal to accept these terms would bring "prompt and utter destruction."[4]

Japan's failure to respond brought the final tragedy of the war, the one that has most troubled posterity. On August 6 the first atomic bomb devastated Hiroshima; three days later a second bomb fell on Nagasaki. Within the American government there was no debate over the decision to drop the bomb; all along, policymakers had assumed that this new weapon would be used to end the war. Insensitive to its revoluntionary character and enveloped by the needs and emotions of the moment, American leaders were unwilling to take political or diplomatic risks to spare the Japanese people further suffering. They calculated that the shock of atomic warfare, along with a Soviet declaration of war, would finally break Japan's will to resist.

---

[3]Cordell Hull, *The Memoirs of Cordell Hull,* 2 vols. (New York, 1948), II, p. 1594.
[4]*Foreign Relations of the United States: The Conference of Berlin: 1945,* 2 vols. (Washington, D.C., 1960), II, p. 1476.

II

In Japan the dramatic early successes of the war brought a wave of patriotism and even euphoria, particularly among intellectuals. At last the ambiguities of the past were swept away and Japan was acting decisively, intent on destroying Western power and culture in Asia and creating a unique new order there. Wartime propaganda shielded most Japanese from the realities of the Pacific struggle, and they were slow to understand that the nation's alleged spiritual superiority could not compensate for America's material advantage. As the conflict progressed, Japan fell back against the gathering might of the United States and confronted irremediable economic and military weaknesses. In 1944 Japan's economic and strategic situation rapidly deteriorated as production declined and the Central Pacific defense line collapsed. By the spring of 1945 Japan was helpless against American air and naval attacks. But the nation persevered, despite the terrifying bombing raids and the extraordinary sacrifices imposed on its people. They still seemed willing to follow wherever they were led.

Japan's leaders desperately searched for an alternative to surrender, until the nation stood on the brink of annihilation. As the war effort disintegrated, the hold of the militarists weakened and more moderate groups began to edge back toward the center of power. Well into 1945, however, the peace faction remained timid and indecisive, while army and navy leaders refused to confront the inevitability of defeat. They hoped for Soviet mediation and a conditional surrender that would preserve some of the military's prestige and authority. Failing that, they were determined to fight on, in a final heroic defense of the homeland. With the nation confronting its greatest crisis, their fanaticism knew no bounds. Those inclined toward peace had to proceed obliquely and could only gradually consolidate their power, wasting precious time exploring Soviet intentions. The Potsdam Declaration disappointed moderates, who could not imagine Japan without the imperial institution, and disputes over its meaning only prolonged the governmental paralysis. Even the first atomic bomb did not break the deadlock. The second finally brought the intervention of the Emperor and tipped the balance toward peace. On August 10 the Japanese government accepted the Potsdam Declaration on the condition that it would not prejudice the prerogatives of the Emperor. The American response did not exclude this possibility, but its lack of a definite assurance brought another stalemate in Tokyo. Once again, Hirohito's intervention produced a consensus and, on August 15, he told the Japanese people that the struggle had ceased. For Japan the decision to end the war had been as agonizing as the decision to begin it.

On September 2 surrender ceremonies took place on the battleship *Missouri*, anchored in Tokyo Bay as a symbol of America's unchallenged power over Japan. Some Americans present took a grim satisfaction in the final conquest and humiliation of Japan. General Joseph W. Stilwell, who arrived in Japan two days before the formal ceremonies, reveled in the extent of the devastation. Aboard the *Missouri*, Stilwell noted the "hard cruel hateful faces" of the Japanese representatives. "No one spoke. We just looked at them . . . for well over ten minutes. It must have seemed ten years to them."[5] But the Supreme Commander for the Allied Powers, General Douglas MacArthur, inspired by the promise of the future, called for a new sense of dedication among both victors and vanquished and hoped that "a better world shall emerge out of the blood and carnage of the past."[6] The long and harsh Pacific war had engendered bitter emotions. Now it had ended, and the destruction had ceased. The two nations had no choice but to proceed along the difficult path of reconciliation.

III

During the war American leaders had given considerable thought to the future of Japan. All agreed that the United States must effect sweeping alterations in Japanese life if that nation was never again to menace the peace of the world. But disputes emerged over the nature and extent of these changes. Experts within the State Department worried over the cohesion of Japa-

---

[5]Quoted in Barbara W. Tuchman, *Stilwell and the American Experience in China, 1911-1945* (New York, 1970), p. 522.
[6]Douglas MacArthur, *A Soldier Speaks: Public Papers and Speeches of General of the Army Douglas MacArthur* (New York, 1965), p. 148.

nese society and insisted on the retention of the Emperor and an indirect occupation that would rule through a reformed governmental bureaucracy. Others, such as Assistant Secretaries of State Dean Acheson and Breckinridge Long, believed that more drastic changes, particularly the abolition of the imperial institution, were essential for the cleansing of Japanese society.

Japan's surrender reinforced the growing conviction of most American officials that the removal of the Emperor might bring a massive instability with which the United States would be ill-prepared to cope. "United States Initial Post-Surrender Policy for Japan," adopted on September 6, called for a "peaceful and responsibile government,"[7] demilitarized and democratized, that would protect individual liberties and human rights. The Supreme Commander for the Allied Powers (SCAP) would exercise his authority through Japanese governmental machinery and would pursue a wide range of policies, including disarmament and the trial of war criminals, the encouragement of democratic processes, and the dissolution of large industrial and banking combinations. The United States would not assume any burden for postwar economic reconstruction. Finally, the document specified that, while the United States would welcome Allied participation, it intended to dominate the occupation of Japan and to administer that nation as one unit. In mid-August the United States had firmly rejected a Soviet request for the occupation of half of Hokkaido, the northernmost of the major islands of the Japanese archipelago.

Mounting tensions in Germany, along with America's dominance of the Pacific war, perhaps justified a unilateral policy, but American policymakers did not envisage Japan as part of the postwar balance of power in East Asia. Japan was to be, as General MacArthur phrased it, the "Switzerland of the Pacific,"[8] while China was to serve as the stabilizing force in that region. While it no longer seemed likely that the Kuomintang could rule the

---

[7] Quoted in Herbert Feis, *Contest Over Japan* (New York, 1967), p. 168.
[8] Quoted in Frederick S. Dunn, *Peace-Making and the Settlement with Japan* (Princeton, 1963), p. 55.

whole of China, it was still possible to believe that China could fulfill its role through a coalition government. Uncertain of the mood of the American people and still hoping for Soviet cooperation, American leaders were reluctant to confront the possibility of a major power vacuum in Asia.

In occupied Japan a curious pattern of rule emerged. From the moment of his dramatic landing at Atsugi airfield on August 30, 1945, when only a handful of American troops were in Japan, General Douglas MacArthur began to impose a highly personal stamp on the occupation. During his years in the Philippines and the Pacific, he had become absorbed in the problems of Asia and convinced that the destiny of Western civilization lay there. MacArthur brought with him an intense sense of mission and of history, a conviction that defeat had swept away the moral and psychological foundations of Japanese life and that he must, more than anything else, lead a "spiritual reformation" that would bring democratic and Christian values to Japan.[9] Sharing many of Washington's objectives, he intended an enlightened occupation designed to achieve its objectives quickly and then to release Japan as a model for the rest of Asia. Aloof and autocratic, remarkably isolated from the land he governed, MacArthur rarely broke his rigid and physically circumscribed routine to leave Tokyo. He sensed the despair and disorientation of the Japanese people and, through his grandiloquent proclamations and carefully calculated symbolic gestures, impressed them with his power and benevolence.

MacArthur supplemented the regular army organization in Japan with a series of sections, each with a specialized function roughly paralleling the subdivisions of the Japanese government. Army observation teams stationed throughout Japan worked with local officials and checked on compliance with occupation directives. The heads of the key SCAP sections were military officers, long-time colleagues of MacArthur's with little knowledge of Japan. Absorbed in the endless problems of reforming a strange and puzzling culture, the American occupation bureaucracy developed

---

[9] Douglas MacArthur, *Reminiscences* (New York, 1964), p. 306.

its own unique perspective, quite different from that in Washington where policymakers, who were Europe-centered by heritage and training, soon relegated occupied Japan to the periphery of their concerns. Even when occupation problems caught their attention, they were cautious about overruling a commander with such strong ties to conservatives in Congress and to the American public.

Thus, Washington's influence was uncertain, filtered through MacArthur's personality and the SCAP hierarchy, while that of the nations that had aided in the war against Japan was virtually nonexistent. In theory the occupation was international and, in December 1945, the United States agreed to the creation of a thirteen-nation Far Eastern Commission and a four-power Allied Council for Japan. The first, situated in Washington, exercised some restraining influence on SCAP; the second, situated in Tokyo, soon became paralyzed by Soviet-American quarrels. Neither in Washington nor in Tokyo were officials willing to allow any genuine Allied participation in the formulation of occupation policy.

Despite the nonmilitary character of MacArthur's duties, he reported to the War Department and the Joint Chiefs of Staff. Both were wary of interfering, while the State Department's representatives in Tokyo, located a mile from SCAP headquarters, were in a subordinate position. Intensely suspicious of diplomats in Washington, MacArthur and his staff felt that State Department cliques sought to undermine their authority. George F. Kennan, who traveled to Japan in February 1948, recalled that liaison between the State Department and SCAP "had been so distant and so full of distrust that my mission was like nothing more than that of an envoy charged with opening up communications and arranging the establishment of diplomatic relations with a hostile and suspicious foreign government."[10]

The first State Department representative in occupied Japan, George Atcheson Jr., was a China specialist who acted both as political adviser to the Supreme Commander and as chief of

---

[10] George F. Kennan, *Memoirs,* 2 vols. (Boston, 1967-1972), I, p. 382.

SCAP's Diplomatic Section. Atcheson cooperated with MacArthur and defended his occupation policies. His successor in September 1947, William J. Sebald, was an Annapolis graduate who had become a Japanese language officer in the navy. In the 1930s Sebald had practiced law in Japan; during the war he served with naval intelligence. He sympathized with most of the occupation policies—though he would have moderated some—and developed considerable rapport with MacArthur. Nevertheless, he was not consulted on key political decisions, nor was he taken by MacArthur on trips outside Japan. Inhibited by his dual and conflicting loyalties, Sebald had to struggle to maintain even minimal prerogatives. Since his communications with the State Department proceeded through army channels, he often found that State Department messages directed to him were opened and acted on by SCAP without his knowledge. For 4 years and 9 months Sebald struggled to win a separate code; by the time he achieved victory, the occupation had largely run its course.

IV

The American conquerors found a beaten and demoralized people, bewildered by the speed with which the nation had collapsed. Fearful and depressed, they struggled for survival in an urban wilderness. Forty percent of Japan's cities were destroyed or seriously damaged; agricultural and industrial production had precipitiously declined, the latter to only one third of the 1934 to 1936 level. The empire was gone, the economy in a shambles, overburdened by the nearly 6 million soldiers and civilians returning from overseas areas. Much of the population verged on starvation, unable to cope with runaway inflation. Americans who had known prewar Japan were shocked by the condition of the land and the people..

The very bleakness of the setting created great opportunities for social change. Fired by a remarkable zeal, the occupation regime set to work, enacting a rash of fundamental reforms. It demobilized Japan's huge military establishment and tried those military and political leaders judged responsible for Japanese aggression. It democratized Japan's political structure through the imposition of a new constitution that guaranteed a whole range of human and legal rights, downgraded the status of the Emperor, created a Western-style parliamentary democracy and, in its famous article nine, renounced "war as a sovereign right of the nation" and pledged that "land, sea, and air forces . . . will never be maintained."[11] Finally, it took steps to reduce the power of Japan's great industrialists and rural landowners and to dismantle the highly concentrated structure of Japanese business and finance. SCAP released political prisoners, stimulated the growth of labor unions, instituted a sweeping purge of Japanese leaders in all walks of life and, in its land reform program, reduced farm tenancy from nearly one half the total of arable land to less than one tenth.

In short, the occupation significantly changed the balance of forces in Japanese society, altering the shape of future elites and their relationship to the people. The military elite, discredited by defeat, was swept away, and many of its civilian collaborators were barred, for varying lengths of time, from positions of political or economic leadership. Government officials were recruited from a broader base in society while business groups, although they remained powerful, now had to compete for influence with labor unions, farmers, intellectuals, and socialists. Occupation reforms accelerated the development of the liberal-democratic strain in Japanese society and brought into positions of authority bureaucrats and politicians who had, during the 1930s, been pushed aside. Members of the prewar Anglo-American clique in the Japanese Foreign Ministry became particularly powerful in the postwar political order.

In many cases the occupation removed roadblocks to reforms long desired by significant groups in Japanese society. Land reforms, women's rights, the civil code, and the union movement, along with the guarantees of individual rights and the broad changes in the political structure, found widespread support and substantial permanency, as did educational and police reforms. The occupation set Japan on a different course in its domestic as well as its international affairs.

---

[11]Quoted in Edwin O. Reischauer, *The United States and Japan,* 3rd ed. (Cambridge, Mass., 1965), p. 351.

The American effort to build a new Japan contained a strong missionary flavor. MacArthur set the tone in his identification of democratization with Christianization and in his frequent calls for Christian missionaries who could create in Japan "a natural base from which in time to advance the cross through all of Asia."[12] MacArthur and the occupation authorities favored Christianity and, as early as December 1945, began to admit American missionaries. Once again the hopes for a Christian Japan, which had ebbed and flowed among American churches since the 1880s, produced an influx of Catholic and Protestant missionaries. But large numbers of missionaries and stirring evangelical campaigns were not enough; Christianity remained a foreign faith, and the Japanese people persisted in their traditional beliefs.

Initially American officials in both Washington and Tokyo were oblivious to the turmoil accompanying the occupation reforms. Washington was preoccupied with other areas of the globe; MacArthur and his top aides, engrossed in the reformation of Japanese society, were actually isolated from conditions in Japan, immersed in an artificial world of easy and constant successes. Occupation authorities did release large quantities of food in order to prevent starvation, but SCAP was not prepared to deal with the problem of economic recovery, nor would it place the economy high on its list of priorities for several years. MacArthur and his advisers appeared unconcerned about the growing power of communist leaders in the labor movement and dismissed the fears of conservative politicians, bureaucrats, and business leaders, who felt weak and exposed. The Japanese government no longer possessed an effective national police force and the depressed economy and fragile psychological condition of the people gave the future a dark hue.

Although Ambassador Sebald and army units in the field warned of a serious communist menace, MacArthur seemed complacent over Japan's internal and external security. In March 1947 he announced that Japan's "spiritual revolution" was complete

---

[12]Quoted in Lawrence S. Wittner, "MacArthur and the Missionaries: God and Man in Occupied Japan," *Pacific Historical Review, XXXX* (1971), p. 79.

and that the time had come to consider a peace treaty. MacArthur argued that the occupation had achieved its objectives and that its rapid termination would stimulate the Japanese economy. He suggested that the United Nations assume the supervision of Japan and assured the press that "the Japanese are relying upon the advanced spirituality of the world to protect them against undue aggression."[13]

In 1947 SCAP finally began to devote some attention to the state of the Japanese economy and the restlessness of the Japanese people. But the Cold War mentality crystallized more slowly among occupation authorities than among those in Washington. SCAP remained self-absorbed, unmoved by the rising communist tide in China and out of touch with the sense of alarm in Washington over apparent Soviet ambitions in Greece, Turkey, and all of Western Europe. The enunciation of the Truman Doctrine did not diminish MacArthur's desire to push ahead with a peace treaty. In April 1947 he told a State Department representative that a conference could be held in Tokyo that summer and that occupation forces could be withdrawn 6 months after the conclusion of a treaty. This proposal aroused little enthusiasm in the United States. Some within the State Department still feared a revival of Japanese militarism, while both the Navy and War Departments wished to continue the occupation, rebuild the Japanese army, and retain complete freedom of movement for American forces in Japan. Secretary of the Navy James V. Forrestal complained about the rigor of MacArthur's reforms and worried over the future security of Japan. Nevertheless, in July 1947, Secretary of State Marshall issued invitations to the members of the Far Eastern Commission to attend a preliminary Japanese peace conference. Apparently worried about congressional criticism of economic aid to Japan and still uncertain of its own intentions, the State Department moved hesitantly toward a settlement. The proposed conference never materialized because of objections from the Soviet Union and Nationalist China over voting procedures.

---

[13] Report of the Government Section, Supreme Commander for the Allied Powers, *Political Reorientation of Japan, September 1945 to September 1948,* 2 vols. (Washington, D. C., 1949), II, p. 765.

Whatever the State Department's motives, by early 1948 officials in Washington had placed Japan within a Cold War framework. As the hope for a unified and friendly China faded, policymakers concluded that America's position in Asia must be based
on a revitalized Japanese society. Late in the summer of 1947
George F. Kennan's Policy Planning Staff shifted its attention from
the European Recovery Program to Japan and promptly rejected
the idea of relinquishing American control over such an enfeebled
nation. Both Kennan and Ambassador Sebald found it inconceiva-
ble that a peace treaty could be considered that contained no
provisions for the internal and external security of Japan. During
his visit to Tokyo in February 1948 Kennan discovered that
MacArthur still minimized the internal communist danger, but
that he did agree on the need for some moderation of occupation
policies. MacArthur, however, was hardly willing to go as far as
Kennan, who felt that the occupation had moved too quickly and
that the purge, police reforms, and reparations deliveries had seriously weakened the fabric of Japanese society. SCAP must slow
down and allow the Japanese to assimilate reforms at their own
pace, reduce the size and costs of its bureaucratic establishment,
and delay any peace treaty until conditions markedly improved.
These views, widely shared throughout the American government, were adopted by the National Security Council in November 1948 and dispatched to Tokyo. The government's alarm was
so great that it urged the creation of a 150,000-man Japanese police
force.

MacArthur had, to some extent, anticipated Washington's
changing view of Japan. But he was responding less to an altered
global perspective than to the troubled situation in Japan itself and
to the complaints of congressional conservatives over socialistic
policies and excessive economic aid. Slowly in 1947, and with
increasing speed in 1948 and 1949, occupation policies shifted
from reform to the rehabilitation of Japan's economy and social
structure. In March 1947 MacArthur acknowledged a serious economic crisis, and SCAP began to lift restrictions on the growth of
Japanese trade and industry; in 1948 SCAP reversed its policy on
economic deconcentration; and in 1949 reparations deliveries
ended as a mission headed by the Detroit banker Joseph M. Dodge

instituted a drastic antiinflationary program. SCAP succeeded in halting inflation and in 1949 the economic picture brightened, but Japan's real economic surge came in 1950, after the outbreak of the Korean War. It was only in 1950 that Japanese industrial production surpassed that of the mid-1930s and not until 1954-1955 that Japan attained prewar per capita levels of productivity, national income, and personal consumption.

Gradually SCAP moved to curb the political left. On February 1, 1947 occupation authorities canceled a general strike and, by early 1949, they were disturbed by widespread railway sabotage and by the increase in communist political strength. SCAP now viewed communism as a direct and immediate threat and instituted a Red purge in the union movement. Nevertheless, it continued to block Washington's plans for a national police force until July 1950, when MacArthur authorized a National Police Reserve of 75,000 men and a Maritime Safety Force of 8000 men.

In the late summer of 1949 the State Department took up the question of a Japanese peace treaty with renewed vigor. Secretary of State Dean Acheson agreed with MacArthur that the occupation was "a rapidly diminishing asset"[14] and that its prolongation would breed unnecessary resentment among the Japanese people. By October 1949 the concept of a harsh, punitive peace had largely vanished within the State Department, and most believed that Japan's sovereignty must be quickly and completely restored. Concerned over instability in Japan, American officials concentrated on the elimination of internal weaknesses, the protection of Japan against Soviet subversion or aggression, and the whole process of converting a former foe into a reliable ally.

Acheson delegated the negotiation of the Japanese peace treaty to the Republican spokesman on foreign policy, John Foster Dulles, who was appointed in April 1950 as Foreign Policy Adviser to the Secretary of State. In part, Dulles' selection represented an effort to exclude Japan from the furor enveloping the administration's East Asian policy; in part, it reflected Acheson's desire to

---

[14] Dean Acheson, *Present at the Creation: My Years in the State Department* (New York, 1969), p. 257.

reserve his own energies for Europe, the area of first priority. Dulles brought to his task a wide range of international experience and a conception of peace with Japan virtually identical with that of the State Department and President Truman. Remembering the failure of the Versailles treaty, he intended to negotiate a moderate, generous peace that would secure Japan against the communist menace in Asia and encourage that nation to become an example for all the peoples of the region. In June 1950, with the coming of war in Korea, Dulles, Acheson, and Truman acquired an even greater sense of urgency. The North Korean invasion suddenly presented the specter of overt communist expansion in Asia and raised the possibility of further probes in Europe as well. From Washington's perspective, Korea was a test of American power and will; it was essential to stand firm and to quiet the apprehensions of Japan's leaders about their nation's security.

Dulles devised a negotiating strategy that maximized American leverage and protected Japan from the extreme demands of America's former allies. Great Britain, although aware of Japan's importance in the Cold War, hoped to encourage Japanese relations with Communist China and to impose certain economic penalties on a liberated Japan. Australia and New Zealand, along with the Philippines and other Asian nations that had endured Japanese occupation, sought heavy reparations and guarantees against future aggression. Dulles, cooperating closely with the British government, turned back these pressures for a punitive peace by dealing separately with each government instead of allowing them to press their demands collectively at a peace conference. The price was a series of security pacts with Australia and New Zealand and the Philippines signed in August and September 1951.

While Dulles conducted the international negotiations, Secretary of State Acheson confronted the fierce opposition of Secretary of Defense Louis A. Johnson and the Joint Chiefs of Staff. They continued to insist that a peace treaty was premature and suggested a variety of proposals that would have allowed only a limited restoration of Japanese sovereignty. The Defense Department also promoted the rapid rearmament of Japan and dispatched a succession of high-level missions to Tokyo to gain MacArthur's support for its program. But MacArthur remained convinced that

Japanese sovereignty must be fully restored and doubted the value of maintaining bases in Japan. He was confident that an American military presence in Okinawa would be sufficient and that Japan would retain strong bonds of friendship with the United States. MacArthur's position, coupled with the growing impatience of Acheson and Truman, brought an agreement in September 1950 between the State and Defense Departments that cleared the way for the negotiation of the treaty.

As early as 1947 Japan's leaders, worried about their nation's vulnerability, had attempted to explore security problems with the American government. At that time Washington's ideas were unformed and the overture failed. In Tokyo continuing internal weakness and growing Soviet-American tension stimulated concern over Japan's fate and raised doubts over the reliability of either a United Nations or a big-power guarantee. Japan's leaders felt they had no choice but to tie their nation's security to the United States, despite the reservations of many Japanese about a peace settlement that excluded the Soviet Union and Communist China and allowed American troops to remain in Japan. Prior to the outbreak of the Korean War, Prime Minister Yoshida Shigeru hoped to win both a clear-cut American commitment to Japan's defense and the removal of all American forces. The Korean War, however, made such an American withdrawal both impossible and undesirable and led Yoshida and his advisers to accept the retention of American bases and troops.

In January 1951, when Dulles and Yoshida began serious negotiations over treaty terms, they found that important differences still separated the two governments. While few disagreements emerged over the general peace treaty, the proposed security pact raised perplexing questions. Dulles, absorbed in the Cold War and concerned over regional stability, insisted that the United States could not specifically guarantee Japan's autonomy unless that nation created an army of 350,000 men and agreed to contribute to the defense of the Pacific region. Yoshida doggedly resisted these demands, which he realized were totally unacceptable to the Japanese people. When MacArthur sided with Yoshida on the impossibility of such large-scale rearmament, Dulles gave way. But the resulting security treaty, while it kept American bases and troops in Japan, did not provide an explicit American guarantee of Japanese independence and expressed the expectation that Japan would "increasingly assume responsibility for its own defense against direct and indirect aggression."[15]

On September 4, 1951, when the peace conference opened in San Francisco, all of the outstanding issues between Japan, the United States, and the bulk of Japan's wartime enemies had been settled. The conference served, by American design, as an imposing symbol of Japan's reentry into the international community. With its conclusion one major task remained—the approval of the peace treaty and security treaty by the United States Senate. In the autumn of 1951 this did not seem a particularly formidable task, for throughout the treaty negotiations Dulles had consulted frequently with Republican senators and had received their assurance, after MacArthur's dismissal in April, that the heated controversy over East Asian policy would not engulf Japan. The American public supported the peace treaty, as did a wide range of powerful organizations such as the American Federation of Labor and the National Association of Manufacturers. In 1945 the public had felt that the surrender terms imposed upon Japan were too lenient, but wartime animosities had rapidly faded and popular confidence in MacArthur's rule had reached remarkably high levels. By 1951 most Americans believed that Japan would be a friendly and dependable ally.

Despite the overwhelming popular approval of the administration's efforts, senatorial consent proved more difficult than either Acheson or Dulles had anticipated. Soon after the conclusion of the San Francisco conference, 56 senators, in a letter to President Truman, warned that they would oppose the peace treaty unless assured that Japan would not recognize Communist China. Prior to the meeting in San Francisco, Great Britain and the United States had agreed that the treaty should mention neither Chinese government and that Japan should ultimately decide the question of recognition. Many Senators, however, were not willing to give

---

[15]Quoted in Martin E. Weinstein, *Japan's Postwar Defense Policy, 1947-1968* (New York, 1971), p. 137.

Japan this choice and, in December 1951, Dulles traveled to Tokyo, accompanied by H. Alexander Smith of New Jersey and John J. Sparkman of Alabama, to explain the Senate's position and to obtain assurances from Prime Minister Yoshida. Yoshida responded with a written pledge that Japan would, in the near future, recognize the Nationalist government on Taiwan, but he did not exclude the possibility, at some distant date, of a Japanese tie with the Chinese People's Republic. Yoshida's letter satisfied most Senators and, on April 28, 1952, despite a small but fierce right-wing opposition, the peace treaty went into effect. After 6 years and 8 months of occupation, Japan was, at last, on the road to full independence.

American leaders were far more sanguine about Japan's future in public than in private. It seemed unlikely that Japan, shorn of its prewar empire, could ever become economically self-sustaining. Secretary of State Acheson told David E. Lilienthal, the former chairman of the Atomic Energy Commission, that he could "see nothing but disaster for us in Japan when the occupation is over,"[16] while John Foster Dulles worried that Japan might gravitate toward Communist China. "Japan can hold out for five or ten years," Dulles commented, "but in the long run the mainland has many attractions of so strong a character that it is hard to visualize Japan and the communist mainland living indefinitely in separate orbits."[17] Preoccupation with Japan's weaknesses obscured, for most policymakers, alternative courses of action and some of the implications of their decisions. Once the Cold War had set in, American officials—with the exception of Kennan—never seriously considered the possibility of a neutralized Japan. Nor did it occur to them that American policy unwittingly heightened Chinese and Soviet fears of a revival of Japanese militarism and perhaps contributed, in some small measure, to the coming of war in Korea and later to Chinese intervention. Finally, American policy-

---

[16]David E. Lilienthal, *The Journals of David E. Lilienthal,* 4 vols. (New York, 1964-1969), III, p. 157.
[17]Quoted in Michael A. Guhin, *John Foster Dulles: A Statesman and His Times* (New York, *1972),* p. 318.

makers did not foresee that the security treaty, whatever its value, was sure to become intertwined with unresolved Japanese feelings about war and peace and national independence.

V

As the new, postoccupation era of Japanese-American relations unfolded, the security treaty became a central factor in Japan's political discourse. Most Japanese had accepted the treaty and were resigned to the continuation of American bases and troops as temporary concessions essential for a restoration of self-rule. Even conservative leaders believed that it would soon be imperative to seek a more equitable arrangement with the United States. They realized, of course, that the treaty brought Japan crucial benefits, such as valuable foreign exchange and the freedom to concentrate on economic growth in an international order guaranteed by American power. But they had no abstract commitment to the defense of the "free world" and were sensitive to the profound anxieties the American tie stirred among the Japanese public. The left wing continuously attacked the treaty, organizing demonstrations against bases and American nuclear tests, and calling for a settlement with the Soviet Union and Communist China. Socialist leaders argued that the treaty abridged Japan's full independence and warned that it might draw the nation into a major war.

From the American perspective this left-wing agitation, however troublesome, was overshadowed by Japan's economic and political progress, and American fears about Japan's future gradually diminished. The early 1950s brought the beginnings of Japan's remarkable economic growth and the consolidation of a two-party system dominated by what later became the Liberal Democratic Party. Under America's sponsorship, Japan reentered international life, negotiating reparations and tariff accords and in 1956 joining the United Nations. Meanwhile, the American government concentrated on completing its Pacific security system by concluding defense pacts with South Korea and Taiwan and, in 1954, capping the whole process with the Southeast Asia Treaty Organization. In East and Southeast Asia American policymakers, attempting to prevent any major alterations in the status quo, were primarily concerned with the French position in Indochina and the safety of Taiwan. The ensuing crises did not directly involve Japan, and it became too easy to regard Japan as a pliable and reasonably reliable protégé.

Nevertheless, throughout the 1950s American officials regarded Japan with a mixture of complacency and anxiety. Secretary of State Dulles and the American military, against the advice of the Tokyo embassy, impatiently prodded the Japanese to build up their defense forces. The Cold War gave them a fresh appreciation of that nation's importance in world affairs, as did the maturation of a new generation of Japan experts within the Department of State. No longer, as in the years before 1932, was the ambassadorship to Japan a dumping ground for political appointees. During the 1950s all three American ambassadors were career diplomats. The first, Robert Murphy, had served largely in Western Europe and, after a brief stay in Tokyo, went on to become an Under Secretary of State for Political Affairs, the third highest policy-making position within the State Department. Neither of the next two ambassadors, John M. Allison or Douglas MacArthur II, reached Murphy's level of achievement, but both were foreign service officers, the first a specialist in Japanese affairs, the second a nephew of General Douglas MacArthur and a former chief of the Division of Western European Affairs. These appointments reflected Japan's new stature in Washington as well as a residue of doubt over its future. Ambassador Allison believed that his basic task was to deter Japan's drift toward an accommodation with the communist bloc, while Ambassador MacArthur warned the President that a failure to work closely with Japan could turn that nation in the wrong direction. In March 1957 Secretary of State Dulles suggested more emphasis on Australia as a defense production base in Asia, since there were "some risks in depending wholly upon Japan."[18]

By the middle of the decade Japanese leaders had achieved more confidence and attempted, in a number of small ways, to establish

[18]Quoted in Dwight D. Eisenhower, *The White House Years*, 2 vols. (New York, 1963-1965), II, p. 142.

a greater degree of independence from the United States. Japan criticized American nuclear testing, restored relations with the Soviet Union, balanced delicately between the two Chinas and, in general, gave the appearance of a more assertive and flexible diplomacy. As early as 1955 the Japanese government raised the subject of treaty revision with the United States. Although firmly rebuffed by Secretary of State Dulles, American alarm over Korea had ebbed and the security policies of the two nations slowly converged. The self-defense force steadily increased in size, totaling 210,000 men by 1959, while the number of American troops stationed in Japan steadily dwindled. In June 1957, when Prime Minister Kishi Nobusuke visited Washington, he and President Dwight D. Eisenhower proclaimed a "new era" in Japanese-American relations,[19] one that involved significant concessions by the United States. The American government agreed to withdraw all ground combat troops from Japan, shift some bases to less populous areas, and fly the Japanese flag alongside the American flag at military installations. American fears of communist military expansion had diminished, and the government no longer pressed Japan for large-scale rearmament and a regional security role. Instead, the United States was eager to strengthen its most valuable relationship in East Asia and, in September 1958, agreed to begin negotiations for a new security treaty.

The nature of the security tie with Japan was not a controversial issue within the American government, nor was it an issue of which the American public was even aware. For the Kishi government and the Liberal Democratic Party, however, it was a matter of life or death for, by the late 1950s, the timidity and uncertainty of the occupation years had passed and a more aggressive, nationalistic mood had arisen among the Japanese people. All Japanese seemed to agree that the time had come to reassess their nation's international position and to recast its relationship with the United States. Profound differences existed, of course, over the nature of these changes but, in January 1960, Prime Minister Kishi

---

[19] Quoted in George R. Packard III, *Protest in Tokyo: The Security Treaty Crisis of 1960* (Princeton, 1966), p. 57.

felt that he had satisfied most of his countrymen when he signed a new security treaty in Washington. In this treaty Japan achieved all of its goals, including a fixed 10-year time limit on the understanding, an explicit guarantee of Japan's external security, a pledge by each nation to settle quarrels in accordance with the United Nation's Charter, and a clause that bound the United States to consult with Japan prior to any major use of American forces, bases, or equipment for a conflict outside of Japan. On the surface, the new security treaty seemed a significant diplomatic victory for the Kishi government and a recognition on the part of the United States of Japan's growing power and prestige.

Kishi's triumph, instead of quieting the discontent within Japan, precipitated a dramatic convulsion that exposed the extraordinary tenseness permeating Japanese society. The spring and early summer of 1960 brought massive demonstrations in Tokyo, a virtual paralysis of the Diet, and the cancellation of President Eisenhower's visit. Kishi had, in fact, lost touch both with his party and with the Japanese people. By entangling his own political fate with the ratification of the treaty and with Eisenhower's visit, he had precipitated a domestic political crisis. Kishi's service in the Tōjō cabinet evoked memories of prewar militarism, and his behavior during the treaty crisis convinced some Japanese that he hoped to restore the brutal, authoritarian ways of the 1930s. Opposing factions within the Liberal Democratic Party, eager to replace Kishi with their own leaders, stood aside while the turmoil mounted.

Whatever Kishi's role had been, the security treaty would have aroused anxieties over a lack of national autonomy and over the danger of being pulled into a war by a bellicose United States. Communist China and the Soviet Union, competing for influence in Japan, launched strident attacks on the Japanese-American alliance and sought to undermine the Kishi government. Their maneuverings increased the appeal of the left wing's contention that Japan's safest course was one of pacifism and neutralism. The notion of Japan as a bridge between East and West had great popular appeal, particularly as Russian technological achievements in the late 1950s led many Japanese to question, for the first time, the preponderance of American power. In May 1960 the eruption of the U-2 incident and the breakup of the Soviet-American summit conference increased nervousness in Japan about both the reliability of American policy and the wisdom of a security tie to the United States. Even conservative defenders of the treaty, convinced that it served the national interest, seemed uncertain of American leadership and uncommitted to the general containment policies of the United States. Their belated and ineffective defense of the treaty encouraged the movement of moderate opinion toward the left and toward a highly emotional, antitreaty position. On June 18 Kishi succeeded in forcing the treaty through the Diet, but the crisis had destroyed his effectiveness and, within a few days, he announced his resignation. The extraordinary outburst against the treaty surprised many Japanese and left Americans uneasy and bewildered over the future course of Japanese-American relations. The most depressing aspect of the security treaty crisis was, as Edwin O. Reischauer wrote, that "after 15 years of massive contact, Americans and Japanese seem to have less real communication than ever."[20]

In Japan the crisis quickly passed. The ratification of the treaty, Kishi's resignation, and the very violence of the demonstrations relieved tensions. Many Japanese apparently concluded that the protestors had gone too far and damaged Japan's standing in the world. Kishi's successor, Ikeda Hayato, adopted a low profile and worked to revitalize the Liberal Democratic Party while focusing the energies of the people on the goal of doubling the national income in a decade. By 1967 Japan's Gross National Product was three and one-half times larger than in 1954 and, in 1968, Japan became the world's third-ranking industrial power. This amazing economic growth brought a new level of affluence in Japan and an increasing interdependence between the Japanese and American economies. Japan drew heavily on American technology and agriculture, while the United States imported Japanese automobiles and household electronic goods. Japan now became America's second largest export market; the two nations had by this time developed the greatest transoceanic trade in the history of the world.

---

[20]Edwin O. Reischauer, "Our Broken Dialogue with Japan," *Foreign Affairs*, XXXIX (1960), p. 11.

In the United States the security treaty crisis brought a greater sensitivity to Japan's needs and a realization, already evident in the last years of Eisenhower's presidency, that the relationship between the two nations must be reassessed. The new administration of John F. Kennedy sought to reassure the Japanese that the United States did not take them for granted and to portray Japan as America's major partner in the construction of a new Pacific community. Kennedy's popularity in Japan made the American alliance more attractive, as did the appointment of Edwin O. Reischauer as ambassador. A leading authority on Japanese history and culture, Reischauer was the first American emissary to Japan who had been born and raised in that country. He hoped to restore the "broken dialogue" between the two peoples,[21] particularly to reach out to intellectuals and left-wing groups that American spokesmen had previously neglected. His energetic campaign did much to improve relations, as did other efforts of the Kennedy administration. In June 1961 Kennedy and Prime Minister Ikeda, meeting in Washington, proclaimed an "equal partnership" between their nations[22] and announced that the two cabinets would begin annual economic consultations. Kennedy also pledged the eventual return of Okinawa to Japanese rule and attempted to ease tension there by increasing local autonomy and American economic aid.

Despite these gestures toward Japan, the United States' concept of an equal partnership remained ill-defined. Official rhetoric recognized Japan's new international status, but American leaders seemed, in fact, unable to come to terms with it. By the mid-1960s Japanese-American relations began, once again, to deteriorate. The American government, mired ever more deeply in Vietnam, focused its attention on Southeast Asia and became less sensitive to other areas of the world. The large-scale bombing of North Vietnam, inaugurated in 1965, made America's involvement in Indochina a prominent issue in Japan. While the Japanese government formally supported American policy, intellectuals and the

---

[21]*Ibid.*

[22]Quoted in Packard, *Protest in Tokyo*, p. 342.

mass media condemned it, and the Japanese people, themselves once victims of American bombing, identified with the North Vietnamese and resented the implicit racism of America's Vietnam crusade. In Washington the feeling grew that the time had come to end Japan's "free ride"[23] and to force that nation to live up to its international responsibilities. American officials urged the Japanese government to undertake a larger political and military role in East Asia, confidently assuming that it would use its power to further America's strategy of containment. In 1966 the replacement of Ambassador Reischauer with U. Alexis Johnson signified this shift toward a tougher policy. Johnson, a high-ranking career officer and specialist in Japanese affairs, was closely identified with American policy in Vietnam. He carried the government's new message to the Japanese.

Commercial problems further complicated Japanese-American relations. Since 1948 the United States had actively promoted the expansion of the Japanese economy and had attempted to integrate Japan into the Western economic community. America's European allies had resisted this policy, while the Japanese had been reluctant to permit American penetration of their unique economic system. By the early 1960s the American position began to harden as government officials and business leaders became less willing to support an unequal economic relationship. In 1965 the United States experienced a major trade deficit with Japan and, in succeeding years, this deficit grew in size as America's world economic position deteriorated. Japan's economic dynamism aroused the fears of some American business groups and led the Nixon administration to adopt temporary, although extreme, countermeasures. The economies of the two industrial giants were heavily dependent on each other, but persistent imbalances led to quarrelsome negotiations. Once Americans had doubted that Japan would ever become economically viable; now they worried over the extent of Japan's economic success.

The reversion of Okinawa in May 1972 removed one long-

---

[23]George R. Packard III, "Living with the Real Japan," *Foreign Affairs*, XXXXVI (1967), p. 195.

standing problem between the two nations and so, in a sense, did America's withdrawal from Southeast Asia. But President Richard M. Nixon and his advisers left the degree of American disengagement undefined, as they did their expectations of America's Asian allies, including Japan. The priority of Japan in official thinking, seldom high, receded in the late 1960s and early 1970s. In 1969 President Nixon appointed Armin Meyer, a career diplomat specializing in Middle Eastern affairs, to the Japanese ambassadorship; 3 years later he chose Robert S. Ingersoll, chairman of the board of the Borg-Warner Corporation, the first American businessman to serve in Tokyo since the 1920s. As in the past, the President's chief foreign policy adviser was an expert in European affairs; his large White House staff did not contain a single authority on Japan. In July 1971 the administration's announcement of the President's trip to China—made after the most perfunctory notification of the Japanese government—vividly revealed the extent to which Japan had slipped to the edge of official consciousness.

The administration's complacency toward Japan seemed dated, a throwback to an earlier era. It was not shared by the foreign policy public, whose level of concern was high. But images of Japan were volatile, a mixture of compassion, fear, and awe. Some agonized over American neglect and Japan's unique dilemma; others harbored dark suspicions of Japan's economic and potentially military aggressiveness; one commentator—Herman Kahn of the Hudson Institute—was euphoric over Japan's future and predicted that it would dominate the twentyfirst century. Few could avoid noticing Japan's growing presence on the world stage and the affluence that brought Japan closer and closer to both the life-style and social ills of America.

In the 1960s many Japanese became aware of the limitations of economic growth and economic diplomacy. It was apparent that the nation's economic surge had produced serious social dislocations and that the government must shift more resources to the public sector. It was also obvious that the nation had failed to achieve an international status commensurate with its great postwar achievements. Much of the accumulating resentment over this fact focused on the United States, which seemd to undervalue its chief Asian ally. Despite the reversion of Okinawa and the lessening number of American troops in Japan—only 30,000 remained in 1972—the partnership was painfully unequal. Comparatively, Americans devoted little attention to Japan and their level of knowledge of that nation was low. American press coverage was often sporadic, preoccupied with the exotic and quaint, and few Americans could identify Japanese political figures.

In contrast, America remained the most important nation for Japan. American popular culture retained its strong appeal, and events in America filled the Japanese mass media. Japanese leaders were acutely aware of these disparities and disturbed both by their nation's dependence on the United States and by American indifference toward Japan. They were highly sensitive to fluctuations in the American economy and in American economic policy and the shifts in America's relationship with China, a country that loomed large on the Japanese horizon. President Nixon's journey to Peking and the swift relaxation of Sino-American tensions produced consternation in Tokyo and a series of frantic efforts (completed in September 1972) to establish a diplomatic tie with Communist China. America's unilateral diplomacy, on an issue of such magnitude for Japan, needlessly embittered relations and increased the feeling that the United States was an unpredictable and untrustworthy ally.

American policy accentuated Japan's sense of aloneness and seemed to indicate that the United States could not aid Japan in its quest for a larger role in world affairs. More and more, Japanese commentators described America's shortcomings, particularly the violence and dissension in American society. Many Japanese emphasized the decline of America's economic and military power and questioned the ability of the United States to maintain its commitments in the Western Pacific. Within the ruling Liberal Democratic Party, criticism of the United States rose along with a conviction that Japan, faced with a fluid international environment in Asia, must pursue a more independent course. The Japanese governing elite, dominated by cautious bureaucrats, businessmen, and conservative politicians, knew the risks of any sharp shifts in foreign policy. While it continued the modest buildup of Japan's military strength and kept open the option to become a nuclear power, it had no concrete plan to satisfy the widespread yearning for more international status. Japan was adrift, dissatisfied with the present, but unwilling to take the initiative in shaping the future.

VI

In the nineteenth century Japan had been a remote, distant object on America's Pacific horizon. By the end of the century it had become an expansionist power, both a threat to America's empire and a hope for civilized development in Asia. Under Theodore Roosevelt's leadership the two nations, in a burst of constructive statesmanship, had reached a realistic accord, only to find it swept away by currents of racism and idealism in America and by Japan's impulsive foreign policy. In the 1920s Japanese and American leaders had tried, once again, to lessen misunderstanding, defining their relationship in terms of the prevailing concepts of international cooperation. These had proved unequal to the test of the great depression and the international anarchy of the 1930s. Both nations had turned inward, losing touch with one another and gradually drifting into a crisis that could only be resolved through war.

Over the years American policy had often lacked coherence and continuity but, beneath the surface confusion, certain attitudes had persisted. With few exceptions, policymakers in Washington and ambassadors in Tokyo had been unable to move beyond the assumptions and preoccupations of their own culture. They had rarely understood the internal workings of the Japanese government or perceived that Japan would follow its own unique course instead of imitate the path of the West. American ethnocentrism had encouraged the belief that Japan, like other non-Western societies, was malleable, eager to assimilate American values and institutions.

The tragedy of the Pacific war had led to the great experiment of the occupation, the apogee of America's faith in its ability to transform Japan. With the end of the occupation came a period in which the two nations shared a massive trans-Pacific trade and a wide range of cultural contacts, as well as a desire to maintain security in the Pacific. But all of these common interests did not fuse into a real closeness; after all the years of interaction, the gap between national attitudes and styles remained immense, as did perceptions of the world. Sensing this, leaders in both nations were apprehensive over the future. The war had brought an era of collaboration that now seemed steadily receding into the past. Possibly it would still stretch out into a permanent rapprochement; it appeared more likely that it would form only an interlude in the long and troubled encounter between the two nations.

Bibliographical Essay

Aᴍᴇʀɪᴄᴀɴ-Jᴀᴘᴀɴᴇsᴇ ʀᴇʟᴀᴛɪᴏɴs ᴄᴀɴ ʙᴇsᴛ ʙᴇ ᴀᴘᴘʀᴏᴀᴄʜᴇᴅ ᴀs ᴘᴀʀᴛ ᴏꜰ ᴛʜᴇ ʟᴀʀɢᴇʀ ᴇɴᴄᴏᴜɴᴛᴇʀ ʙᴇᴛᴡᴇᴇɴ ᴛʜᴇ Uɴɪᴛᴇᴅ Sᴛᴀᴛᴇs ᴀɴᴅ Eᴀsᴛ Asɪᴀ. One should begin with Akira Iriye, *Across The Pacific: An Inner History of American-East Asian Relations* (New York, 1967), an outstanding study of the interplay between China, Japan, and America, and move on to Ernest R. May and James C. Thomson, Jr., eds., *American-East Asian Relations: A Survey* (Cambridge, Mass., 1972), a series of authoritative essays outlining the conclusions of previous scholars and suggesting opportunities for future ones. William L. Neumann, *America Encounters Japan: From Perry to MacArthur* (Baltimore, 1963) was a pathbreaking effort, now dated, while Edwin O. Reischauer, *The United States and Japan*, 3rd ed. (Cambridge, Mass., 1965), rich in its analysis of Japanese character and society, devotes little space to the evolution of American governmental policy, the primary focus of this book. Richard W. Van Alstyne, *The United States and East Asia* (New York, 1973), is a recent, brief survey.

During the nineteenth century, American contact with Japan was a small event on the panorama of American expansion. In understanding the nation's westward surge, Albert K. Weinberg, *Manifest Destiny: A Study of Nationalist Expansionism in American History* (Baltimore, 1935) and Henry Nash Smith, *Virgin Land: The American West as Symbol and Myth* (Cambridge, Mass., 1950) remain immensely useful. Frederick Merk, *Manifest Destiny and Mission in American History: A Reinterpretation* (New York, 1963) reexamines old themes, while Glyndon G. Van Deusen, *William Henry Seward* (New York, 1967) and Ernest N. Paolino, *The Foundations of the American Empire: William Henry Seward and U.S. Foreign Policy* (Ithaca, 1973) reassess one of the most significant mid-century statesmen. The work of William H. Goetzmann, particularly his *Exploration and Empire: The Explorer and the Scientist in the Winning of the American West* (New York, 1967), greatly enlarged my knowledge of Westward expansion.

On American relations with Japan, Foster Rhea Dulles, *Yankees and Samurai: America's Role in the Emergence of Modern Japan, 1791-1900* (New York, 1965) is a competent synthesis; Payson J. Treat, *Diplomatic Relations Between the United States and Japan, 1853-1905*, 3 vols. (Stanford, 1932-1938) provides lengthy quotations from State Department archives; and Tyler Dennett, *Americans in Eastern Asia* (New York, 1922) is an indispensable guide to the activities of American diplomats and missionaries in the Orient. There is a large literature on the American opening of Japan. Arthur C. Walworth, *Black Ships off Japan: The Story of Commodore Perry's Expedition* (New York, 1946) provides a good general account, and Samuel Elliot Morison, *"Old Bruin": Commodore Matthew C. Perry, 1794-1858* (Boston, 1967) traces the career of the central actor. The thoughts of the first American diplomat in Japan can be followed in Mario Emilio Cosenza, ed., *The Complete Journal of Townsend Harris, First American Consul General and Minister to Japan* (New York, 1930); those of a later American minister, Richard B. Hubbard, in his *The United States in the Far East: Or, Modern Japan and the Orient* (Richmond, 1899). For an understanding of the complex negotiations over extraterritorial rights, one still turns to F. C. Jones, *Extraterritoriality in Japan, and the Diplomatic Relations Resulting in its Abolition, 1853-1899* (New York, 1931). Important comparative perspective is found in Grace Fox, *Britain and Japan, 1858-1883* (London, 1969) and James A. Field, Jr., *America and the Mediterranean World, 1776-1882* (Princeton, 1969).

Unfortunately, American missionaries in Japan have been studied only by church historians. Charles W. Iglehart, *A Century of Protestant Christianity in Japan* (Rutland, Vermont, 1959) and Winburn T. Thomas, *Protestant Beginnings in Japan: The First Three Decades, 1859-1889* (Tokyo, 1959) give only a bare factual outline. The influence of missionaries on governmental policy is obscure, but one biography, Evarts Boutell Green, *A New-Englander in Japan: Daniel Crosby Greene* (Boston, 1927) provides some scattered insights.

Of the many books dealing with American foreign policy in the late nineteenth and early twentieth centuries, several are particularly helpful in establishing a context for Japanese-American relations. Richard Hofstadter, *Social Darwinism in American Thought*, rev. ed. (Boston, 1955) is excellent on racism and imperialism; Mira Wilkins, *The Emergence of Multinational Enterprise: American Business*

Abroad from the Colonial Era to 1914 (Cambridge, Mass., 1970) gathers much data on economic expansion; C. Roland Marchand, *The American Peace Movement and Social Reform, 1898-1918* (Princeton, 1972) is the best and most recent study of this important phenomenon; and Robert H. Wiebe, *The Search For Order, 1877-1920* (New York, 1967) analyzes the organizational revolution in American society and suggests some of its profound implications for foreign policy.

The background of the first crisis between the two governments is developed by Hilary Conroy in *The Japanese Frontier in Hawaii, 1868-1898* (Berkeley and Los Angeles, 1953), and evidence of the growing resentment toward Japan can be found in Fred Harvey Harrington, *God, Mammon, and the Japanese: Dr. Horace N. Allen and Korean-American Relations, 1884-1905* (Madison, 1944) and in Herbert Croly, *Willard Straight* (New York, 1925). John Morton Blum, *The Republican Roosevelt* (Cambridge, Mass., 1954) and Howard K. Beale, *Theodore Roosevelt and the Rise of American to World Power* (Baltimore, 1956) are general guides to Theodore Roosevelt's foreign policy. Blum's interpretation, however, is too Roosevelt-centered, while Beale's obsession with China hopelessly confuses his assessment of East Asian policy. Many of Roosevelt's own letters—to be used with caution—are in Elting E. Morison, ed., *The Letters of Theodore Roosevelt*, 8 vols. (Cambridge, Mass., 1951-1954). Three books examining Roosevelt's diplomacy during the Russo-Japanese War are Raymond A. Esthus, *Theodore Roosevelt and Japan* (Seattle, 1966), Eugene P. Trani, *The Treaty of Portsmouth: An Adventure in American Diplomacy* (Lexington, Kentucky, 1969), and John Albert White, *The Diplomacy of the Russo-Japanese War* (Princeton, 1964). Charles E. Neu, "Theodore Roosevelt and American Involvement in the Far East, 1901-1909," *Pacific Historical Review, XXXV* (1966) views the whole of Roosevelt's East Asian policy, and his *An Uncertain Friendship: Theodore Roosevelt and Japan, 1906-1909* (Cambridge, Mass., 1967) studies intensively the Japanese-American crisis of those years. Akira Iriye, *Pacific Estrangement: Japanese and American Expansion, 1897-1911)* (Cambridge, Mass., 1972) is a unique analysis of the interaction of expansionist thought. Peter W. Stanley, *A Nation in the Making: The Philippines and the United States, 1899-1921* (Cambridge, Mass., 1974) and Michael H. Hunt, *The Frontier Defense and the Open*

Door: Manchuria in Chinese-American Relations, 1895-1911 (New Haven, 1973) both develop important but neglected topics. The evolution of naval and military strategy can be followed in William Reynolds Braisted, *The United States Navy in the Pacific, 1897-1909* (Austin, 1958) and Richard D. Challener, *Admirals, Generals, and American Foreign Policy, 1898-1914* (Princeton, 1973). Two general discussions of racism, John Higham, *Strangers in the Land: Patterns of American Nativism, 1860-1925* (New Brunswick, 1955) and Oscar Handlin, *Race and Nationality in American Life* (Boston, 1950), recreate the atmosphere that spawned it. For an understanding of anti-Japanese sentiment, one must turn to Roger Daniels, *The Politics of Prejudice: The Anti-Japanese Movement in California and the Struggle for Japanese Exclusion* (Berkeley and Los Angeles, 1962).

On the Japanese side, Shumpei Okamoto, *The Japanese Oligarchy and the Russo-Japanese War* (New York, 1970) penetrates the workings of the Japanese ruling elite, and Roger F. Hackett, *Yamagata Aritomo in the Rise of Modern Japan, 1838-1922* (Cambridge, Mass., 1971) tells the story of its dominant member. There is also a stimulating essay by Marius B. Jansen on "Modernization and Foreign Policy in Meiji Japan," in Robert E. Ward, ed., *Political Development in Modern Japan* (Princeton, 1968). George W. Monger, *The End of Isolation: British Foreign Policy, 1900-1907* (London, 1963) touches on Great Britain's tie with Japan, while Ian H. Nish, *The Anglo-Japanese Alliance: The Diplomacy of Two Island Empires, 1894-1907* (London, 1966) examines it in great detail.

The Taft years are relatively unexplored. I have summed up my own impressions in an essay dealing with the period from 1906 to 1913 in Ernest R. May and James C. Thomson, Jr., eds., *American-East Asian Relations: A Survey* (Cambridge, Mass., 1972). Donald F. Anderson, *William Howard Taft: A Conservative's Conception of the Presidency* (Ithaca, 1973) and Paolo E. Coletta, *The Presidency of William Howard Taft* (Lawrence, 1973) examine Taft's philosophy and style of leadership. Charles Vevier, *The United States and China, 1906-1913: A Study of Finance and Diplomacy* (New Brunswick, 1955) sees American policy as economically motivated, and Walter V. Scholes and Marie V. Scholes, *The Foreign Policies of the Taft Administration* (Columbia, 1970) add details but no new interpretations. Francis M. Huntington-Wilson, *Memoirs of an Ex-Diplomat* (Boston, 1945) records the views of Knox's right-hand man and expert on East Asia, and Peter Lowe, *Great Britain and Japan, 1911-1915: A Study of British Far Eastern Policy* (London, 1969) analyzes some aspects of British policy. But the fullest, most satisfactory studies—still unpublished—are two Ph.D. dissertations, Paige Elliott Mulhollan, "Philander C. Knox and Dollar Diplomacy, 1909-1913" (University of Texas, 1966) and Teruko Okada Kachi, "The Treaty of 1911 and the Immigration and Alien Land Law Issue between the United States and Japan, 1911-1913" (University of Chicago, 1957).

For an understanding of Woodrow Wilson's East Asian policy, Roy W. Curry, *Woodrow Wilson and Far Eastern Policy, 1913-1921* (New York, 1957) and Burton F. Beers, *Vain Endeavor: Robert Lansing's Attempts to End the American-Japanese Rivalry* (Durham, 1962) are a beginning, but there is much additional information in Paolo E. Coletta, *William Jennings Bryan: Progressive Politician and Moral Statesman, 1909-1915* (Lincoln, 1969) and Arthur S. Link, *Wilson: The New Freedom* (Princeton, 1956) and *Wilson: The Struggle for Neutrality, 1914-1915* (Princeton, 1960). Madeleine Sung-Chun Chi, *China Diplomacy, 1914-1918* (Cambridge, Mass., 1970) is broader than its title suggests, and Sadao Asada's unpublished Ph.D. dissertation, "Japan and the United States, 1915-1925" (Yale University, 1963) is indispensable. George F. Kennan, *Russia Leaves the War* (Princeton, 1956) and *The Decision to Intervene* (Princeton, 1958) are reliable and eloquent guides through the large and controversial literature on American intervention in Russia.

Issues at the Paris Peace Conference are covered by Russell H. Fifield, *Woodrow Wilson and the Far East: The Diplomacy of the Shantung Question* (New York, 1952); those relating to naval policy by William Reynolds Braisted, *The United States Navy in the Pacific, 1909-1922* (Austin, 1971). Two well-constructed monographs, Peter Duus, *Party Rivalry and Political Change in Taishō Japan* (Cambridge, Mass., 1968) and Tetsuo Nagita, *Hara Kei in the Politics of Compromise, 1905-1915* (Cambridge, Mass., 1967) chart changes in Japan's domestic polity. Marius B. Jansen, *The Japanese and Sun Yat-sen* (Cambridge, Mass., 1954) probes Japan's reaction to the Chinese revolution, and James W. Morley, *The Japanese Thrust into Siberia, 1918* (New York, 1957) explains the complex motivations behind Japan's Siberian expedition. Ishii Kikujirō, *Diplomatic Commentaries* (Baltimore, 1936) gives a prominent Japanese diplomat's view of the Lansing-Ishii negotiations.

Scholars have devoted much attention to the early 1920s, a period that brought a superficial resolution of problems between Japan and the United States. Various dimensions of the Washington Conference are explored in Thomas H. Buckley, *The United States and the Washington Conference, 1921-1922* (Knoxville, 1970); Harold and Margaret Sprout, *Toward a New Order of Sea Power: American Naval Policy and the World Scene, 1918-1922*, 2nd ed. (Princeton, 1943); and John C. Vinson, *The Parchment Peace: The United States Senate and the Washington Conference, 1921-1922* (Athens, 1956). Sadao Asada, "Japan's 'Special interests' and the Washington Conference, 1912-1922," *American Historical Review, LXVII* (1961), along with his previously cited dissertation, are penetrating studies of Japan's approach to the Washington Conference, and Ernest R. May's forthcoming book on that gathering analyzes bureaucratic politics in Great Britain, Japan, and the United States. Hughes' reminiscences on foreign policy can be found in David J. Danelski and Joseph S. Tulchin, eds., *The Autobiographical Notes of Charles Evans Hughes* (Cambridge, Mass., 1973). Robert K. Murray, *The Harding Era: Warren G. Harding and His Administration* (Minneapolis, 1969) provides new information on Harding's role in foreign policy. His Secretary of State, Charles Evans Hughes, has been neglected by historians. Merlo J. Pusey, *Charles Evans Hughes*, 2 vols. (New York, 1951) and Dexter Perkins, *Charles Evans Hughes and American Democratic Statesmanship* (Boston, 1956) are superficial, while Betty Glad, *Charles Evans Hughes and the Illusions of Innocence: A Study in American Diplomacy* (Urbana, 1966) contains some insight but no sustained analysis. The role of the business community is examined in Joan Hoff Wilson, *American Business and Foreign Policy, 1920-1933* (Lexington, 1971); that of the navy in Raymond G. O'Connor, *Perilous Equilibrium: The United States and the London Naval Conference of 1930* (Lawrence, 1962), Thaddeus V. Tuleja, *Statesmen and Admirals: The Quest for a Far Eastern Naval Policy* (New York, 1963), and Gerald E. Wheeler, *Prelude to Pearl Harbor: The United States Navy and the Far East, 1921-1931* (Columbia, 1963). William L. Neumann, "Franklin D. Roosevelt and Japan, 1913-1933," *Pacific Historical Review, XXII* (1953) is useful, as is Rodman W. Paul, *The Abrogation of the Gent-*

lemen's Agreement (Cambridge, Mass., 1936). We need to know much more about events in the middle and late 1920s and about the influence of East Asian experts and American ambassadors to Japan.

The diplomacy of the great powers in East Asia is surveyed in Akira Iriye, *After Imperialism: The Search for a New Order in the Far East, 1921-1931* (Cambridge, Mass., 1965), and the illusions of Japanese policymakers are exposed in his forthcoming essay, "The Failure of Economic Expansionism, 1918-1931." British policy is scrutinized in Ian H. Nish, *Alliance in Decline: A Study in Anglo-Japanese Relations* (London, 1972), Stephen Roskill, *Naval Policy Between the Wars, I: The Period of Anglo-American Antagonism, 1919-1929* (London, 1968), and William Roger Louis, *British Strategy in the Far East, 1919-1939 (London, 1971).*

The first major challenge of the interwar peace structure came in Manchuria. The origins of the crisis there can be traced in Takehiko Yoshihashi, *Conspiracy at Mukden: The Rise of the Japanese Military* (New Haven, 1963) and in Sadako N. Ogata, *Defiance in Manchuria: The Making of Japanese Foreign Policy, 1931-1932* (Berkeley and Los Angeles, 1964). For the American reaction Armin Rappaport, *Henry L. Stimson and Japan, 1931-33* (Chicago, 1963) and Elting E. Morison, *Turmoil and Tradition: A Study of the Life and Times of Henry L. Stimson* (Boston, 1960) are helpful, along with Henry L. Stimson, *The Far Eastern Crisis: Recollections and Observations* (New York, 1936) and *On Active Service in Peace and War* (New York, 1957). One should note, however, Richard N. Current's bitterly critical *Secretary Stimson: A Study in Statecraft* (New Brunswick, 1954) and Herbert Hoover's account in *The Cabinet and the Presidency, 1920-1933* (New York, 1951). Christopher Thorne, *The Limits of Foreign Policy: The West, the League and the Far Eastern Crisis of 1931-1933* (New York, 1973) is a major reassessment. The middle years of the decade are covered by Dorothy Borg's monumental *The United States and the Far Eastern Crisis of 1933-1938: From the Manchurian Incident Through the Initial Stage of the Undeclared Sino-Japanese War* (Cambridge, Mass., 1964). Manny T. Koginos, *The Panay Incident: Prelude to War* (Lafayette, 1967) and Hamilton Darby Perry, *The Panay Incident: Prelude to Pearl Harbor* (New York, 1969) describe a potentially dangerous incident.

The literature on the mounting Japanese-American crisis after

1937 is full, but no single book suffices. Herbert Feis, *The Road to Pearl Harbor: The Coming of the War Between the United States and Japan* (Princeton, 1950) is based too narrowly on State Department archives, while Paul W. Schroeder, *The Axis Alliance and Japanese-American Relations: 1941* (Ithaca, 1958) overstates its revisionist thesis. Waldo H. Heinrichs, Jr., *American Ambassador: Joseph C. Grew and the Development of the United States Diplomatic Tradition* (Boston, 1966) is perceptive, particularly on the difficulties of comprehending Japanese policy. One can read Grew's own assessment in *Turbulent Era: A Diplomatic Record of Forty Years, 1904-1945*, 2 vols. (Boston, 1952). William L. Langer and S. Everett Gleason, *The Challenge to Isolation: 1939-1940* (New York, 1952) and *The Undeclared War: 1940-1941* (New York, 1953) remain important sources, and two articles by Robert J. C. Butow, "The Hull-Nomura Conversation: A Fundamental Misconception," *American Historical Review, LXV* (1960) and "Backdoor Diplomacy in the Pacific: The Proposal for a Konoye-Roosevelt Meeting: 1941," *Journal of American History, LIX* (1972) add crucial details to our knowledge of the final negotiations. Stephen E. Pelz, *Race to Pearl Harbor: The Failure of the Second London Naval Conference and the Onset of World War II* (Cambridge, Mass., 1974) is a new study, based on Japanese materials, as is Dorothy Borg and Shumpei Okamoto, eds., *Pearl Harbor As history: Japanese-American Relations, 1931-1941* (New York, 1973), a volume of essays by Japanese and American historians that, through its exploration of the institutional dimensions of foreign policy, adds enormously to our understanding of the coming of war. Among the memoirs of American participants, I found John Morton Blum, *From The Morgenthau Diaries: Years of Urgency, 1938-1941* (Boston, 1965), and Cordell Hull, *The Memoirs of Cordell Hull,* 2 vols. (New York, 1948) especially revealing. Two biographies of Americans in China, Russell D. Buhite, *Nelson T. Johnson and American Policy Toward China, 1925-1941* (East Lansing, 1968) and Barbara W. Tuchman, *Stilwell and the American Experience in China, 1911-1945* (New York, 1970), tell of the response to Japanese depredations there. American prewar planning is conveniently summarized in Forrest C. Pogue, *George C. Marshall: Ordeal and Hope, 1939-1942* (New York, 1966), while the perspective of Americans in the Philippines is party recreated in D. Clayton James, *The Years of MacArthur: Volume I, 1880-1941* (Boston, 1970).

The literature on Pearl Harbor is voluminous. Charles Callan Tansill, *Back Door to War: The Roosevelt Foreign Policy, 1933-1941* (Chicago, 1952) and Robert A. Theobald, *The Final Secret of Pearl Harbor: The Washington Contribution to the Japanese Attack* (New York, 1954) are typical of the books that accuse Roosevelt of deliberately seeking war with Japan. Ladislas Farago, *The Broken Seal: The Story of "Operation Magic" and the Pearl Harbor Disaster* (New York, 1967) and Walter Lord, *Day of Infamy* (New York, 1957) are highly readable accounts that emphasize dramatic details. But the only study that offers a convincing explanation of how the tragedy occurred is Roberta Wohlstetter, *Pearl Harbor: Warning and Decision* (Stanford, 1962).

In assessing Japanese expansionism, one can begin with three older works: F. C. Jones, *Japan's New Order in East Asia: Its Rise and Fall, 1937-1945* (New York, 1954); David J. Lu, *From the Marco Polo Bridge to Pearl Harbor: Japan's Entry into World War II* (Washington, D.C., 1961); and Robert J. C. Butow, *Tojo and the Coming of the War* (Princeton, 1961). James B. Crowley, *Japan's Quest for Autonomy: National Security and Foreign Policy, 1930-1938* (Princeton, 1966) adds much new information on army thinking, but advances some questionable interpretations. John Hunter Boyle, *China and Japan at War, 1937-1945: The Politics of Collaboration* (Stanford, 1972) traces the twists and turns of Japan's China policy. Two collections of essays, George M. Wilson, ed., *Crisis Politics in Prewar Japan: Institutional and Ideological Problems of the 1930's* (Tokyo, 1970) and James W. Morley, ed., *Dilemmas of Growth in Prewar Japan* (Princeton, 1971) focus on domestic aspects of Japanese policy, while one popular account, John Toland, *The Rising Sun: The Decline and Fall of the Japanese Empire, 1936-1945* (New York, 1970) skims across the surface of events. David Bergamini, *Japan's Imperial Conspiracy* (New York, 1971) sees Hirohito as the villain. Japan's tie with Germany is examined in Frank W. Iklé, *German-Japanese Relations, 1936-1940* (New York, 1956), Johanna Menzel Meskill, *Hitler and Japan: The Hollow Alliance* (New York, 1966), and Ernst J. Presseisen, *Germany and Japan: A Study in Totalitarian Diplomacy, 1933-1941* (The Hague, 1958). James V. Compton, *The Swastika and the Eagle: Hitler, the United States and the Origins of World War II* (Boston, 1967) and Norman Rich, *Hitler's War Aims: Ideology, the Nazi State, and the Course of Expansion* (New York,

1973) put German-Japanese collaboration in the context of Hitler's broader aims.

During the 1930s British East Asian policy was, as always, intertwined with that of the United States. Nicholas R. Clifford, *Retreat From China: British Policy in the Far East, 1937-1941* (Seattle, 1967), Malcolm D. Kennedy, *The Estrangement of Great Britain and Japan, 1917-1935* (Berkeley and Los Angeles, 1969), and Bradford A. Lee, *Britain and the Sino-Japanese War, 1937-1939* (Stanford, 1973) help in understanding it, as does Sir Llewellyn Woodward, *British Foreign Policy in the Second World War*, 3 vols. (London, 1970-1972).

World War II brought a confrontation between Japanese and Americans on many levels. Forrest C. Pogue, *George C. Marshall: Organizer of Victory, 1943-1945* (New York, 1973) outlines the dilemmas of Pacific strategy; Herbert Feis, *Churchill, Roosevelt, Stalin: The War They Waged and the Peace They Sought* (Princeton, 1957) records the Allied decisions on Japan taken at wartime conferences; and Roger Daniels, *Concentration Camps USA: Japanese Americans and World War II* (New York, 1971) discusses the evacuation of Japanese-Americans from the Pacific Coast. On this issue, one should also consult Stetson Conn, "The Decision to Evacuate the Japanese from the Pacific Coast," in Kent Roberts Greenfield, ed., *Command Decisions* (Washington, D.C., 1960) and Audrie Girdner and Anne Loftis, *The Great Betrayal: The Evacuation of the Japanese-Americans During World War II* (New York, 1969), which dwells on the personal experiences of the Japanese. The best accounts of decisions made in Tokyo and Washington in the summer of 1945 are Robert J. C. Butow, *Japan's Decision to Surrender* (Stanford, 1954) and Herbert Feis, *The Atomic Bomb and the End of World War II* (Princeton, 1966). A different point of view is in Gabriel Kolko, *The Politics of War: The World and United States Foreign Policy, 1943-1945* (New York, 1968).

The American occupation of Japan is a rich field for further study, one that historians have largely ignored. Kazuo Kawai, *Japan's American Interlude* (Chicago, 1960) gives a good overview, while Harry Emerson Wildes, *Typhoon in Tokyo: The Occupation and Its Aftermath* (New York, 1954) is much more sketchy and critical. Joyce and Gabriel Kolko, *The Limits of Power: The World and United States Foreign Policy, 1945-1954* (New York, 1972) has several chapters on Japanese-American relations. Three important memoirs dealing with the occupation are George F. Kennan, *Memoirs, 1925-1950* (Boston, 1967), William J. Sebald, *With MacArthur in Japan: A Personal History of the Occupation* (London, 1965), and Douglas MacArthur, *Reminiscences* (New York, 1964). MacArthur remains a puzzle, but Lawrence S. Wittner, "MacArthur and the Missionaries: God and Man in Occupied Japan," *Pacific Historical Review, XXXX* (1971) shows the kinds of insights that archival research can bring. Chalmers Johnson, *Conspiracy at Matsukawa* (Berkeley and Los Angeles, 1972) adds interesting information on conditions in Japan, and Herbert Feis, *Contest Over Japan* (New York, 1967) traces Soviet-American rivalry there. For the peace treaty, Frederick S. Dunn, *Peace-Making and the Settlement with Japan* (Princeton, 1963) is essential; Bernard C. Cohen, *The Political Process and Foreign Policy: The Making of the Japanese Peace Settlement* (Princeton, 1957) focuses on public and congressional opinion; and Dean Acheson, *Present at the Creation: My Years in the State Department* (New York, 1969) recreates some of the concerns of American policymakers. Sigeru Yoshida, *The Yoshida Memoirs: The Story of Japan in Crisis* (Boston, 1962) presents one Japanese perspective.

The literature on Japanese-American relations in the postoccupation period is vast but one-sided. It analyzes Japan's domestic and foreign policies at great length, but says little about the perceptions of Americans policymakers. For those, one must turn to a miscellany of sources, such as Robert Murphy, *Diplomat Among Warriors* (New York, 1964), John M. Allison, *Ambassador From the Prairie or Allison Wonderland* (Boston, 1973), and Michael A. Guhin, *John Foster Dulles: A Statesman and His Times* (New York, 1972). Martin E. Weinstein, *Japan's Postwar Defense Policy, 1947-1968* (New York, 1971) is useful for security negotiations, and George R. Packard III, *Protest in Tokyo: The Security Treaty Crisis of 1960* (Princeton, 1966) touches on American policy in the 1950s and provides an excellent analysis of the Japanese reaction to it. Of the many books dealing with current relations, Herbert Passim, ed., *The United States and Japan* (New York, 1966) and Gerald L. Curtis, ed., *Japanese-American Relations in the 1970's* (Washington, D.C., 1970) are products of the American Assembly; Robert E. Osgood, *The Weary and the Wary: U.S. and Japanese Security Policies in Transition* (Baltimore, 1972) contains the thoughtful speculations of a political scientist; and Zbigniew Brzezinski, *The Fragile Blossom: Crisis and Change in Japan* (New York, 1972) embodies the efforts of an expert on Soviet affairs to understand Japan. Albert Axelbank, *Black Star Over Japan: Rising Forces of Militarism* (New York, 1972) and Herman Kahn, *The Emerging Japanese Superstate: Challenge and Response* (New York, 1970) represent the two poles of American reaction to Japan's emergence as a great economic power. Edwin O. Reischauer, "Fateful Triangle—The United States, Japan and China," *New York Times Magazine*, September 19, 1971, is a fine example of contemporary history.

On the Japanese side, Nathaniel B. Thayer, *How the Conservatives Rule Japan* (Princeton, 1969) helps to explain the surface stability of Japanese politics. Japan's changing international position is assessed in John K. Emmerson, *Arms, Yen and Power: The Japanese Dilemma* (New York, 1971), Donald C. Hellmann, *Japan and East Asia: The New International Order* (New York, 1972), and Lawrence Olson, *Japan in Post-War Asia* (New York, 1970). The essays in James William Morley, ed., *Forecast For Japan: Security in the 1970's* (Princeton, 1972) seek to predict the future, while the stimulating journalistic effort by the staff of the Asahi Shimbun, *The Pacific Rivals: A Japanese View of Japanese-American Relations* (New York and Tokyo, 1972) catches much of the pathos and turmoil of the past.

Index